# Rocky Mountain Constitution Making, 1850–1912

**Recent Titles in Contributions in Legal Studies**
***Series Editor: Paul L. Murphy***

The Network of Control: State Supreme Courts and State Security Statutes, 1920-1970
*Carol E. Jenson*

Drugs and Information Control: The Role of Men and Manipulation in the Control of Drug Trafficking
*Jerald W. Cloyd*

State Supreme Courts: Policymakers in the Federal System
*Mary Cornelia Porter and G. Alan Tarr, editors*

The Future of Our Liberties: Perspectives on the Bill of Rights
*Stephen C. Halpern, editor*

Tightening the Reins of Justice in America: A Comparative Analysis of the Criminal Jury Trial in England and the United States
*Michael H. Graham*

The Development of Law on the Rocky Mountain Frontier: Civil Law and Society, 1850-1912
*Gordon Morris Bakken*

Clients and Lawyers: Securing the Rights of Disabled Persons
*Susan M. Olson*

The New High Priests: Lawyers in Post-Civil War America
*Gerard W. Gawalt, editor*

The Little Rock Crisis: A Constitutional Interpretation
*Tony Freyer*

Nuclear Weapons and Law
*Arthur Selwyn Miller and Martin Feinrider, editors*

Native American Aliens: Disloyalty and the Renunciation of Citizenship by Japanese Americans during World War II
*Donald E. Collins*

Corwin's Constitution: Essays and Insights of Edward S. Corwin
*Kenneth D. Crews, editor*

The Role of State Supreme Courts in the New Judicial Federalism
*Susan P. Fino*

Church-State Relationships in America
*Gerard F. Bradley*

# ROCKY MOUNTAIN CONSTITUTION MAKING, 1850–1912

GORDON MORRIS BAKKEN

Contributions in Legal Studies, Number 35

GREENWOOD PRESS
New York • Westport, Connecticut • London

**Library of Congress Cataloging-in-Publication Data**

Bakken, Gordon Morris.
Rocky Mountain constitution making, 1850-1912.

(Contributions in legal studies, ISSN 0147-1074 ; no. 35)
Bibliography: p.
Includes index.
1. West (U.S.)—Constitutional history. I. Title. II. Series.
KF4541.B18 1987 342.78'029 86-12143
347.80229
ISBN 0-313-25538-5 (lib. bdg. : alk. paper)



Library of Congress Catalog Card Number: 86-12143
ISBN: 0-313-25538-5
ISSN: 0147-1074

First published in 1987

Greenwood Press, Inc.
88 Post Road West, Westport, Connecticut 06881

Printed in the United States of America

The paper used in this book complies with the Permanent Paper Standard issued by the National Information Standards Organization (Z39.48-1984).

10 9 8 7 6 5 4 3 2 1

To the memory of my pioneer forebears:

Halvor Jacobson (1829-98) and Johanne Bug (1836-1928)

Jacob Martinius Jacobson (1858-1928) and Anne Lande (1860-1955)

Mildred Jacobson (1886-1984) and Nordahl Anderson (1885-1971)

and

To my parents

Evelyn Anderson and Elwood S. Bakken (1915-1969)

# Contents

# Acknowledgments

In the course of research and writing, a historian accumulates numerous professional and financial debts. My only hope is that this brief section and this book can compensate partially those who have invested time and money.

Parts of this book grew out of a seminar conducted by Stanley I. Kutler. For his patience and long suffering, I am deeply indebted. Allan G. Bogue helped me develop other aspects of the book and gave generously of his time and insights.

The support of my research has been most generous. The University of Wisconsin Graduate School provided computer-time funds for voting analysis. The Ford Foundation provided funds through the University of Wisconsin fellowship program for a summer of writing. The Penrose Fund of the American Philosophical Society made a most generous grant that liberated me from summer teaching. Finally, the Russell Sage Foundation granted funds for a year of residency at the University of Wisconsin Law School, providing me with an opportunity to work with Willard Hurst. Professor Hurst has influenced both the nature and the exactitude of my inquiry.

My gratitude to my wife, Erika, is more than double for this book as it is both a product of her labor and patience. But for her expert computer manipulation of the text, this book would not have been seen print. To my children, Angela and Jeffrey my thanks. To Angela for her patience with a father too often busy to answer questions and to Jeffrey for his indulgence with my lack of time to watch him shred a killer tube.

Very special thanks for this and my two previous books goes to Mary Yount. Mary has edited all three books with the love of learning and expertise of language that has given me great joy and a feeling of comfort. Mary's work on these books has been remarkable both because she has given so much of her time to them and because she has helped me to grow so much as an author. Her gentle, "Dr. Bakken, do you really want to say this?" has made me think, "What would Mary say?" often enough to give language life and history a sense of living. My stumbling style, I hope, has matured to a readable level of prose in no small measure due to Mary's gentle hand.

Before we begin, a word, gentle reader, about the prose that will follow. My first book, *The Development of Law in the Rocky Mountain Frontier, 1850-1912* (1983), received reviews that questioned my style, but not my parentage. My second book, *The Development of Law in Frontier California, 1850-1890*, was an attempt to out-pun Lawrence Friedman and to wrench from John P. Reid the aura of making legal history fun. Because John Reid has privately indicated that my best prose can be found in Little League newsletters, in this book I am attempting to write in the serious style befitting a scholar, but with sufficient wit to keep John's title in jeopardy. I will allow my reviewers to decide where this book properly belongs in literature as well as in historiography.

# Rocky Mountain Constitution Making, 1850–1912

# Introduction

One oft-stated tenet of the creation of the American republic was that the people must have frequent recurrence to fundamental principles. One form of that recurrence to fundamental principles was the state constitutional convention. In the Rocky Mountain states, constitution makers faced the burden of stating fundamental principles for their respective states and of dealing with the demands of time and place. As Thomas Jefferson observed, the times belonged "to the living generation," and that generation's constitution was to "go hand in hand with the progress of the human mind."(1) Inherently tension existed between the Founders' documents and demands of changed times. What was fundamental law? What principles must be restated without contemporary gloss? How far should the hand of government reach into the personal or business affairs of mankind? Should a state constitution be an instrument of change or one of stability? In searching for answers to these questions, constitutional convention delegates looked to the Declaration of Independence, the Constitution, the Bill of Rights, and the Northwest Ordinance.(2) They also turned to constituent politics to find convention consensus.

The issues before these constitutional conventions were fundamental public law concerns. First, delegates had to deal with the command aspects of their documents. They had to focus upon the public policy issues of resource allocation through taxation, the definition of interests in property, and the role of corporations in the socioeconomic life of the community. Second, the delegates had to express emerging shared values in their constitutions. They had to articulate personal rights and liberties, concepts of equality, and the limits of government discretion. In analyzing their work we must ask how, when, and among whom consensus emerged. Third, the delegates had to wrestle with the concept of the public good. They had to decide when government could use its force to fix the terms of socioeconomic operations for its citizen. Further, delegates also could decide to fix those terms in the constitution itself and thwart future government attempts to act. Finally, delegates had to decide whether to allow the process of interest bargaining to operate as a means to a legal and social order that was efficient and fair. Was that process to operate in the constitutional convention, to decide the issues then and there? Was it better to leave the issues to future generations operating in future legislatures?

This volume explores these questions in the contexts of eight constitutional conventions and their legal heritage. The important questions are really twofold. First, how, when, and among whom did consensus emerge on these questions? Second, how did that issue consensus reflect the fundamental principles of the founding period and the demands of the time and place? In analyzing these issues, I have focused upon topics of broad constitutional import and general regional concern.(3) Some topics of single-state or isolated interest await future study, but this book is about our constitutional heritage and the stamp of a region on a then living generation of Americans. What flows from this study, then, is both constitutional history and the history of the American West. In the conventions we find both recurring to the roots of the republic and the fibre of the frontier.

# 1

# A Rocky Mountain Constitution Making Heritage

The Rocky Mountain territories inherited a long tradition of state constitution making. The Northwest Ordinance had prescribed specific stages of self-determination. The third stage offered a congressional enabling act for the writing of a constitution when the population reached 60,000. Prior to 1850, the strict requirements of the third stage fell into disuse. Congress allowed the territories to petition for statehood, or an enabling act, without the requisite 60,000 population. Enabling acts ceased to be authorizations for constitution making; rather, they became devices to legitimate statehood movements in many territories. As such, territorials were free to initiate constitutional conventions and petition Congress for admission. Frontiersmen often called constitutional conventions when their control of an area was assured, hoping to avoid the territorial system. They drew up constitutions that reflected their belief in republican government and affirmed contemporary concepts of law.

Ohio set the general pattern in 1802, petitioning Congress for authorization to write a constitution and elect a state government. Congress responded with an enabling act that established rules for the election of delegates to the constitutional convention, the date of the election and convention, and restrictions upon the substance of the constitution regarding federal interests. Ohio, Indiana, Illinois, Alabama, Mississippi, Missouri, and Louisiana followed this procedure to statehood. Between 1836 and 1848 Congress admitted five territories--Arkansas, Michigan, Iowa, Florida, and Wisconsin--but only issued an enabling act to Wisconsin. This absence of enabling acts corresponded to the congressional democratization of the territorial system itself. Congress shifted the primary responsibility for statehood to the territorial inhabitants in the 1830s and 1840s. In this same period Congress made major changes in the territorial system that extended home rule.(1) The net result was a laissez-faire attitude in Congress and great latitude for territorial action.

Congressional action on enabling acts varied in the remaining years of the 19th century. California, Oregon, and Kansas wrote constitutions and organized state governments without enabling acts; Nebraska and Minnesota petitioned Congress and obtained authorizations before establishing state government; Nevada received an enabling act amidst her haste to attain statehood and the electoral college. Congress avoided bitter floor fights in bypassing enabling acts before the Civil War. The California statehood scheme was a political expedient. Similarly, in granting an enabling act to Nevada, Congress gave federal sanction to the statehood movement and three electoral votes to Abraham Lincoln. Whether partisan or national interest was served, the enabling act question was only procedural in nature.

In contrast to Congress' view of the enabling act, territorials assumed that an enabling act was necessary to any statehood movement and to the validity of any constitution. The Colorado statehood movement, for example, waned after the voters defeated the 1865 constitution, in part because its leaders, having once failed under the 1864 Enabling Act, seemed to think that they could not reconvene or call a new convention to write another constitution unless Congress provided a new law.(2) When other statehood forces contemplated action, it was the political wisdom of acting without an enabling act, not the legality, that was questioned.(3) Small groups of dedicated men motivated statehood movements to overcome local apathy and interest group opposition.(4) Often, the enabling act was the key to their programs of persuasion.

Part of any statehood movement was overcoming objection to statehood. Most frequently territorials feared that statehood would be too expensive. They foresaw burdensome taxation and unwise legislative fiscal policy as a probable reality. Some territorial office holders naturally feared the loss of their jobs. Expense and taxation were the prevalent fears. Fiscal policy became important in the constitutional-convention deliberations of state constitutional offices and their salaries and in the taxation of mining property.

New Mexico and Utah, the first territories of the Rocky Mountain West, reacted to their acquisition by the United States with constitutional conventions. The Mexican War brought federal authority and the prospect of territorial government. Both New Mexico and Utah held constitutional conventions and applied for statehood. Multiple factors prevented their acceptance into the Union, but their efforts did illustrate the operation of statehood movements and their concepts of constitution making.

Utah was not faced with a military presence in 1849 when its constitutional convention met, but the opportunity for autonomy and the prospects of territorial vassalage spurred church leaders to act. Brigham Young and other church leaders acted quickly after the signing of the Treaty of Guadalupe Hidalgo in 1848. Early in 1849 the church council meeting in Heber C. Kimball's home announced that a convention would be held on March 5. On that date Daniel Spencer called the delegates together, and a committee of ten reported a complete state constitution in three days.(5) The document was similar in many respects to the

Illinois constitution of 1818.(6) The structure of government was conventional, providing for a bicameral legislature, a governor and lieutenant governor, and a three-judge supreme court. The constitution also provided for elections, a militia, and a bill of rights. It was a borrowed document, based on republican principles, and was outwardly inoffensive. It was a document reflecting the reality of Deseret, not a conscious design for future fundamental law development.

The implementation of the constitution betrayed the purpose of its creation and the intentions of the framers. Brigham Young was elected governor; Willard Richards was secretary of state; Heber C. Kimball, Newell K. Whitney, and John Taylor were supreme court justices. All were either members of the First Presidency or Apostles. The legislature was similarly all-Mormon. The State of Deseret was a constitutional theocracy whose purpose was the entrenchment of the church. As a document, the constitution did not betray the purpose of Mormon domination. However, the effort to gain statehood failed for national political reasons, and Utah became a territory as part of the "Compromise of 1850." This first failure at least gave the Mormons more time for studied reflection on the nature of a constitution. But this failure coupled with subsequent ones produced a growing degree of anxiety. When the 1895 constitutional convention met with an enabling act, many delegates saw that this convention offered a golden opportunity for statehood. This attitude gave credence to conservatives in the 1895 convention who argued that a radical document could result in continued territorial vassalage.

Military rule was a fact in New Mexico, and statehood was a means to home rule and political power. Native New Mexicans saw in statehood a chance for home rule, but Americans were more interested in the federal and state offices that would be created. With the blessing of President Zachary Taylor, the statehood forces started their campaign in November 1849 under the leadership of James S. Calhoun. Calhoun was Taylor's agent in Santa Fe and a former Whig congressman from Georgia. Richard Hanson Weightman provided the political ability and, with Calhoun, formed the nucleus of the movement.(7) Manuel Alvarez, former American consul at Santa Fe; Dr. Henry Connelly, a resident politico; Donaciano Vigil, another native and political office holder; and Joab Houghton, a lawyer and political opportunist, joined the statehood forces with hopes for political gain. This group opposed a territorialist faction. During the ensuing political battle, Vigil and Houghton drifted away from the statehood forces; when the constitutional convention convened, they were in control posing as statehood men.(8) The relative merits of statehood or territorial status were only arguments of political convenience, and opportunists used both if the political climate seemed right.

A Houghton majority controlled the convention and approved a constitution written by Joab Houghton and others after a ten-day session. The constitution sketched a standard institutional pattern: a bicameral legislature, governor, lieutenant governor, four-member supreme court, circuit courts, and militia.(9) The convention declared itself against slavery, but kept the suffrage white and male although "all men [were] born equally free and independent." It naturally followed that no person could be held by law to serve any person as a servant, slave or apprentice after he attained the age of 21.(10) The proviso was then attached, "unless they be bound by their own consent after they arrive at such age." In the New Mexican mind of 1850, the abolition of slavery as a political and anti-Texan device(11) was distinct from the local desire to maintain peonage and child labor.

The election of state officers reflected the political battle leading to the convention. Henry Connelly and Manual Alvarez were elected governor and lieutenant governor by large majorities. Connelly was allied with Houghton and Alvarez with Weightman, but both worked with the statehood men led by Calhoun.(12) William S. Messervy, formerly of Massachusetts and a prominent merchant, won election as representative to Congress on the Weightman ticket. The legislature elected Weightman to the Senate. The statehood supporters who pushed the issue received the spoils of office and entrenched their political interests in the state institutions. Their victory was short-lived as all hopes of statehood died with Zachary Taylor. Although the constitution failed and territorial government ensued, the experience did demonstrate the use of the constitutional convention as a political forum. This characteristic was evident in later conventions as delegates used the convention floors to further political aspirations.

In both Utah and New Mexico, statehood was a means for political gain pushed by the power structure of the region. The motivation of home rule existed for both areas, and the constitutions gave the framework for that operation--but political power was the prize. The opportunity to seize political power by controlling the legal system in a period of flux was the prime motive for statehood. The federal authority was nominal in Utah with the Mormon hierarchy in complete control while military government in New Mexico was complete. The recognition in New Mexico that civil government was imminent was common among the military and civilians alike. Statehood allowed local elections rather than carpetbag appointments. The constitutional conventions were dominated by the politicos, and their constitutions offered Congress a palatable continuity with other states. The failure of these movements was not due to a lack of domestic approbation, but resulted from national political opposition. These characteristics were similar to those of the final constitutional conventions. Later personnel was usually composed of the first-rank politicians and interest group leaders. The single distinction was that statehood was a more immediate reality for the delegates.

The political motivation was covert in terms of entreaties to Congress, while the home rule issue was the overt argument for statehood. Richard Hanson Weightman's communication to Congress in 1850 was representative of this home rule sentiment.(13) He complained to Congress of the harshness of the military rule, the Indian troubles, outlaws, and damage to private property in general. Here he implicitly argued that the residents of the area were best equipped by experience to handle domestic problems. Beyond the grounds of expediency, Weightman argued that statehood was a constitutional right derived specifically from the Constitution in general and the Northwest Ordinance in particular. The rights of American citizens included the right of self-government within a republican frame of government. The right of self-determination was paramount for the frontier American arguing for statehood.

Nevada and Colorado also held constitutional conventions in their periods of first settlement. Both areas were settled due to the mineral strikes made in the late 1850s. Both were nominally under the jurisdiction of a territorial government. The Utah territorial administration extended into Nevada's turbulent mining camps as did Kansas' into Colorado's. But the relative effectiveness of the two systems was great. Utah courts and administrative officials in the Carson Valley were extremely active while Kansas officials were absent. Colorado miners had relative independence of action and used local self-government based on the mining district in lieu of federal institutions. Yet both territories had recourse to constitutional conventions in these periods of sparse settlement and unsettled times.

The first Nevada convention was a reaction to Mormon rule within the territorial system. Nevada settlers found the Mormons in control of the Carson Valley with ambitions for further administrative control. There was an immediate confrontation between the Gentile miner-settler and the Mormon establishment. The Gentiles naturally objected to church control of secular affairs. More importantly, they objected to the Mormon control of the administration of justice in the area.(14) The Gentiles vehemently protested to Washington against the Mormon government that "so [mixed] together church and state that a man [could not] obtain justice in any of its courts." Stating their grievances, they significantly fell back on their constitutional rights: "The Constitution guarantees to us our rights and if we cannot obtain them by peaceable measures, we shall maintain them as our fathers did."(15) This sentiment, coupled with the emergence of a Gentile majority of 1859, led to a constitutional convention in that year. The recourse to the methods of their forefathers included a declaration of separation from Utah's tyranny and a constitution for their provisional government.(16)

The convention met and quickly produced fundamental law. The constitution called for the standard institutions of government, less a supreme court which was left to the discretion of the legislature. The document reflected a faith in the democratic process, a dislike of executive power, faith in the legislative body, and a dislike of corporations.(17) The convention then memorialized Congress to extend territorial status to Nevada to relieve it of the tyrannies of Utah. Sentiment for separation and federal territorial status was almost unanimous, but a minority protested the use of a constitutional convention as a vehicle of change. They felt that "the framing of a Constitution was an unwarranted assumption of power."(18) There was a clear distinction between the making and use of a constitution and the application for territorial status. The majority saw the constitution as a device for the establishment of de facto, non-Mormon government. The electorate agreed and ratified the convention's work.(19) Statehood does not appear to have been a popular issue at the time. Again, constitution making was a device to escape an onerous system of government. The Nevada pioneers wanted self-government but were not particularly concerned with the form so long as Mormons were excluded.

Statehood in Colorado dramatically failed at the same time. From the beginning it was clear that a majority of the first settlers envisaged themselves as making up a territory separate from Kansas or Nebraska.(20) Their efforts to secure territorial status failed, and in April 1859 a constitutional convention was called to write the fundamental law for the "State of Jefferson." The convention met in June and reconvened on August 1 to adopt the constitution. The people rejected the innocuous document a month later by a three-to-one vote, basically because of the perception that statehood was too expensive.(21) In October the more ambitious politicians met and wrote the organic act for the territory of Jefferson. This met with the miners' approval, and a government swiftly formed. The legislature took over the reigns of government in November and enacted a civil and criminal code.(22) It also organized a county and court system and petitioned Congress for territorial organization. Calling itself "territorial," government was in operation petitioning Congress for its blessing and funds. Statehood as a device had failed.

In contrast to the statehood campaigns in Utah and New Mexico, the failure of statehood in Colorado and the acceptance of constitutional provisional government in Nevada reflected differences in basic conditions. All were united in their desire for self-determination or, more historically phrased, popular sovereignty. Each territory in its turn made the argument, and convention delegates wrote their beliefs into fundamental law. Each sought to escape from an immediate threat and, in so doing, to gain something. Military rule in New Mexico was as real a threat to self-determination as Mormon probate courts were in Nevada. The imposition of the alien territorial system upon the saints of Utah was equally terrifying. Colorado miners wanted an end to lawlessness and uncertainty in the marketplace. Government could provide both through the enforcement of criminal law and mining regulations. In all cases, government attuned to the needs of the domestic populace was sought as a means to order. It also provided a means to political and economic gain that individuals voraciously sought. What separated the final means, statehood or territorial status, lay in the political and economic environment of the area concerned.

Statehood as an acceptable device developed in a society having an established population and at least the beginnings of sophisticated political organization. New Mexico's population was established, and the American and Mexican political factions had been in operation prior to military occupation. The United States' control provided the favorable political environment for a popular campaign for statehood. The established nature of the economy made statehood financially attainable.

Utah's political organization was a fact of saintly life and Utah economic development a spectacular achievement. The catalyst of federal interference in Mormon business spurred statehood plans.

These conditions did not, relatively speaking, exist in Nevada or Colorado. There, the populations were transient and the economies uncertain. Politics existed in a factional sense. The desire for government was strong, but the ability and will to have it pay its own way was lacking. Their definition of self-determination included the right of territorials to elect their own officials, to legislate on all issues affecting the territory, and generally to control their own destiny with the federal government picking up the tab. In each case, the government paid the bills, but restricted territorial popular sovereignty.

After initial failures to achieve statehood, some territories periodically held constitutional conventions and applied again to Congress. Utah repeated the ritual six more times before gaining admission. New Mexico held conventions in 1872 and 1890 before succeeding in 1910. Nevada, although becoming a state in 1864, wrote a total of three constitutions. Colorado wrote two more before joining the union in 1876. Arizona wrote a provisional constitution similar to Nevada's in 1860 as a device to gain home rule and territorial organization.(23) Statehood devotees met in Phoenix in 1891, wrote a constitution, and were rebuffed by Congress. The pattern was general where political organization was sufficient, and this provided a general heritage of constitution making for the territories. It provided not only a heritage, but also actual documents for constitutional conventions to draw upon in their deliberations.

These territorial constitutions reflected their times and situations. Utah and New Mexico wrote simple constitutions outlining the basic structure and duties of government in 1850. Nevada's 1859 constitution was of a similar mold. The legislature was given almost complete freedom to act.(24) There were few attempts to write specific legislation into the 1859 Nevada constitution.(25) Delegates borrowed constitutional language in whole or in part from other states.(26) The lack of specific legislation in the constitutions reflected the newness of the situation and the absence of developed problems.(27) It also reflected the political inability of special interests to gain specific concessions in the constitutions. As time passed and new conventions were held, convention delegates looked first to their own past and then to the experience of the region for guidance. In Utah, for example, the 1856 and 1862 constitutions were similar to their first.(28) The 1872 Utah constitution used the Nevada constitution of 1864 as reference.(29) The 1882 constitution was essentially the same as the 1872 document, and the 1887 convention used the 1882 constitution as a model.(30)

Similar practice can be found in the other territories. New Mexico looked to contemporary constitutions for guidance in 1872, but new features started to appear. Railroads were declared public highways, and there was a new awareness of the changing complexion of marketplace operations. The corporation received more convention consideration.(31) In the 1890s, territorial constitutions took on a "progressive character."(32) For example, in Arizona, the Phoenix constitution of 1891 evidenced a Jeffersonian concept of government, but also reflected current national and local problems. The sentiment against vested interests and monopolies was reflected in clauses that not only prevented wildcat corporation schemes, but also abolished all dormant and exclusive charters.(33) The female suffrage issue was partially confronted by allowing women to vote in school elections. The constitution also included a water rights clause favorable to irrigation companies. The progressive spirit was general in the document, but so too were concessions on suffrage and water rights. These issues would later plague Arizona delegates when they again convened in 1910.

Constitutional convention delegates had a long tradition of constitution making to draw upon when they convened in their respective territories. The tradition was one of borrowed provision and periodic innovation reflective of contemporary concerns. There was a tradition of political party and individual action precedent to, and within, constitutional conventions. Dynamic personalities made their presence felt from time to time. Statehood movements were initiated by individuals and factions. The stamp of a single man or group was often found on a provision or a whole constitution. Party, bloc, economic interest, and personality--all had a role in the making of Rocky Mountain constitutions.

# 2

# The Conventions and Their Delegates

In the Rocky Mountain constitutional conventions, personality, procedural maneuver, and rhetorical flourish often influenced the votes that ultimately determined the nature of the constitutions. The delegates to the conventions represented a cross-section of territorial interests. The relatively unsophisticated organization of many of the territorial political parties caused personality to play a significant role in delegate behavior.

The dominant delegates in each convention represented a variety of interests and territorial experiences. There were professional politicians serving a variety of interest groups. They came to the conventions seeking public office while performing their public duty. The economic interest groups served themselves in hopes of special constitutional concessions. Cattlemen, miners, farmers, and merchant-capitalists came to the conventions in varying strengths. Ethnic and religious interests also were present. Hispanics went to several conventions to represent their cultural interests. Mormons and the Mormon "problem" were significant in the Utah and Idaho conventions. A survey of the key figures and the interest groups in the constitution-making process affords an overview of the forces at work.

The western politician who polished his skills in the territorial period, used the constitutional convention as a campaign forum, and gained public office thereafter was a key figure in most conventions. His status as a party leader played a key role in marshaling votes. Moreover, his ability to assert his personality in a parliamentary context was important in breaking convention deadlock.

Although not a member of the 1864 Nevada convention, William Morris Stewart was representative of the tough western politician who gained national office. Stewart was a member of the 1863 convention that fashioned the document used as a model by the 1864 convention. He went to the U.S. Senate when Nevada became a state. In the Senate, Stewart was the author of crucial 1866 and 1872 mining legislation that became the 19th-century guideline for the industry and remains the basic law of the land today. The strong pro-mining record that Stewart established was carried on in the Nevada convention by Samuel A. Chapin and J. S. Crosman.(1)

William A. Clark of Montana was another pro-mining delegate who ultimately reached the Senate. Clark was a pioneer in the Montana copper industry and acquired a fortune from his mining, freighting, and mercantile enterprises. In the convention he was a leading spokesman for the mining interests of the western part of the state. Clark's political activity in later years brought a great deal of notoriety to him and the system of senatorial appointment in general. The blatant legislative jobbery conducted in Montana presented the country with the stark corruption of the system. This, of course, gave later progressive politicians ammunition for their reforms.(2)

Clarence D. Clark of Wyoming was prominent in Republican state and national politics. In the convention Clark was a spokesman for the western section of the state. When statehood arrived, he won election to Congress for two terms and later appointment to the Senate. Clark was among a great number of delegates to state conventions who continued their political careers on the national level.

Weldon Brinton Heyburn of Idaho also was prominent in state and national Republican politics. Heyburn was a lawyer with considerable practice before the federal courts before coming to Idaho in 1883. He was a delegate to several Republican national conventions and was elected to the U.S. Senate in 1902. In the Senate, Heyburn was a chief architect of the National Pure Food Act and chairman of the joint committee of Congress that codified federal law. In the convention, Heyburn brought his high level of legal talent to bear on technical matters of law.(3)

Other state politicians went from the convention to the statehouse. George W. P. Hunt of Arizona was a leader of the Progressive Party (Arizona Democratic variety) and its delegation in the convention. Hunt was a businessman of diverse interests. He was instrumental in the success of the Old Dominion Commercial Company, a pioneer mercantile firm in southern Arizona, and he published the Daily Globe. When the convention met, he became its president and was the spokesman for the Progressive party. With statehood, Hunt was Arizona's first governor and guided the legislative program that fulfilled some of the promises of the constitution.(4)

Other delegates had long records in territorial politics and service in various state posts. George Ainslie of Idaho, a Pike's Peak miner and lawyer who came to Idaho in 1862, entered actively into territorial politics. From 1869 to 1873, in addition to his legal practice, he edited the Idaho World, the only Democratic newspaper in the territory. Ainslie served in the legislature, on the county level, and as delegate to Congress. In the convention, Ainslie was a key figure on the Democratic side of the aisle. With statehood, Ainslie turned his talents to his legal practice and to the organization of transit and water companies in Boise. Many of the members of the conventions had long records of political activity and office holding. New Mexico's delegation was particularly heavy with major and minor politicos.(5)

State political parties were represented by most of their abler members. The Santa Fe Ring was well represented in the New Mexico convention. Charles A. Spiess, Albert Fall of Teapot Dome fame, and Thomas Benton Catron kept their delegation under a tight rein. Charles A. Spiess, "the Black Eagle of San Miguel County," was elected president of the convention. He was a law partner of Catron and a territorial legislator. Thomas Benton Catron was the leader of the Santa Fe Ring. Albert Fall was a long-time political intriguer in the territory. These men represented the close-knit political organization that ran territorial politics, and they came to convention to ensure their continuance in power. When statehood was achieved, both Catron and Fall became U.S. senators. The political control exercised by these men in the convention assured a Republican constitution for New Mexico.

The Mormons exercised similar control in Utah with a preponderance of voting strength and the hierarchy's programs ably supported by George M. Cannon. Cannon was a native of Utah, born in 1861, and worked his way up through the Mormon economic and political system. He was extremely popular with the Mormon Republicans and was their floor leader.(6) Cannon was aided at times by Brigham Roberts, a Mormon Democrat. Roberts was a gifted orator and writer and was a member of the First Council of the Seventy of the Church. With statehood, Roberts was elected to Congress, but was refused his seat because of a previous conviction on a polygamy charge. Robert's case touched off the Reed Smoot investigation by Congress and the concurrent national crusade against the church. The Mormons had numerous other spokesmen in the convention. Many, like Apostle John Henry Smith, already had power as leaders in the church.(7)

For many the convention was another platform from which to voice their campaign oratory. It was also a political arena in which old antagonisms were fought again. Party control in a parliamentary situation was an important function of the politicos who came to make fundamental law. Even more than political philosophy, these same men oftentimes represented economic interests. The parties themselves were usually representative of the interest bargains that were struck in territorial politics.

The cattlemen were well represented in several conventions. Wyoming's convention had a strong cattlemen's delegation. DeForest Richards, who held extensive livestock and mercantile interests around Douglas, was one of cattlemen's spokesmen and was later governor of the state. Hubert E. Teschemacher was educated at Harvard University and came to Wyoming in 1879. He accumulated large cattle holdings, was active in the Wyoming Stock Growers' Association, and was a territorial legislator. Robert C. Butler and his brother held range land that extended across two counties in southern Wyoming. Richards, Teschemacher, Butler, and others used their votes to aid the cattle interests of their state.(8) The cattlemen used bloc voting to achieve their policy goals in the convention.

The range-cattle industry was dominant in six Montana counties. Delegations there worked constantly to offset the influence of the mining counties in the convention. They were joined by other rancher delegates in the debates. Conrad Kohrs was one of the territory's earliest cattlemen. Kohrs helped form the Montana Stock Growers' Association and was a territorial legislator. Edward Cardwell, S. S. Hobson, Charles H. Loud, Samuel L. Mitchell, Alfred Myers, and William R. Ramsdell were other stock growers at the convention. Together they voted their first interest... cattle.(9) The Montana cattlemen joined together on economic issues related to their interest, but, of equal importance, they were part of a sectional bloc opposed to Western Montana miners' aspirations.

Miners generally were well represented in the conventions. The miners who went to the conventions were usually mine owners or supervisory personnel. The mine laborer was not influential in convention deliberations although occasionally present. During the period 1850-1912, the region experienced a fundamental transformation in the mining industry. The strikes and rushes quickly ended and were replaced by corporate organization, structured labor systems, and economic and human dignity struggles. Exotic tales of gold and silver and fortunes won and lost were replaced by reports of copper and coal production. Although the transitions were dramatic, mining interests, both corporate and labor, found the constitutional convention an important vehicle. William A. Clark of Montana was the leader of the corporate mining faction in convention. Nevada's delegation was salted with miners representing both the San Francisco and the local interests. Samuel A. Chapin, J. S. Crosman, W. W. Belden, Israel Crawford, and E. F. Dunn ably led this faction against a strong "cow-county" group. Idaho's convention had a strong miners' delegation as did Colorado's in an earlier period.(10) The Rocky Mountain territories owed much of their economic growth to the mines, and in each convention at least a nominal group of miners were present.

Sheep ranching was well represented in the Arizona and New Mexico conventions. The range-cattle industry had passed from the western scene with the winter of 1887, and sheep ranching had made steady progress in the Southwest for decades. In the Arizona convention, Charles C. Hutchinson was representative of frontier sheepmen. A Dartmouth College graduate, he came to Arizona in the 1880s and organized the Grand Canyon Sheep Company, the Hutchinson Sheep Company, and numerous other similar sheep and cattle companies that he used to develop a fortune. Hutchinson was a pioneer in breeding techniques that produced a better market lamb. Unlike many of his counterparts in the convention, he was not an office seeker. His election to the convention was honorary and a vote of confidence in his ability to represent the sheep interest. Solomon Luna of New Mexico similarly abstained from taking major political office to maintain his reign as "sheep king" of New Mexico. Luna's activities were extremely varied in territorial New Mexico, being a vice president of the First National Bank of Albuquerque and on the board of an insurance company. Luna also had vast real estate interests unrelated to his huge sheep holdings. He was a staunch Republican and protected his deep Hispanic interest in the convention. Both

Hutchinson and Luna held sheep and voted that interest, but their politics went beyond economics. Luna was the nominal leader of the Hispanic delegation to the New Mexico convention and used his influence to offset the power of the Anglos and the Santa Fe Ring.(11)

Hispanics constituted were significant factions in several conventions. Colorado, Arizona, and New Mexico had appreciable Hispanic populations when the gringos arrived. In the territorial periods, Hispanics struggled to maintain their political and economic control, but it gradually slipped away under an Anglo-Saxon system of government. A few of their number were politically aware enough to take advantage of the system and work within it to develop political power. It was this upwardly mobile Hispanic who represented the faction in the respective constitutional conventions. For example, Casimiro Barela came to Colorado in 1867, established extensive ranch holdings, and won election to the territorial assembly. Barela developed power within the legislature, being returned continually during statehood, and was elected president pro tem of the senate in 1894. He used his forceful character and superb English to work well both with his Anglo peers and with his constituents. Carlos C. Jacome gave the Hispanics their token representative in the Arizona convention. Jacome was a successful Tucson merchant, but he was in the Republican minority. The Hispanic with the greatest power was Solomon Luna. The New Mexico convention had 32 Hispanic and 68 Anglo delegates; except for Luna, this minority power was compromised by the established power of the Santa Fe Ring.(12) Like other minorities in the convention, Luna had limited power. Hispanics played a minor, but continuing, part in the making of Rocky Mountain constitutions.

Various professions were present in most constitutional conventions. Doctors and lawyers were the most numerous. Lawyers comprised one-fourth to one-third of the total membership of the conventions excepting Utah's, in which only 15 of the 107 delegates were members of the bar. Newspapermen also were in attendance in prominent positions. George W. P. Hunt of Arizona and George Ainslie of Idaho were powerful editors of prominent state papers. Wilbur F. Stone was editor of two Colorado newspapers. Stone was a classics and law graduate of Indiana State University and a practicing lawyer in Indiana before coming to Colorado in 1859. He was elected to the legislature and was a district attorney before the convention. Stone also had a long public service record on charitable and educational boards in Denver. Stone's colleague, Henry P. H. Bromwell, had a publishing and public service record. Bromwell published the _Age of Steam and Fire_ in Illinois from 1853 to 1856. Elected to Congress from Illinois, he served from 1865 to 1869. He was a delegate to the Illinois constitutional convention of 1869 and then moved to Denver in 1870. Bromwell quickly involved himself in politics and won a seat on the territorial council. In 1874 he ran unsuccessfully for delegate to Congress, but in 1875 he won election to the constitutional convention. There he led the "granger" faction and introduced numerous measures gleaned from his Illinois experience.(13) The editor delegates were often experienced politicians and superb propagandists for their views. In and out of conventions they played important roles in molding opinion.

Lawyers were the most numerous professional in each of the conventions. Law was a nominal occupation of many pioneers; not surprisingly, many lawyers were also miners, ranchers, merchants, and the like. The biographies of men like William Stewart of Nevada or George Ainslie of Idaho bear out this occupational diversity. Many of the delegates from the bar were also jurists at one time or another. For example, John T. Morgan of Idaho and Asbury B. Conaway of Wyoming were territorial supreme court justices when their conventions met. This fusion of economic pursuits and the varying levels of professional proficiency made the conventions a forum for legal as well as political debates. The lawyers debated the finer points of law; in general, they also were the spokesmen for varying economic interests. Their profession required that they be articulate, and this ability was obvious in convention debates. Importantly, their function as theorists for hard interest politics helped develop conceptual lines for compromise. Equally, their ability to dispassionately argue a constituency's wishes allowed them tactically to become the devil's advocate.

All of these economic, political, and cultural interest groups operated in the parliamentary confines of the constitutional convention. How they interacted to produce fundamental law was revealed in their debates, their votes, and the constitutions they produced. The debates are a matter of public record except in New Mexico where lawmakers decided that published discussion was too expensive or revealing. Colorado's record is largely procedural, but the newspapers provided some material from the convention floors. Arizona's convention debates still languish in manuscript awaiting the editor's pen and a legislative appropriation. The votes of all the conventions are available in varying forms. The roll call vote was the most positive record of delegate attitude, but the show of unnamed hands and the voice vote were often tools of convenience and anonymity. This record gives context and meaning to their deliberations.

The voting behavior of delegates can be described quantitatively through the use of a few simple devices and the computer.(14) One technique of identifying groups of delegates that act in concert is cluster bloc analysis.(15) If we record the number of times that each delegate votes with every other delegate, we can find groups of like-minded individuals by fitting the pair-agreement scores into a matrix with the highest agreements in the upper left corner. Delegate groups derived by this process are called cluster blocs. The Guttman scaleogram program is another technique of description. It deals with association among delegates in a different way. This variety of scaling procedure isolates a roll call in which a small group of delegates vote against the rest of the members and then adds to this roll call others in which the members of the small group are in agreement but are joined, roll call by roll call, by other delegates who vote with the original minority on subsequent votes. Because they could find few who shared their opinion on the original roll call, the members of the initial small group are assumed to have held an extreme or radical position on a particular subject. The added roll calls express increasingly moderate views on the same area of controversy, until the last roll call added may contain perhaps only a small group in opposition to the original minority--a group whose members are utterly opposed to any concession whatsoever on the subject at issue. Roll calls arranged in this way, therefore, form a scale that ranks delegates according to their attitude on a particular problem.

Both techniques have limitations. The cluster bloc analysis may not reveal the shifting patterns of agreement among delegates over time and gives no hint of the relative extremeness in attitude of group members in comparison with the positions taken by members of other groups. It may require the researcher to make arbitrary decisions concerning the outer limits of the clusters. The scaleogram masks but does not completely destroy temporal relationships, does not isolate the members of self-conscious groups, and discards roll calls that will not scale. Also involved in scaling is the assumption that delegates will vote for measures that in their minds represent only half-a-loaf because half is, after all, better than none. Not all delegates were so logical; some, in frustration, voted against measures because they deemed them too weak. This behavior was apparent in mining taxation and water rights law votes in some conventions. But, in general, the principle holds. Several Nevada miner delegates verbalized the feeling in the final vote on the taxation article. Compromise was a dominant feature of constitutional issues that evenly divided a convention. In sum, neither the cluster bloc technique nor the Guttman scale is perfect or all-revealing; however, if used together in conjunction with the debates and the tactics of parliamentary procedures, these methods can reveal the constituent factors that produced Rocky Mountain constitutions.

In addition to inherent mechanical limitations of the two programs, the sources impose an additional limitation on the use of quantification. New Mexico's convention roll calls reveal the obvious pattern of Republican versus Democrat, with the Santa Fe Ring using the Republican caucus as a vehicle for writing the constitution and maintaining uniform voting strength. As a result, quantification would only reveal the obvious: a Republican constitution or, as the Democrats put it, "a gang-made constitution." Thus New Mexico's roll call votes were not analyzed by computer. Another problem of a similar nature presented itself in other conventions. The votes that determined the structure of a section or article often were not recorded as roll calls. There was a definite limitation on the number of roll calls available. On the other hand, some roll calls were excluded as they contained no substantive issues and revealed a straight party line vote. In other conventions, the same issue produced identical voting patterns the inclusion of which would only reinforce that single pattern. Even with these limitations, the use of the computer can graphically delineate the patterns that determined the law and aid the historian in describing the processes that produced the respective constitutions.

Before dealing with specific issues as they came before the respective conventions, a general description of the voting patterns is useful as background for the behavior of delegates in specific areas of constitution making. This generalized view of delegate behavior is constructed of roll calls on five issues with varying numbers of roll call votes within each. These same votes were used for Guttman and cluster bloc analysis. The issues for each convention vary because of availability and the procedural desire of delegates to avoid a roll call on issues in certain conventions.

The Nevada delegates divided along economic and geographical lines. In general, the miners voted together against the cow-county delegates. Samuel A. Chapin, a Storey County miner, led the radical miners, and the cow-county delegates followed the lead of Albert T. Hawley, a Douglas County attorney. The cow-county delegation received support from a Carson City group led by John H. Kinkead, a Carson City merchant and member of both the 1863 and 1864 conventions. John A. Collins, a Storey County miner, led the moderates and often was instrumental in securing compromise. Political party affiliations were largely meaningless in 1864 because all members were "unionists."(16)

Colorado's convention was dominated by Republican voting power as evidenced by the dispensation of patronage offices in the convention, but the party membership was divided by Henry P. H. Bromwell who led a "granger faction." The Republicans could afford the division with a 24-to-15 voting edge, but the state was split on sectional lines between the English-speaking North and Spanish-speaking South. Bromwell led a group of from six to nine stalwarts in the convention. These men proposed the radical granger approach to constitution making and gave the Democrats under George E. Pease a good target for criticism. Pease was a Yale lawyer and forceful personality in the convention. There was also a generation gap in politics. Wilbur F. Stone, Henry C. Thatcher, Casimiro Barela, and LaFayette Head were the only members of the old guard in the convention. A younger generation of politicians was numerically dominant in the convention. The sectional split on cultural grounds also was exacerbated by an urban-rural split that was apparent in revenue and irrigation matters. The Denver delegates were isolated by a coalition of farmers and ranchers. These aforementioned cleavages in the voting attitudes worked within a general context of Republican grangers at one extreme and Pease Democrats at the other extremity. The compromises that made the constitution possible were made by the moderate Republicans who voted between the extremes.(17)

Wyoming's constitutional convention voting patterns reflected much of her political history. An early sectional split was evident in Wyoming politics with Laramie and Albany counties in the populous southeast battling the western counties of Carbon, Sweetwater, and Uinta. The northern counties all worked against these southern ones and in the convention voted with the western delegates to secure favorable apportionment and tax provisions. Wyoming politics also was based on personalities rather than ideology, and this too was evident in the convention. Cluster blocs and Guttman analysis reveal no dominant role of political parties. Rather factions revolved around dominant personalities like Hubert Teschemacher or around sectional interests. Uinta and Sweetwater delegates had a high degree of cohesion against the Laramie and Albany County votes.(18)

Montana's convention was similarly split. William A. Clark led a group of miners and western county delegates, and Conrad Kohrs headed the cattlemen's faction. Party was not an important factor in voting behavior as each group was evenly divided politically. Importantly, a third group existed within the convention that often decided the nature of the constitution. Martin Maginnis led a center coalition of miners, laborers, and minor capitalists. This group often managed to tip the balance for the eastern interests in the convention. Maginnis had been territorial delegate since 1873 and was a powerful figure in the Democratic party.(19)

The Idaho delegates voted along economics interest lines with party affiliation being personally oriented. Weldon B. Heyburn led the Republican side of the non-miner delegation and was joined by George Ainslie on the Democratic side of the aisle. Former chief justice of the territorial supreme court John T. Morgan and William Horace Claggett, a Shoshone County lawyer, led the miners in the convention. They were both Republicans, but received bipartisan support from mining counties. Political factions formed around personalities, or lacking a dominant figure in a particular delegation, county delegations voted their economic interest.(20) Generally, the Republicans voted as a block as did the Democrats; however, the cohesion of the Democrats was comparatively low.

The Utah convention was fragmented by religion, politics, economics, and sectionalism. There was the obvious Mormon-Gentile conflict, but the Gentiles wisely joined with political and economic interest factions to avoid impotent isolation in the convention. The political split was decreed by the hierarchy in 1890 to facilitate federal approval of Utah's government. Supposedly this took the onus of religion out of state politics. In the convention political blocs were very evident and far from unified. Rather they split on an economic and sectional basis following a particular leader. As with other conventions, political faction followed personality. The major cleavage in the convention was between the agricultural and the mining interests. Joel Ricks, a Sevier County railroad agent, was often spokesman for the agrarian point of view, but the group also tended to be liberal. One of its number, Theodore Brandley, was the single advocate for the referendum in the convention. William F. James, a Salt Lake City miner, led the other end of the spectrum. This group was supported by numerous "capitalists" and mining county delegates. Between these two extremes, the political factions operated. Most closely associated with the Ricks faction was a group of 15 Republicans led by Dennis Eichnor, a Salt Lake City attorney. Eichnor, a Gentile, was joined by six others. Brigham Roberts was spokesman for a small group of Democrats who also voted along the liberal line.

The determinative voting power in the Utah convention was with the Mormon hierarchy. George Cannon marshaled Mormon Republicans when needed in conjunction with William Creer's Democrats. Together they had 40 percent of the convention. Both men were dependable Mormons and orators. Their attitudinal voting behavior varied from the moderate to the conservative side of most issues. The key to the passage of an issue often depended upon the ability of these men to draw over other factions.(21)

Democrats dominated the Arizona convention, but the party was fragmented. George W. P. Hunt led the Progressives, but unity was not a feature of the Democratic majority. Conservatives, led by the prosperous rancher Wilfred T. Webb, voted a firm ideological line. Webb later worked against Hunt in a governor's race. The middle ground was occupied by a merchant-capitalist, Morris Goldwater. A man with a successful Phoenix mercantile establishment behind him, Goldwater was active in territorial politics. He was mayor of Prescott and served as a territorial legislator. Goldwater's moderate faction became the key to progressive success as its votes swung many issues. It was among these factions that the form of fundamental law was fought as the Republicans could muster only 11 votes.(22)

Republicans controlled the New Mexico convention. The Santa Fe Ring within the Republican delegation used the caucus system to quiet insurgents. The Democrats were isolated in the convention and had little practical impact. When the document was completed, many Democrats worked to have it defeated at the polls charging that it was "gang-made" and a "gold-brick."

These general voting patterns were predominant on most convention issues with certain controversial issues altering patterns. Voting alignments only provide a generalized background for the activities of the conventions as procedure, personality, and overall tactics played a most important part in making Rocky Mountain constitutions.

Finally, the fact that these eight constitutional conventions made fundamental law over a half century creates a conceptual problem of time and sequence. Nevada's delegates met during the Civil War amid a Republican ascendancy. Colorado, Idaho, Montana, and Wyoming delegates felt the Populist press for human rights as well as constituent interests. Arizona's Progressives rode the tide of reform into their convention. But New Mexico's convention did not flow with the current politics of progressivism. Rather New Mexico's convention reflected the entrenched interest politics that developed with celestial certainty over the decades. So too Utah's convention was more a part of its peculiar heritage than the national political scene. The conventions were united by many factors, but not all by the national drift of the times. Some conventions followed and others led on issues like female suffrage. The periods of debate as well as the factions are matters for careful scrutiny although not always susceptible to easy categorization.

# 3

# A Rocky Mountain Bill of Rights

When the constitutional convention delegates assembled to write their respective bills of rights, they drew upon a tradition older than the Constitution, made or attempted reforms reflective of the times, and introduced new fundamental rights peculiar to their environment. Congress created a tradition of enumerating the fundamental rights of citizens in the Northwest Ordinance. This enumeration was continued in subsequent territorial organic acts. Previous state and federal experience foretold a multitude of proposals and a melting of issues into fundamental concepts. The respective periods of authorship also offered specific proposals. The late 19th century was a period of growing agitation over the administration of justice. Many assailed the grand and petit juries as institutional devices. Criminal law reform was ongoing. Delegates picked up these issues and debated them hotly. Their resolution usually reflected the temper of the particular convention and more generally of the times. Constitution makers also proposed new rights. Delegates introduced the right to water or, more precisely stated, the right of private eminent domain as a right of necessity on the arid frontier. The bill of rights for the conventions was the first battleground for the issues of tradition and innovation and for the nature of the constitution itself.

The agreed-upon axioms of fundamental rights as guaranteed in the Constitution and the territorial organic acts stimulated little debate. The conventions accepted the free exercise of religion, speech, assembly, press, and petition. Delegates generally included the right to keep and bear arms although the militia often received a separate article. Fourth and Fifth Amendment freedoms won inclusion and elaboration as did those relating to criminal prosecutions, procedures, and trials. In general, these fundamental concepts received attention only in terms of an interpretative gloss. In the Wyoming convention, delegate Henry G. Hay, a cattleman and later state treasurer, offered an amendment to the bill of rights article providing for a strict construction. Delegate George C. Smith, a Rawlins attorney, quickly pointed out that the enumerated rights should be given a liberal reading "as intended." Hay immediately withdrew his amendment.(1) A liberal construction and a complete enumeration of rights were prevalent features of the Rocky Mountain bills of rights.

An exception to this general trend of concern was the matter of religion. Not religion in general, but Mormonism in particular, was the issue laced into the consideration of liberty of conscience. Delegates debated the inclusion of religious tests, the abolition of polygamy, and the place of the Bible. The Idaho constitution was unique in its provisions relating to religion. Delegates deliberately included anti-Mormon clauses because of strong antagonisms dating back to 1872, an anti-Mormon Republican majority in the convention, and a firm belief that the delegates had to "deal" with the "Mormon problem."(2) The newspapers railed at the delegates, continually reminding them of their obligation to "crush out its illegal practices with the strong arm of the law."(3) The convention responded with a gloss on the freedom of religion not "justify[ing] polygamy," disfranchisement, and non-sectarian school instruction.(4) Some delegates wanted Bible readings in the schools to promote morality; others quickly responded with visions of a Mormon takeover and Catholic, Jewish, and Protestant squabbling over which version of the Bible to use.(5) To the distress of many outside the convention, the measure lost.(6) In general, religious toleration was a good concept as long as Mormons were excluded. This attitude was prevalent in Idaho and the nation. By the turn of the century the religious storm passed, and Mormons joined the Idaho political community.

In this same period of relative sufferance, Utah held its convention and pondered the meaning of religious toleration. The Mormon majority offered a lengthy section that completely covered the field, even guaranteeing that no church would dominate the state.(7) Unfortunately, regarding a religious test for voting, the author of the section also included property qualifications that stimulated lengthy debate. Charles S. Varian, a Gentile and former U.S. attorney who prosecuted polygamous Mormons, reminded the convention that only "necessary" restrictions be placed in the constitution.(8) J. F. Chidester, a Mormon attorney, agreed, observing that "if we continue to adopt such measures as this we will have the whole Constitution in our bill of rights."(9) This suffrage issue soon melted into a discussion of the taxation of church property over the protests of those who said the issue was a matter of taxation and not of fundamental right.(10) Each delegate tried to outdo the other in establishing the absolute separation of church and state in Utah. This cluttered the document with needless phrases, but the delegates hoped it would satisfy a hostile Congress. Religious toleration as a concept was current, but delegates lost their focus in an effort to please the readers of their document in Washington. Utah's convention best illustrated the self-conscious effort to write fundamental law that would not antagonize a Congress suspicious of its goals. As we will see, Arizona's convention delegates threw caution to the wind with its recall provisions knowing Washington to be antagonistic.

The convention discussions over the contents of respective bills of rights illustrated variances in delegate concepts of the document that they were constructing and their roles. The fundamental rights were borrowed from a century of American history and practice. If the meaning of traditional American fundamental rights was in conflict with local experience, then the constitution reflected a delegate awareness and largely negative response. Mormonism, or more particularly polygamy, was not to be part of constitutional law if it posed an actual threat. Idaho delegates reacted with extreme negativism to the "Mormon problem." Utah delegates, being predominantly Mormon, reacted with a tempered negativism to please Congress. Both conventions operated in a national temper of anti-Mormonism,(11) and each reacted to peculiar local circumstances. By 1910 the "Mormon problem" had faded, and religious toleration sections contained only vague references to it.(12) Delegate action on this issue followed conservative American tradition and was responsive to community interests. Temperance for Utah was as politically expedient as was extremism in Idaho. Each reflected a dominant interest of its respective area and constituency. Constitutionalism also served as a conservative brake. Many found the inclusion of multitudinous issues in the bill of rights repugnant, but delegates' desires to satisfy their constituency and fulfill a regional or interest need often overcame this objection.

The inclusion of new "rights" and the reform of older ones illustrated the working atmosphere of the conventions. Jury reform was an issue of the times and a nagging problem in the mining and irrigation areas because of prolonged litigation. Reform took various shapes. Convention delegates modified or abolished the grand jury, provided for non-unanimous civil jury verdicts, and debated criminal jury verdicts. Delegates questioned both substantive and procedural law. The constitutional products were conservative and reflected a dominant concern for economics. Some conventions revised civil verdicts so that hung juries could not stand in the way of market processes. The market and more particularly the peculiar economics of the region gave birth to new "rights." Eminent domain powers appeared among the fundamental rights of citizens. Again, the delegates worked with prevalent community opinion for definite marketplace objectives. The changes were made possible because a majority in each convention was able to act on the issues. Activists used the territorial experience as a compelling argument for including new rights in bills of rights.

The reform or abolition of the grand jury as a means of instituting criminal prosecutions reflected a growing dissatisfaction with institutional process of the territorial period. Too often the delegates had seen the grand jury being used as an inquisitorial tool of an economic or political interest group. The delegate concern about this issue largely reflected the times of conventions or the nature of political or interest control of the convention. Nevada, with little experience, a tendency to borrow, and no sense of urgency, retained the grand jury system in 1864.(13) New Mexico, operating amid urgent political demands for abolition, also retained the system.(14) Apathy and the inertia of tradition in Nevada and the massive, conservative control of the Santa Fe Ring in New Mexico produced similar results. These factors worked against reform in the other conventions resulting in half-a-loaf compromises. Colorado delegates limited the grand jury to 12 men, required nine votes for an indictment, and provided that the legislature could abolish or regulate the institution.(15) Where abolition proved politically impossible, the initiative was turned over to the legislature or the institution was constitutionally regulated.(16)

The Montana experience was representative of the course of constitutional debates and the force of issues involved. Delegates debated issues in the context of public discussions. Abolitionists saw the grand jury as "cumbersome, obsolete, and expensive" and observed that "when the reason for...an institution [had] passed away, the...institution should go with it."(17) Conservatives saw abolition as "a hazardous experiment" and characterized the grand jury as the common man's hedge against political influence in the criminal justice system.(18) The opposition refuted the allegations of utility with accusations of bribery, uneducated deliberations, and general obsolescence.(19) The charges of corruption and characterizations were similar on both sides of the argument. The central issues were who was to control the process and what procedural advantages would be derived for the criminally accused.

The convention delegates debated the issue along the pattern existent in the public at large. Political liberals and conservatives alike damned the institution as "inquisitorial," "a relic of the dark ages," and "a black spot and a disgrace upon the escutcheon of our country."(20) Institutional conservatives reminded the convention of the grand jury's utility as a "check" against "time serving district attorneys."(21) Moderates admitted the force of the arguments on both sides; being reluctant to abolish the grand jury, they advocated compromise solutions.(22) The compromise passed in a form allowing both information and indictment, a limited grand jury, and the calling of a grand jury by the district judge. Prosecution by information came only after "examination and conviction by a magistrate." The Helena Daily Herald commented that this "reduced if not removed" the "evils of the grand jury system."(23)

The relative benefits such revision provided to the criminally accused were amplified in the Arizona convention of 1910. The information provided the accused with the elements of the crime he was accused of and a hearing before a magistrate, forcing the prosecutor to display enough evidence to establish probable cause to believe that the accused had committed a crime. The grand jury met in secret, and the accused had little idea of the evidence against him. The next step came in Arizona: elevating the preliminary hearing to constitutional status. Progressives flocked to the aid of the proposal calling it a "protective law."(24) The proposal became part of the bill of rights, but was limited to information prosecutions for felonies.(25) The delegates then debated the related problem of technical errors in criminal cases.

Frontiersmen found technical errors thwarting substantial justice repugnant in the territorial period. Delegates brought that atmosphere to the convention and resolved it in specific terms. The Progressives offered a section to the judiciary act that stated that no criminal case could be reversed because of technical error where substantial justice had been done. Goldwater Democrats, more conservative in philosophy, led by M. G. Cunniff, a Yavapai County mine operator, joined in support, calling the measure "a protection for the public and...the accused man." The Democrats, both Progressive and conservative, agreed that this measure would promote speedy trials and secure justice.(26) As such, it became constitutional law.(27) This proposition became law because of the evil that had been previously experienced. The Democrats who held the votes agreed on the issue, and the solution was not considered radical.

When a proposal that confessions illegally extorted be inadmissible as evidence hit the convention floor, the factors needed to secure reform dissolved. James E. Crutchfield, a Maricopa County minister and spokesman for the Hunt Progressives, proposed that the the third degree be abolished in Arizona. He characterized the proposal as one of "the fundamental principles connected with the rights and liberties of the human race." Extorting confessions from prisoners under the influence of mental anguish was a rank injustice, he continued. A. C. Baker, also a Maricopa County Progressive, denounced the proposal as "absolutely wild and crazy." He then asked the rhetorical question: "Do you intend in this constitutional convention to array yourselves on the side of criminals; do you intend to put the State of Arizona on the line protecting criminals?"(28) The Hunt Progressives were split; the issue was not immediate enough and far too radical. It lost and had to wait half a century before a man named Miranda came before the national bar of justice and made it national constitutional law.

In considering the institutions of the criminal process and the rights of the accused, the convention delegates reflected their times and conservative nature. The grand jury generally survived, but reform was instituted by way of prosecution by information and the use of the preliminary hearing. The structure of the system changed to facilitate current concepts of criminal justice. The system had to be open. Delegates found the secrecy of the grand jury repugnant and minimized it by providing an alternative route for the criminal process to take. This preserved the institution but allowed the process to bypass it. Such a compromise was conservative of institutional tradition as it evinced a desire to expand the limits of personal liberties. The limit to this desire for greater equity or justice in the system was reached when delegates sensed inordinate innovation. A "Miranda warning" in 1910 would have astounded the nation as it did Arizona delegates.

This spirit of conserving the institutional form while altering procedure was also evident in the convention debates on civil jury verdicts. Public expectation of reform was prevalent, and delegates drew heavily on the public rhetoric and discontent with hung juries.(29) Mining and water rights litigation constituted the bulk of judicial business in the late 19th century, and the hung jury tied up economic progress by increasing the costs of justice. More important, the practical fact of stagnating resources cost the states money in lost wages and underdeveloped wealth. Delegates used the rhetoric of economy as a device to stimulate support for eliminating the unanimous verdict on a superficial level. The underlying interest in stimulating economic growth gave this issue vitality. The constitutional convention delegates responded positively to popular demands for change and their own parochial concepts of aiding their respective economies.

The origins of the three-fourths civil jury verdict in the region was Nevada's 1864 constitutional provision.(30) The delegates recognized their peculiar environmental situation, their specific need for a three-fourths verdict provision, and its experimental nature.(31) Advocates argued that, although the proposal was experimental, Nevada was "the very country to try it in."(32) The environment required new procedures. Practical experience of "interests of enormous magnitude" being involved in mining cases worth millions required a speedy and just system of resolution. One delegate found precedent in Scottish law, but the majority found economic necessity a better rationale. Over the cow-county protests of improper and experimental legislating in the constitution, the three-fourths civil jury verdict became law.(33)

The convention delegates looked to their regional experience for guidance on this question. William H. Claggett, leader of the reform in Idaho, directly cited the Nevada experience in advocating the three-fourths verdict proposal. He also noted California's and Montana's acceptance of the proposal.(34) Again over the protests of continuity, common-law tradition, and justice, the advocates used economy and pragmatism arguments to win approval.(35) The Montana Bar Association gave its pre-convention blessing based on the California experience with a similar proposal. Delegates readily approved the civil side verdict proposal, but attempts to have the same apply to criminal cases muddied the waters. The bulk of mining business and the millions involved easily persuaded Montana delegates.(36) Utah delegates, hypersensitive about innovation, saw precedent in Wyoming's provision so that they "would not be the first to break the established order."(37) Once over this hump, Utah delegates readily agreed that justice was best at the least expense to the taxpayers. The three-fourths verdict was a cost-cutting expedient for a new state in their minds.(38) Regional agreement on the expedient and inexpensive nature of the reform won it rapid approval. Economic motivations were primary for the states due to their previous experience with prolonged litigation. Reform as such was a device delegates thought would aid economic development in a peculiar regional environment.

Jury reform that altered fundamental rights for economic reasons was paralleled by the growing sentiment for a new fundamental right: private eminent domain. Private eminent domain rights originated in territorial law based on the peculiar economic necessity of the region. Local mining district regulations had allowed rights of way for tailings and water ditches. Irrigation law had recognized the right to construct ditches across another's property. Territorial law gave force to custom; with increased usage of water, government began to regulate. Constitutional convention delegates drew upon this tradition and, where mining and irrigation company interests were strongest, pushed for additional power. Territorial law had declared certain acts of taking private property to be a public use. What constituted a public use was the first issue extremists tried to strain beyond traditional bounds. Then delegates debated the taking of private property for a private use. All recognized that provision for private eminent domain was necessary in the arid West, but most disagreed on the terms of that provision. In final form delegates extended the right, satisfying their concepts of necessity and fundamental law.

The contours of the debates spanned the issues involved, reflected the times, and evidenced the strength of interests in the conventions. Eminent domain was the power of the sovereign government to appropriate real property for a public use or for the general welfare. When such property was taken, the owner was entitled to just compensation. Rocky Mountain convention delegates recognized this scope and the additional necessity of conferring such powers upon private persons for ways of necessity. These included water ditches, reservoirs, ways for tailing, and the like. Without such extraordinary powers, mining and irrigation were impossible. The question of balancing this essentially market-oriented power against the vested interest in private property grated on delegate sensibilities. To insure a balance, some conventions required that just compensation be rendered before the taking. Others enumerated what they considered a public use in detail to prevent abusive use. In general, all were willing to extend this custom to constitutional sanctity based on their belief in its economic necessity and distrust of legislative process.

Nevada closely followed the federal model on the issue and expanded the interpretation of just compensation. As a matter of course, the delegates agreed that private property could not be taken without just compensation, but the time of payment presented a problem. Proponents had the best of the issue as only a feeble minority argued against it. Albert T. Hawley, cow-county delegation spokesman, offered an amendment that would have given specific power to the legislature to define a public use. Miners who controlled the convention immediately defeated the proposal, and the convention adopted a broad section that specified that compensation be rendered before the taking.(39) The compensation section was conservative in the light of further developments; as the issue was one among miners rather than between farmers and miners, delegates were jealous of their particular interests. Specificity was not necessary where dominant mining interests controlled and assumed the operation of law mainly among miners.

Colorado's experience was similar, but the whole convention atmosphere was different. Colorado stood at a crossroads in economic history as the age of enterprise was flexing its muscles, conveying its promises, yet alienating certain segments of society. Market processes had to be promoted, but, as the balance of bargaining power shifted away from the individual, delegates recognized that rampant capitalism needed limits. The Granger element, led by H. P. H. Bromwell, verbalized this need for restraint and succeeded in part. In broad terms the convention forbade the taking of private property for private use, then listed numerous exceptions. Private ways of necessity, reservoirs, drains, flumes, and ditches found exception if for agricultural, mining, milling, domestic, or sanitary purposes. The extensive exceptions and practical realities of their application limited the broad prohibition. Conceding the necessity of the provision, the delegates balanced the right by having the damages ascertained by a board of commissioners of three or more freeholders, or a jury. Until the damages were paid, the property could not be "needlessly" disturbed. Questions of "public use" were specifically delegated to the judiciary "without regard to any legislative assertion."(40)

Colorado's response indicated a growing concern in the West for maintaining the fluidity of market processes unhampered by what delegates considered unwarranted interference by interests operating in the legal system. At the same time, the delegates recognized the limits of their power in that the fluidity had to be operative within a legal framework. The right of eminent domain for ways of necessity was a statement of economic belief, and its constitutional regulation was a response to experience and future apprehensions. In terms of determining damages, the balancing process maintained discretion in the normal channels. This marginally allayed fears of corporate lawyers dominating legal proceedings and, more importantly, speeded the whole eminent domain process by establishing the board of commissioners. The delegation of power to the courts to decide the issue of "public use" removed the question from the political caprice of the legislature. In theory, the convention promoted market processes and equity.

The Idaho convention delegates drew directly on their territorial heritage and the Colorado precedent in debating the merits of private eminent domain; but more than a decade of American economic history separated the conventions, and the populist critique now had more vitality. The delegates divided into two major groups on this issue: miners and non-miners. Within each group factions existed who based their voting support on broader grounds: whether private power should be subject to public power in the sphere of mining and agricultural development. On this level, delegates debated the proper locus of economic decision making. The coalition of miners and free enterprise delegates dominated the convention but, due to significant opposition, resorted to parliamentary maneuver to write constitutional law.

Idaho delegates came to these convention debates with a long territorial heritage and constant reminders of the significance of the issue by the press. Idaho territorial law and the federal mining laws of 1866 and 1872 had provided for the taking of private property for ways of necessity for miners.(41) The availability of statute, however, did not retard the sentiment for a constitutional right. The Idaho Daily Statesman called for a positive use of the state's power of eminent domain in private hands to promote mineral and agricultural development. The paper characterized the issue as one of vested rights versus state power.(42) The positive assertion of the right in the constitution guaranteed Idaho's growth, according to the *Statesman*. Delegates were in agreement on this point. The constitutional right was necessary due to environmental conditions and was a proper means of stimulating economic growth. Delegates disagreed, however, on the extent to which the sovereign power of the state should be delegated to the private sector. Interest groups coalesced on these issues and waged parliamentary war to write fundamental law.

Miner and non-miner delegates rallied behind specific proposals and fought over their merits in interest terms. Led by Shoshone County lawyer Weldon Heyburn and Ketchum lawyer Orlando Batten, non-miners advocated the adoption of the Colorado constitution provisions. These provisions, they argued, were proven by time and provided sufficient safeguards against the uncompensated taking of private property. The miners, on the other hand, disregarded the taking issue and pushed for a broad grant of power. Led by William H. Claggett, the convention president, the miners parried these arguments with statements on the nature of state power, the "necessities of our country," and the interests of miners.(43) Each characterized his particular proposal in terms of its benefit either to agriculture or mining. Moderates, operating between these poles of opinion, emphasized the importance of irrigation; but they specifically tried to strike a balance by tempering the miner's proposal with limiting clauses directly from the Colorado constitution.

The efforts at compromise early in the debates failed because of the unwillingness of the extremists to compromise. Non-mining interest delegates characterized the miners' proposal as "thievery" and a "tool of monopolists."(44) Miners warned that if their proposal did not pass the whole constitution could be lost. Overwhelming passage of the committee proposal written by the miners ended the rhetorical deadlock.(45) When the measure came up for final consideration, the opposition renewed its thievery theme, and one delegate dramatized his disgust by walking out.(46) The miners tried to soothe opposition feelings by demonstrating that their measure had precedent in other state constitutions; whereupon, Batten again offered the Colorado sections, opening the debate anew.(47) Former territorial chief justice John T. Morgan, who had previously advocated compromise, now voiced the miners' argument of necessity. In the intervening time, the miners had made Morgan aware of the necessity of their position, and he now joined them.(48)

With the miner/non-miner battle lines firmly drawn, delegates invoked the issue of constitutionalism as the measure was pushed to a vote. James Wesley Reid, former North Carolina congressman and a Lewiston lawyer, objected to the miners' version on the grounds that it contained no limits for power. Property could be taken, he asserted, for "any purpose on God's green earth," and that in itself was unconstitutional.(49) This broad power, its opponents vehemently claimed, subjected all property owners to arbitrary power contrary to any concept of constitutionalism.(50) H. S. Hampton, a Cassia County lawyer, replied for the miners. The Colorado constitution provisions were too narrow, he argued, as the miners wanted something that would "cover every industry."(51) This argument was discredited quickly as an open-ended invitation to rank injustice.(52) Seeing their fortunes dwindling, the miners forced Batten's Colorado model section to a vote. This lost by a wide margin, 14 to 33. But the non-miners engaged in an amendment fight based on their constitutional arguments. Reid offered an amendment limiting the definition of a necessary purpose. This lost 17 to 31. George Ainslie, a Boise lawyer, immediately offered a similar amendment that lost 22 to 27. Seeing their majority fading before the onslaught of offensive amendments, the miners resorted to a parliamentary power play. With Morgan in the chair, the miners rammed the section through on a voice vote. The non-miners received their defeat with resignation, a frequent occurrence in the Idaho convention.(53) The constitutional arguments drew votes, but the preponderance of miners with their economic arguments carried the day and wrote fundamental law.(54)

The Idaho experience represented an extreme in constitution making on eminent domain. Although implicitly recognized as legislation, all delegates agreed that something was required on the subject in the constitution. This assertion of power, as in Colorado, deprived the legislature of its function as policymaker. Delegates' fears were solely with court interpretations, but only in minimal terms. Economic considerations were weighted more heavily than constitutional arguments in shifting votes and in orienting debate. As such, fundamental rights as defined in a bill of rights were traditional in a historical and economic sense. Economic necessity called for, and delegates responded with, a right of eminent domain similar to the one existent in territorial law.

The debate of this issue in the Montana convention followed a similar pattern, but delegates emphasized the law of new conditions more extensively. Hiram Knowles, a Butte lawyer, noted that the provisions for the taking of private property for the private use of a way of necessity was "a departure from the ancient landmarks." "But," he continued, "we live in a different country, and are surrounded by a different climate and a different soil from that which exists where the common law had its birth."(55) Knowles was joined by others who all agreed that America was different and that English common law had to be changed to meet the needs of the arid frontier.(56) The delegates, cognizant of their territorial law heritage in this realm, then moved to define the uses they considered necessary.

The idea of using the term "private use" proved offensive as it defied the language of the federal Constitution. So, as other conventions had done previously, the private use was termed "public" and these uses defined.(57) Once over this conceptual hump, the delegates assumed their prerogative to define, once and for all, what a public use was.

Having assumed the power to define a public use, the delegates went directly to the heart of their purpose. Joseph K. Toole, a Helena lawyer and later state governor, voiced general delegate concern in stating that they were "directly interested in promoting, by every constitutional method, the storage and disposition of water."(58) This interest included uses for agricultural and mining purposes and was phrased broadly enough to receive support from all interests. Fears of restrictive interpretations disappeared when Knowles observed that the courts had previously seen environmental need and altered law to suit it.(59) With general support based on the obvious state need and the broad language of the provision, it became part of the constitution. The ends, defined in specific economic terms, justified overt legislation as a constitutional means of achieving continued economic progress viewed in the parochial terms of the Montana delegates of 1889.

Wyoming's convention delegates accepted without significant debate similar sections in their bill of rights. The sections contained the usual provision for ways of necessities for "reservoirs, drains, flumes, or ditches" for "agricultural, mining, milling, domestic or sanitary purposes."(60) In the two decades that followed the Nevada convention, the private use of the power of eminent domain had become an accepted article of faith in the arid West. It had been elevated from legislative status to a constitutional right based on the recognized economic needs of the region and delegate distrust of legislatures.

After 1889 the contours of this right had definition, but Utah and New Mexico refrained from including eminent domain in their bill of rights. Arizona put the right into its bill of rights and, as Colorado had done, made the determination of a public use a judicial question.(61) Utah, fearing congressional rejection and trusting Mormon legislative majorities, adopted the federal model. New Mexico did the same and included the specific ways of necessity provision in its water rights article. New Mexico's caucus system insured the passage of the federal model without debate. But the debates of the Utah convention did reveal new concerns in the arid West.

Utah delegates were most concerned with its use by railroads and municipalities. This concern reflected the growing dissatisfaction with corporate abuse of power and the growing pains of Salt Lake City urban life. The centers of controversy were the time of compensation whether it should be before or after the taking, and the inclusion of "or damaged" in the section.(62) Delegates feared that requiring the paying of damages before the work started would hamper economic growth and play into the hands of obstructionists.(63) Some delegates feared that the inclusion of "or damaged" would "bankrupt cities."(64) This fear came from actual experience with street grading in Salt Lake City and other municipalities. The raising of the street level severely decreased the value of abutting property, but the debates never got to the next question of whether this action was a "taking" to bring it under the law. They were far too concerned with the possibility of decreased property values in urban Utah.

The convention resolved the issues in favor of the federal model due to an existent system in territorial law, a viable application of that law based on environmental considerations, and the inability of mining delegates to overcome these and other arguments. Franklin S. Richards, a Salt Lake City attorney and spokesman for the Mormon Democrats, reminded the convention of the existence of territorial law on the subject. The system provided that a bond be posted before work was commenced, and the courts then assessed damages.(65) This system provided a compromise between property rights and the needs of a rapidly expanding economy in a peculiar environmental circumstance. William F. James, a Salt Lake City miner and "one of the most substantial businessmen in the Territory,"(66) feared possible delays in enterprise and evoked the demands of the Great Basin environment as evidence.(67) Others quickly took up this environmental analysis as justification for broad powers for specific uses. These included the typical ones as found in the Idaho and Wyoming constitutions.(68) Charles S. Varian, leading Gentile spokesman and able constitutional lawyer from Salt Lake City, found the very breadth of the proposals objectionable. He exploded, charging an invasion of "the rights of the private citizen in these particulars named. Where are you going to stop?" he asked rhetorically.(69)

Ingwald C. Thoreson, a Cache County teacher, lawyer, and spokesman for the regular Democrats, answered Varian's argument with a broad assertion of delegate power. According to Thoreson and his fellow Democrats, the delegates were vested with absolute power from the people to "guard their interests, guard their lives, their liberty and their property, and...restrict the Legislature upon this very point and upon all such points."(70) Joseph Murdock, a stake president and Mormon Democrat, tried to blunt the argument by asserting that only powers to prescribe boundaries for legislative action rather than legislating were granted.(71) The arguments for delegate power were persuasive but faulted by the concept of constitutionalism that delegates assumed.

Varian answered his critics in constitutional terms and defeated them with rhetoric and reason. He asserted that compensation had to be rendered for the taking of private property for a public use. This was fundamental, a proposition beyond the power of delegates to change. Second, Varian maintained that private property could not be taken for private uses at all. The notion that delegates had unlimited power was "in violation of the principles upon which this government rests." This higher law he saw embodied in the 14th Amendment. In this context, it was "upon the judiciary that the weight of determination [of what constituted a public use] fell." As the question of necessity was a shifting one, "the question of public use must finally be determined by the courts."(72) This constitutional argument, coupled with its faith in the courts and the existing law, carried the day against later miner attempts at amendment.(73) The faith in courts first and the confidence in a Mormon legislature second allowed the section to become fundamental law.

In dealing with their respective bills of rights, convention delegates looked first to tradition and copied it; second, they looked to their environmental situation and made law to confront it. Quantitatively, their use of traditional verbiage outweighed change. Even the inclusion of new fundamental rights had historical lineage in territorial law. But taken together, the bills of rights manifested a growing willingness to extend experience into constitutional provision, to define rights rather than trusting to legislatures, and to trust the judicial system to maintain these rights once defined. In this tendency, bills of rights became essays in specificity and overt legislation rather than broad affirmations of fundamental belief.(74)

In so exercising their power, the delegates affirmed their belief in the need to act affirmatively. Action itself was change because it withdrew traditional legislative functions. The delegates assumed the power to define a public use and to change the structure of a grand jury. Both acts were innovative in some respects, but delegates based their prerogative on environmental necessity. This recognition of environmental uniqueness was coupled with a sense of regional identity. Rocky Mountain precedent was far more persuasive than eastern law. The three-fourths verdict in civil cases and the right of private eminent domain resulted. These products evidenced a deep concern for property as opposed to personal rights. The delegates were trying to balance economic power in the marketplace and to smooth its processes. In putting these considerations first, few delegates considered their actions legislation. Specificity was needed to protect immediate interests and preserve them, a function territorial legislatures had not adequately performed.

Once defined as a matter of right, delegates saw their fundamental freedoms being protected by the court system. Delegates repeatedly paid tribute to the work of the territorial courts in keeping territorial law viable in a changing environment. This heritage assured delegates of an equitable administration of the propositions that became fundamental rights.

# 4

# State Institutions

Rocky Mountain constitution makers retained traditional government institutions. They maintained the triumvirate of legislature, executive, and judiciary, although they varied their relative powers with time and convention. In general, convention delegates demonstrated little concern for institutional forms. Their central problem was financial. State government, they conceded, would cost more than territorial status; therefore, jobs and salaries were important issues. In the last quarter of the 19th century another problem grew from the disaffection of a growing minority. The levers of government had seemingly been wrested from the people, according to these "progressives." The constitutional convention provided them with another forum to plead their case. Voting power and a growing sympathy for their arguments did produce results, especially in Arizona. The initiative and referendum became the means through which they sought to obtain home rule and alternatives to regular legislative processes.

All delegates recognized the increased financial burden of statehood. The problem presented convention delegates with several alternatives. Constitutional offices could be severely limited in number or the salaries reduced to match potential revenues. Alternatively, the tax rate or base could be expanded to provide for adequate salaries and officers. Corporate interest opposed increased tax rates and expansion of the tax base. Advocates of "good government" favored higher salaries irrespective of the sources of revenue. Delegates also had the option of leaving salary considerations to future legislatures, but the clash of sentiment often forced objective settlement in the constitution itself. Economy-in-government proponents were joined by political minorities and anti-statehood forces who tried to achieve their ends through scare tactics. The weapon was persuasive when political blocs were evenly matched or majority arguments tenuous. The issue continually pervaded debate on the institutions of government in the conventions.(1)

The territorial governor generally had been a carpetbagger of the majority party then in Washington. The governor sometimes developed local political parties if his tenure were lengthy enough.(2) As an outsider and political adventurer, local politicos held him in low repute and worked to delimit his power. Territorial experience often led delegates to reduce executive salaries but to maintain traditional functions and powers. This was due to a general attitude of complacent copying of institutional forms. Only when pocketbook politics were involved did delegates battle one another.

The institutional structure of the executive department won inclusion with little debate. Nevada copied its previous constitutional verbiage. Colorado delegates debated the governor's term heatedly, but all agreed his function should be a check against ill-advised legislation. Montana delegates passed section after section of the executive article until they came to the salary schedule. Salaries, too, were the single most debated subject in Idaho with executive appointive power a secondary concern. Only the governor's veto power detained Wyoming delegates in their debates. Utah delegates passed on executive powers with little debate. Arizona and New Mexico convention delegates also gave the office short shrift in debates.(3) The institutional form and structure of the executive held little delegate attention.

As bill of rights issues had illustrated, delegates were concerned about fiscal affairs and economic growth. Executive salaries were matters of fiscal affairs. Many delegates posited economy in government as the obverse of good government. Taxation and indebtedness limitations were closely associated issues, and voting patterns developed that spilled over into the taxation issue. In general, the conventions fixed executive department salaries at low levels subject to legislative change. Legislative, judicial, and other salaried departments received similar treatment. Countering the specificity of fixing salaries at all were delegates who saw the issue best resolved by the legislature. This sentiment was strongest in Colorado where delegates gave the legislature complete authority. New Mexico's convention, in contrast, prohibited legislative tampering for ten years. The convention exchanges on these issues were sharp and votes were counted closely. Each convention displayed peculiarities of its own, but all saw economy as a key issue.

The Colorado and New Mexico conventions were structured in political terms. The Republicans held at least a three-to-two margin in each, but party organization and latitude for dissent varied markedly. The Republican caucus system controlled the New Mexico convention with an iron fist. A working alliance among Republican leaders quelled insurgents and presented Democrats with no grounds for compromise.(4) Colorado's political organization was less well developed; although partisanship was evident in the convention, meaningful compromise was possible.(5) The Granger faction led by H. P. H. Bromwell was able to secure significant concessions that allowed greater popular control of government salaries. Legislative prerogative to alter salaries as well as county commission control of county salaries found fruition.(6) The Colorado constitution was more responsive to popular will thereby than the New Mexico document that conceded nothing to the people for ten years.

The Colorado convention evidenced a rural-urban split on this issue that also was prevalent in other conventions. Proponents of higher salaries and legislative discretion were in the northern urban area, while opponents were south and east of Denver. Montana delegates produced a similar voting pattern. Southwestern delegates from Butte, Anaconda, and Missoula advocated high salaries. Delegates from the eastern part of the territory, the cattle-county delegates, and strict constructionist advocates were opposed. The proponents were also oriented toward business and mining and represented established political or economic positions.(7) Wyoming delegates aligned themselves on the salary issue with western opposing eastern delegates from Laramie and Cheyenne. The eastern delegates had the voting power and imposed their will upon the cow counties.(8) Similarly, Idaho's convention split with delegates from the Boise area and Shoshone County advocating higher salaries, and non-mining county areas opposing them.(9) In Utah, Salt Lake City and County delegates formed the nucleus of the group that advocated the highest government salaries. They consistently lost to delegates from rural counties.(10) High salary advocates were generally those in political control of the future state and were assured of at least immediate occupation of the offices that they were creating. Rural delegates were political minorities in the relative terms of state politics, but they had a vested interest in avoiding increased tax burdens that would fall on them first. Thus, farmers and miners were joined in opposition to high salaries for constitutional officials for pocketbook reasons.

Economy also posed a problem in the creation of state judiciaries. An independent supreme court necessitated additional salaries as did the increased number of district judges. This economic problem carried over fiscal conservatives from the salary debates. Laymen also questioned the bar closely on the necessity for extra courts and judges. Aside from the pocketbook issues posed, delegates uniformly accepted the judiciary's key role in the lawmaking process. Although occasionally castigating selected territorial judges, delegates were willing to maintain judicial power at territorial levels or expand it to deal with state problems that they foresaw. The problem of crowded dockets and vast economic interests at stake in litigation generally pushed conventions into expanding the judicial institution and its powers.

Nevada's territorial experience with its courts had not been a happy one, and its constitution reflected this experience. William Stewart's conflict with the territorial supreme court over mining cases resulted in the physical destruction of that court.(11) Stewart had personally conducted the campaign and had left a heritage of distrust and apprehension of the judicial institution. The attitude was manifested in the impeachment and removal section of the Nevada constitution which provided for the removal of judges "for any reasonable cause...which may or may not be sufficient grounds for impeachment."(12) Proponents of this section argued that "a stupid judge [was] as bad as a dishonest one" and without such a provision only a "wrongful act" would allow removal.(13) Liberal members of the bar rebutted the argument with visions of turbulent fights in the legislature over trifles.(14) But the mine owner's lawyers, joined by other Comstock Lode delegates, easily overwhelmed the cow-county delegates and liberal bar.(15) The removal provision, although requiring a two-thirds vote of the legislature, put into constitutional law the means mining lawyers like Stewart needed to eliminate unfavorable judicial opinion.

Although Nevada delegates passed a broad removal provision, they proceeded to grant their judiciary broad powers directed at solving current problems. The convention created an independent supreme judiciary, lacking in the territorial system, with three justices instead of a proposed five. Delegates obtained economy in three justices and independence for appellate jurisdiction eliminating the old problem of a judge sitting twice on a cause.(16) The document provided for district courts and gave them broad jurisdiction including probate. This effectively eliminated the hated probate courts run by Utah's Mormons previous to 1861.(17) But several delegates noted that this placed too much institutional weight on the side of deciding mining cases at the expense of inferior courts.(18) Mining delegates retorted that this was intended "to suit our own particular wants." A compromise solution gave discretion to the legislature on the establishment of justices' courts, but the convention specifically excluded jurisdiction over mining claims and title to real estate.(19) The convention gave courts of record broad jurisdiction that evinced a general confidence in the efficacy of the judicial institution but limited the discretion of justices' courts. The fear of bad judicial decision hedged by removal was coupled with a general confidence in the courts as arbiters of the prosperity of Nevada.

Overloaded court dockets and a growing Granger agitation to do something about the railroads faced the Colorado convention delegates when they met to consider a judicial department. The *Rocky Mountain Daily News* reminded the delegates of the perilous situation that existed. Territorial court dockets were overloaded, judges were overworked, and millions of dollars were at stake.(20) The *News* also advocated an appointive supreme judiciary, but delegates never seriously questioned the appropriateness of an elected judiciary.(21) Delegates tried to clear dockets by creating new courts, but they failed to give the legislature adequate discretion to continue their work. The supreme court was restricted to three members and the number of district courts specified in the constitution. This inflexibility evidenced a distrust of the legislature and resulted in the continuation of the problem delegates sought to relieve, overcrowded dockets.(22) The Grangers, led by H. P. H. Bromwell, who had been a member of the 1870 Illinois constitutional convention, attempted to give the supreme court original jurisdiction over railroad controversies and the power to set reasonable rates.(23) This effort lost, the victim of business oriented delegates who believed the provision would frighten away capital. The dominant attitude of the convention prevailed, and Colorado was made safe for business. Although restricted to appellate jurisdiction, the supreme court was independent which cured the territorial evil of judges sitting on two levels in the system.(24) The efforts to increase its power did demonstrate a confidence in the institution and the willingness of some to expand its power.

Montana delegates worked to strike a balance between expense and efficiency in the judicial system but created no impediments to the exercise of judicial power. The expense of the judicial system and the distribution of district courts dominated convention debates. The preponderance of southwestern voting strength dictated moderate salaries and the allocation of judicial districts.(25) Although delegates cut the size and number of courts to a minimum, they did not impair the power of the courts to act.

Wyoming's convention went to the "verge of calamity" on the question of an independent supreme judiciary. The opponents of an independent supreme court charged that the proposal was a lawyers' conspiracy to bankrupt the state. Delegates and the territorial press continually forecast fiscal doom.(26) Proponents replied that the cost was well worth it because it eliminated district judges sitting on the same case on the appellate level, and the vast interests coming before Wyoming courts required studied consideration by a detached tribunal.(27) After lengthy and vehement debate, the independent judiciary men won by four votes.(28) Delegates debated institutional structure, but gave jurisdiction relatively short shrift. Judicial power was not restrained but confidently allowed to find its own course. Delegates reminded one another that men like Willis Van Devanter would always grace the bench to give Wyoming quality adjudication. The Wyoming convention displayed confidence in its bench and only altered the structural arrangement.

Idaho's judiciary article illustrated the growing tendency to legislate in constitutions, but the broad outline of an elected, independent supreme court with expansive jurisdiction remained. Idaho delegates spent most of their time debating details of form rather than the conceptual role for their supreme court. Delegates prohibited certain forms of action that had been abolished already by Idaho territorial law.(29) Delegates fervently argued the merits of judicial salaries and finally included a general statement in the article.(30) The most serious division arose over the election of judges. The press warned the convention against legislative appointment, and former judges foresaw political caucus control of elections; but the majority found the wisdom of the people the best guardian of the institution and impartial judgment.(31) The convention delineated the details of the institutional structure for all time with legislative discretion allowed for lower courts. Again, form was prominent and power delegated without extensive debate. Idaho's fundamental law included chaff that other conventions allowed to blow away.

Utah's convention wrote a judicial article that surpassed Idaho's in specificity. Delegates prescribed judicial procedure, passed an anti-nepotism section, and elevated the lower court system to constitutional status. In the process it created a bevy of offices and gave the legislature the authority to create more. This raised the ire of the press and fiscally minded delegates, but the Mormons prevailed.(32) In the dominant mood of caution, the delegates assured the Congress that relatives would not sit on causes of one another and that clerks would not be "within the degree of first cousin." At the same time, they assured each other that "our judges will be different from those who have been sent here from Washington."(33) The Mormons carefully beat back attempts to have the probate courts included in the constitution, thus assuring the elimination of another symbol of conflict.(34) Although littered with special sections, the Utah judicial department retained the elected, independent supreme court with broad jurisdiction. The close attention paid to the judicial article was due to the territorial past. The delegates recognized the need to placate Congress with an anti-nepotism section. Regarding judicial power, they refrained from altering institutions that previously had been onerous because, with statehood, they could control the membership of the bench.

When Arizona and New Mexico delegates met to consider the state judiciary, their conventions were the testing grounds for progressive arguments. The growing sense that courts had exceeded their authority with their intervention in the state and national economy permeated the Arizona convention and was evidenced by the Democratic minority in New Mexico.(35) In New Mexico the Republican caucus produced the judicial article and, with slight concessions, secured its passage. The judicial system was composed of an elected supreme judiciary and district, probate, and justice courts. The article prohibited structural change for ten years. The court system was conservative in structure, traditional in jurisdiction, and unresponsive to legislative or popular restructuring.(36)

Arizona's, in contrast, maintained a traditional structure and provided for institutional expansion to meet immediate needs. In general, Arizona delegates tried to limit judicial power in specific areas by delineating procedure and by giving the people the power of recall. The specificity used was directed at procedure and jurisdiction. Judges could charge a jury only on matters of law. The harmless error rule directed at technical errors became constitutional law. Delegates carefully described the jurisdiction of the various courts. Finally, progressives incorporated recall to insure compliance and public harmony. The specificity used by Arizona delegates was directed both at legislative and judicial power. The enumeration of jurisdictional limits withdrew the power from the legislature. The technical error rule was a judicial invention, and convention inclusion only insured its continuance. The limitations were conservative of judicial power although specific in enumerating its boundaries.

The recall of judges passed under national pressure, amid partisan debate, and with internal party conflict. President Taft warned a Phoenix audience against a "crank constitution," while Theodore Roosevelt toured the country cautioning the nation against measures that eroded popular control of government.(37) Arizona delegates saw the need to rid their legal system of the "conditions of corruption." Beyond election and specific constitutional limitations, recall became the progressive argument for "clean government." Recall was only an extension of the Progressive goal of bringing government closer to the people.(38) Although Progressives disagreed among themselves on the appropriateness and the practicality of the measure, recall was adopted to complete the Progressive program designed to give greater popular control of government.

Although Rocky Mountain judiciaries differed in particulars, all were headed by elected, independent supreme courts with broad jurisdiction. The popular confidence displayed in the judicial institution was maintained. Only eccentricities derivative of individual territorial experiences distinguished judicial power and structure. The articles became longer, more verbose, and more specific as the tendency to legislate became more manifest. Specificity solidified 19th-century judgments in constitutions, which were too often not readily amendable. Fiscal considerations frequently disallowed legislative discretion in judicial or executives' salaries. Some of the territorial chaff was discarded. Except in New Mexico, probate courts lost favor. Some states expanded lower court systems to meet contemporary demands and allowed legislative discretion to create more courts when needed. The territorial experience with courts did not significantly limit the exercise of judicial power in the states.

When the Rocky Mountain constitutional conventions debated the nature of their respective legislatures, many of the issues associated with other institutions dominated discussion. Economy in government was a theme throughout convention debates. Delegates limited legislative discretion with procedural and substantive devices designed to curb previous practices. These efforts were intended, in general, to bring legislation in tune with contemporary public needs and to eliminate corruption. When territorials found that enumerated prohibitions did not materially affect practice, they turned to direct legislation as an alternative. This issue was hotly debated in the late 19th century and found fruition in Arizona. It represented not only a clash of political ideology but also an effort at home rule. The home rule issue pointed up the growing distance people felt from government, and Progressives used this sense of lost communication to push their legislative package.

Nevada's constitutional convention delegates spent more time debating the merits of the Pacific railroad than the legislative department. The thrust of their action was negative, prohibiting franchises, special legislation, and the like. Abolishing special legislation would minimize corruption and increase private incentive, they argued. But legislative power, outside of enumerated prohibitions and procedural safeguards like single subject bills, three readings of bills, and the keeping of journals, was allowed substantial latitude.(39) The delegates assumed the legislative function themselves when delineating legislative power. They put a homestead and women's separate property act in the legislative article and commanded the legislature to implement them. Similarly, they spent hours on the Pacific railroad, but only allowed counties and municipalities to pledge their credit to the grand adventure.(40) Significantly, the delegates saw no essential difference between their acting to pledge the state's credit and allowing the legislature to do it. Fearing the consequences of massive debt and high taxes, they refused to act and forebade the legislature to extend the state's credit to other than educational or charitable organizations. Legislative power was merged in the convention with the immediate prerogative to act once and for all for the good of the state. This attitude of static constitutional legislative power froze 19th-century concepts in fundamental law proposed to last for centuries.

This enumeration of limitations on legislative power was representative of the general delegate willingness to limit the exercise of institutional power. The delegate faith in the operations of the marketplace dictated that contractual relationships be minimally encumbered. The prohibition of special legislation functioned to promote the broadest participation in the marketplace without legislative aid being dispensed to favored parties.

Merged with legislative power was the issue of who would exercise such power. Nevada delegates debated apportionment along wealth versus population lines and resolved this issue with minor difficulties. They distributed senatorial representation along compromise lines but did not arbitrarily give each county a senator.(41)

Increasingly, conventions delegated power to their legislatures, apportioned the state approximately along county lines for the senate, and froze the proportional balance of house and senate.(42) By 1889 the question of apportionment overshadowed all other legislative department issues when convention delegates met to formulate fundamental law. The substantive limitations on legislative power as enumerated in the special legislation prohibitions section had become standardized inclusions. Now the issue was the exercise of power within the institution by the political interest group.

The Montana convention debates revealed a new cynicism on the efficacy of the legislative institution. Delegates distrusted the legislature as a policymaker for the future state. They made no distinction between the territorial and state legislatures of the future. These attitudes resulted in the absence of resolve to reform the institution. Thus posited, the issue was simply one of combatting one interest group with another through representation to assure some sense of compromise.(43) The main floor fight became one of east versus west, or farmer-cattleman versus miner on the one-senator-per-county provision.(44) It also had party overtones as the Democrats used their instant majority to bulldoze, as the Butte Daily Intermountain put it, the one-senator section through the convention.(45) The delegates assumed prerogatives of legislative power, but the locus of political power became the critical issue. The polarity of interests in the convention was that of territorial days. The convention deadlock forced many political bargains and apportionment was only one. Helena became the capital to which each cow county sent a senator.

Wyoming's delegates also accepted traditional legislative powers enumerating substantive and procedural limitations and concentrated on the issue of whether one house should represent something other than people. The usual lines were drawn early in the debate. Hubert E. Teschemacher, a Harvard-educated cattleman, reduced the argument of the cow counties to the absurd at the outset. He offered a section giving each county and county subsequently created by the legislature a senator. Elliott S. N. Morgan, a fellow Laramie County Republican, added to Teschemacher's argument, claiming that every man was free, independent, and entitled to representation.(46) The liberals wanted Wyoming apportioned according to population so that the people rather than the economic interests would have sway in the legislature. This sentiment also was that of the urban east, which feared the continued rural domination of the state.

The cow-county delegates argued the radical consequences of proportional representation focusing upon the opportunities for abuse. Frederick H. Harvey, a University of Iowa LLB and Douglas lawyer, stated the cow-county position: "If you have two houses based upon the same rule of apportionment you make no distinction, [and] the only excuse in the world for having two houses is that one should be a check upon the other, because it is absolutely necessary to restrain the majority."(47) This argument was buoyed up by others who recalled the abuses of the territorial legislature. Still others characterized representation on a population basis as "an inducement to rascality."(48) Some delegates raised the expense issue to complicate the matter, but what emerged was a northern dissatisfaction with previous experience.(49) The mining and railroad counties of the south, the northerners claimed, used fraudulent voting rolls to gain power. The convention finally resolved the issue with a compromise solution and passed the matter on to future legislatures.

Several Wyoming delegates argued that a population basis for both houses of the legislature negated the need for a senate. One Idaho delegate used the same argument and proposed to abolish the senate in Idaho, but found himself the only member voting "aye."(50) Idaho delegates then debated the Montana model of one senator per county. Several delegates attacked the measure as representing interests and not people.(51) Apportionment based on the last election for delegates assured a legislature safe for democracy, and free of Mormons. Alternatively, a one-senator-per-county apportionment gave "the Mormon Counties" too "large an amount of representation."(52) Subsequently, each county was assured one representative and senatorial districts were left to the province of the first (and Gentile) legislature. The one-senator plan received substantial support for the same reasons it had in Montana and Wyoming, but the specter of Mormonism proved too horrible for a majority of delegates to tolerate. Thus the state senate in a growing number of states became the bastion of interests other than population, at least on paper. In fact, this reality did give inordinate influence to rural and corporate interests. The late-19th-century politician then started to seek new avenues to escape the legislative domination of an interest contrary to those of his constituents.

Utah's convention maintained its conservative tenor on apportionment, but the dissatisfaction with previous legislative process was evident. Theodore Brandley, a Mormon farmer, brashly suggested to the Utah convention that the referendum was a form of legislation closer to the people, but his words were lost in committee and the clash of debate.(53) Utah's delegates were not prone to experiment but were concerned about the outcome of their floor fight. One-senator proponents waved copies of the Montana constitution before the convention and conjured up all the familiar arguments.(54) The rhetorical question was immediately asked, "If you adopt that principle [of representation] for all time, why not include the cities?" The cities, they argued, were as much part of the economy as the counties.(55) The retort came directly from the territorial experience as one delegate reminded the convention that Salt Lake City had "a tendency to forget that there was any other part of the State."(56) Proponents resolved one senator per county into a one-representative- per-county section. This measure succeeded over the protests of Salt Lake City Gentiles and Sanpete County Mormons who, for their own reasons, opposed apportionment by the hierarchy led by George M. Cannon and associates.(57) Religious and peculiar sectional antagonisms muddied the rural-urban split of delegates. Significantly, Utah followed old, timeworn paths to apportionment and buried the referendum without debate.

The Utah convention did reflect the growing concern with corporate influence in government and private affairs in the new state. First, delegates argued vociferously for adequate salaries for legislators to prevent the corruption they saw running rampant in eastern cities. Next, to prevent the scandalous ruin associated with aid to railroads, several delegates fought for and won a prohibition against the lending of the state's credit.(58) In general the tactics of substantive limitation on legislative discretion dominated, but several delegates questioned the efficacy of withdrawing public issues from the arena of public debate by embodying them in a constitution. A small minority voiced this protest against inordinate legislation in the constitution, but the majority saw immediate and permanent decision on controversial issues as more palatable.

This internal questioning of the wisdom of legislating in constitutional conventions was paralleled by dissatisfaction with the growing distance between popular desires and legislative actions. As Brandley had offered the referendum as a possible answer to closing the gap, so too did Arizona and New Mexico delegates advocate procedural change in legislating for their new states.

The two conventions resolved these issues in marked contrast. Arizona's progressive Democrats captured their convention and easily passed the initiative, referendum, and recall, while New Mexico progressives were able only to wrench a token referendum from the Republican majority. Arizona progressives characterized their program as "a simple and ever-ready means to test the popular will on any subject." Those progressive devices, they claimed, would prevent corporations from filling the statute books with legislation and put government back in the hands of the people.(59) Several Democrats thought that the principles should be extended to "cities, towns, and counties" and give "absolute home rule." Ranchers and miners from the less populous counties voiced this sentiment and gained some support from other rural delegates. The Hunt progressives quashed this intraparty rebellion by quickly associating the prohibition issue with home rule and using the fear of conflicts of state and municipal laws to defeat the movement.(60

Home rule for political subdivisions was as dangerous as legislative corruption, but the expression of sentiment did illustrate a rural dissatisfaction with the course of previous legislation. The initiative, referendum, and recall provided a viable alternative for the people to legislative jobbery, but popular will did not relieve grievances in the cow counties.

The progressives' argument for self-determination for the people was directed against corporate interests, but rural delegates saw it as a device to ameliorate the impact of urban influences on public policy. As with Utah, rural delegates felt abused by the political power of urban areas. Exactly the opposite happened in Colorado when Denver progressives escaped the clutches of the rural state legislature in a home rule amendment. The critique of legislative power was motivated by interest abuses, but the coalition of progressives varied with the locus of power in the respective states.

New Mexico progressives never had a chance of getting any meaningful part of their program into fundamental law. Harvey Butler Fergusson led the fruitless campaign for progressive reform in the convention. Fergusson was a leader in the New Mexico bar, one of the few liberal members of that organization. He had been special assistant to the U.S. attorney general in suits against New Mexico corporations, a delegate to Congress, and author of the Fergusson Act of 1898 which donated five million acres for schools. His politics were always Democratic, being a member of the Democratic National Committee for 14 years and private secretary to William Jennings Bryan.(61) Against the Republican "stone wall," Fergusson could not prevail. The _Santa Fe New Mexican_ characterized the initiative and referendum as "latter day socialism" and "subversive."(62) This expressed dominant Republican thought, but the Republican caucus did produce a referendum as a sop to the progressive protest.(63) Fergusson labeled the referendum "a gold brick" and launched a drive to defeat the constitution, but failed.(64) Statehood was more compelling to the electorate than the form of government. The Santa Fe Ring was safe, and political reality defeated progressivism in New Mexico.

The Rocky Mountain convention deliberations on state institutions evidenced the influence of the territorial experience and the desire to place limitations on the exercise of institutional power. The carpetbag heritage of territorial officials combined with fears of fiscal irresponsibility based on previous experience produced specificity in the constitutions. It also directed attention to particular institutional problems of the past. The deliberations produced traditional institutional forms and limitations on the exercise of power.

The carpetbag heritage was evident when the delegates debated the executive. Although they realized that the territorial features would be removed with statehood, the delegates had little interest in expanding his powers. Not only had the previous experience been poor, but also the delegates did not want to extend inordinately institutional power into marketplace functions.

The conventions displayed a hypersensitive fiscal consciousness. The territorial system had given government a free ride on federal funds. This was exacerbated by legislative irresponsibility. The experience soured delegates both on legislative ability and the fiscal stewardship of government in general. This failure of the territorial system to make government pay its own way and to hold all its officials accountable to the people at the polls rather than to Washington deepened cynicism about institutional government. The increased taxes needed to support state government drew opposition for economic reasons, but cumulatively the territorial experience led delegates to lowering the costs of government in general. Delegates slashed salaries and often froze them in constitutions. They limited offices in number except in New Mexico, where the Santa Fe Ring found the opportunity to entrench the faithful. Statehood was a precious thing to the delegates, but they wanted it at discount prices.

Judicial power remained unfettered excepting fiscal considerations that reduced the size of some lower court systems. Delegates did not object to the exercise of judicial power in the territorial period, but they found its form abhorrent. They reformed the structure by creating an independent supreme judiciary. This was accomplished even at the increased costs to the system. This cost factor demonstrated the delegates' dislike of the territorial system and their belief in the efficacy of their state judicial system. Except for isolated threats to the system such as Nevada's removal section or Arizona's recall provision, Rocky Mountain delegates expressed confidence in their courts' past and future. They saw them as a positive influence in the contract society and as a necessary instrument in the marketplace.

Delegate concern with the marketplace resulted in limitations on the exercise of institutional power. The enumeration of prohibited legislative activity was the usual vehicle of limitation. This was coupled with procedural rules that only guaranteed the regularity of the legislative process. With the close of the 19th century, delegates became more concerned with balancing political and economic interests within the system. This balancing program was aimed at limiting interest influence within the institution. Apportionment was a device for the accomplishment of this goal.(65) However, progressive devices became more popular by the turn of the century. Delegates sought to increase popular influence in the legal process through the initiative, referendum, and recall. These devices were aimed at limiting the exercise of institutional power so that the marketplace functions could continue without government favoritism. The progressive package was devised as a means of home rule for the people as opposed to institutions. Theoretically this gave the operatives in the marketplace the power to define a public policy most closely attuned to their needs. Specificity in the constitutions was the most pervasive limitation. The delegates legislated where the interest blocs were able and the issues amenable.

# 5

# Taxation of Mineral Wealth

Constitutional convention deliberations of the taxation of mineral wealth drew heavily upon the territorial experience and regional precedents and demonstrated the impact of convention procedure on constitution making. The final product of each convention reflected the power of economic interests and the influence of the evolution of legal thought on mining.

The territorial experience with mining resulted in definite delegate concepts. Most believed that the industry was environmentally unique, needed encouragement, and required marketplace stability. These goals, most delegates felt, could be obtained through a taxation program.

The tax program that delegates deliberated was complicated by fiscal considerations. All delegates recognized that statehood would necessitate increased tax burdens. As mineral wealth was an appropriate object for taxation, the delegates were forced to consider the relative burden for that industry.

The locus of tax burdens was an economic interest issue. Agricultural, cattle, and irrigation interests also sought favorable tax treatment. Delegates were aware of a public distaste for tax favoritism; hence, they began to question the policy of tax exemptions and the equities of the whole system. This direction of debate found fruition in Arizona, but was minimal in other conventions.

The interest contours of convention debates demonstrated the impact of bloc voting and the uses of parliamentary maneuver. Economic interest polarization of the taxation issue often led to stalemate in the conventions. Moderates, who in several conventions held the necessary votes, enabled compromise.

Convention resolution of the issue generally found precise language. Despite convention deadlock that often led to abdication of power to future legislatures, delegates wrote specifics into their constitutions. This behavior indicated their distrust of legislative action and their assumption of a policymaking role for the new state. It also reflected the ability of economic interest blocs to act in concert to attain specific goals.

The taxation of mineral wealth was a critical issue for many conventions. Many delegates saw their miner constituency scrutinizing their deliberations and threatening rejection of the whole constitution if adverse sections won inclusion. Within the conventions, bloc-lock often generated a crisis atmosphere. In this context, delegates bargained for compromise and a constitution. Although the issue declined in importance by the turn of the century, the convention deliberations most graphically displayed the impact of procedure and bloc voting in the making of fundamental law.

Nevada's experience with its 1863 constitution demonstrated the critical nature of the mining tax. The 1863 document, providing for a tax on all mines whether productive or not, was resoundingly rejected by the people.(1) When the delegates reassembled in 1864, they produced a constitution that remedied this political indiscretion.(2) But change was not without opposition. The failure to tax the mines, the opponents asserted, would result in rejection at the polls as surely as complete taxation had.(3) This polarization of opinion and the unfortunate experience of 1863 influenced other conventions. Montana's Walter A. Burleigh, former Dakota territory delegate, foresaw a public "gnashing of teeth" when the taxation article was unveiled.(4) Similarly, John K. Jeffrey, a Cheyenne banker, implored the Wyoming convention not to evince "any intention whatever either of legislation for or against property" as it would lead to popular discontent and economic disaster.(5) One Idaho delegate characterized a pro-mining tax provision as "anti-democratic" and a "crime against the people." The Colorado constitution of 1876 which unhesitatingly exempted mines from taxation for ten years coupled with the Nevada experience gave these delegates grave cause for concern.(6) The specter of miners creating a tax island infuriated cattlemen and farmers who ostensibly wanted to do the same.

Many delegates questioned the appropriateness of doing more than extending the power to act to future legislatures. It was politically expedient to avoid fixing a mining tax in the constitution, but 19th-century delegates were prone to legislate rather than assign power to legislatures already found untrustworthy. A compromise in the form of constitutional legislation also was as expedient as deferring to future legislatures. When deadlock was evident in Nevada's convention, J. S. Crosman, a Lyon County miner, proposed a compromise that he thought appeared "like legislation," but was "no more so than many things which we have already adopted." But other delegates rebutted his argument with condemnations of unconstitutional tinkering with fundamental law.(7) The concept of delegate role drew lines of conflict, but constitutional activists were generally miners and opponents cattlemen. Delegates acted on concrete, immediate interests rather than constitutional scruples.

The Colorado territorial press continually reminded delegates to avoid legislation, trifles, and newfangled schemes, but the business of the convention was exactly that, interest legislation. The Denver Daily Times noted that several delegates had forgotten their function and were making "statutory enactments." Other papers castigated the convention for delays and their failure to "only enact fundamental law."(8) But the delegates were concerned with more than propriety. They had to combat each other's programs in a parliamentary arena to produce an organic act for their new state.

The cow-county delegates of Montana took up the "legislation" cry against the miners. Led by Walter A. Burleigh, they reminded the convention that the constitution was "an organic act, the framework for the legislation to fill up," prescribing "a limitation of power and nothing else." Burleigh found no justification for legislating for mines any more than for cattle. The territorial press agreed. Using the arguments of Thomas Cooley, famous Michigan jurist and constitutional lawyer, the press condemned the convention for legislating too much.(9)

Wyoming convention delegates overcame their apprehension about legislating in the constitution because they feared the corruption of the state legislature more. The taxation debate was touched off by the introduction of a Colorado model section. This was immediately branded "special legislation," but the cow-county delegates reminded each other that legislation was necessary if it had their stamp upon it. Melville C. Brown, a Laramie lawyer and president of the convention, struck responsive chords when he characterized legislators as men wearing the "brass collars" of "monied corporations." Brown agreed that it was "not wise to legislate in forming a constitution," but "necessary to limit the action of the legislature" to prevent "the spectacle of seeing men wearing the brass collars of these companies coming into the legislature, and doing their bidding." The territorial press mimicked this schizoid tendency by chastizing the convention for legislating too much, but demanding that it do something to tax the mines.(10) Legislation in the constitution, delegates and the press believed, was better than leaving it to the state legislature.

Idaho and Utah delegates proceeded to act without excessive fears of legislating too much, but the growing complexity of constitutional law did present problems. James H. Beatty, an Idaho lawyer, chief justice of the state supreme court and later U.S. federal district judge, observed that "a man must read it [the mining property taxation section] 20 times to see what it means." John T. Morgan, territorial supreme court chief justice and later justice of the state supreme court, implored the convention to stop legislating as territorial law was already adequate on the subject. But the majority wanted ironclad assurances of continuing tax immunities.(11) Similarly, Utah's delegates quickly adopted a section modeled on Montana's with little apprehension. Both territorial presses pleaded for "broad" provisions and cited Thomas Cooley for support, but went unheeded.(12)

The unconstitutional legislation argument was a tool of convention dissent and an affirmation of a role concept. The minority of any convention used the legislation charge as a device to prevent the entrenchment of a vested interest. The legislation issue was tied to specificity, but both were devices of opposition. However, constitutional conservatives argued similarly in denouncing specificity. They thought their role to be framers of general policy goals and institutional structure. To them, the constitution was only a guide for future generations and not a specific set of rules for interest entrenchment.

The reality of a foreign-capitalized industry caused many delegates to question the wisdom of tax policy. The locus of tax benefits troubled delegates because they were caught between the need for foreign capital and their parochial sense of keeping dollars at home. The distance and traditional insensitivity of unseen investors controlling local affairs grated the sensibilities of many delegates. In the Nevada convention, John A. Collins, himself a miner, blasted the contention that tax incentives benefited the "poor miner." "The truth [was]," he contended, "that the miners who [were] proposed to be protected in this way, [were] those men who never had any interest in our community--men who [did] not live [there], at all.")13) Albert T. Hawley, leader of the cow-county delegates, agreed, adding that it created a "privileged class." A. J. Lockwood, an Ormsby County mechanic, equally wanted "to make those gentlemen who [were] rolling in wealth in San Francisco, pay something for the support of our government."(14) The alliance of farmer and labor delegates formed early in the debates with substantial support coming from small-mine owners and mine laborers.(15) This alliance was economically oriented; more important, it opposed the California control of the domestic economy.

Wyoming's delegates similarly attacked foreign capitalists. Melville C. Brown noted that a Colorado provision would result in "the wealth [being] carried from the state (as it had been in Colorado) and [put] in the hands of non-residents." Clarence D. Clark, an Evanston lawyer and later U.S. senator, condemned a Colorado provision as a "special tax" for the benefit of capitalists. Anthony C. Campbell, U.S. attorney for Wyoming, reminded the convention that "persons in New York [had] succeeded in getting title to a large body of coal land for...speculation, and they [proposed] to let those lands lie there, without undertaking to develop them."(16) Wyoming too had a foreign-capitalized mining industry, and delegates reacted against it. Wyoming delegates also had another specific target, the Union Pacific, which held large coal tracts.

Several Idaho delegates attacked the inequities of the territorial mining tax, but others thought additional taxation a double burden. Judge John T. Morgan caustically noted that a "vast amount of money [had] been taken out of [the] territory and almost no taxes [had] been paid upon it at all." Others feared that the taxation of net proceeds from mines was an income tax or at least double taxation.(17) The double taxation argument was part of the debate over the propriety of taxing mining property, but it gave mine owners a rhetorical tool to defend themselves against parochial appeals to local self-interest.

Utah's delegates used the same arguments of equity and double taxation, but the Mormon preponderance in votes mooted the debates. George M. Cannon, the hierarchy's spokesman, announced the taxation committee's draft section. Charles S. Varian, leading Gentile delegate, attacked the section on its failure to provide equity and its obvious favoritism of certain property. David Evans, Gentile attorney from Provo and territorial legislator, reminded delegates of mining's favored position noting that "some men [had] amassed great wealth from the products and yet [had] paid nothing whatever toward the support of the territory." Anthony W. Ivins, a Mormon cattle rancher and legislator, feared that tax exemptions which had resulted in the "onslaught" of "the moneyed interests" in territorial politics would likewise corrupt the state. But after the opposition had vented its spleen, the committee version, copied from the Montana constitution, passed.(18) The Mormon delegates wanted conformity and tradition to pervade their fundamental law, and equity could be delayed for the consideration of future generations.

The delegate attitude toward alien ownership developed in the territorial period and flourished in the conventions. It was an emotional appeal to nativist sentiment and the obvious inequities of the past. However, the argument failed to acknowledge the economic factors inherent in the issue. The encouragement policy had been popular on the national and the local level. This had produced abhorrent results, but the delegates were pressed for viable alternatives. Their sole appeal was to emotion, encouraging others to impose at least minimal tax burdens on the mines.

As the past experience with mining taxation had been inequitable, most delegates thought that mining required protection in its infancy and that it should be encouraged to expand. This was part of their resource allocation function and their belief that the constitution was an economic instrument. But delegates who were discontent with an extractive industry, colonial economics, and obvious inequities forced explicit evaluation of the issues.

Nevada delegates questioned the uniqueness of mines and proposed that farms too be taxed only on their net proceeds. Others wanted ad valorem taxation of all property without discrimination. Miners countered with claims of unique economic problems and long expositions on indirect benefits.(19) But all agreed that mines had to be taxed for political and economic reasons. Excepting Colorado, which exempted mines for ten years, a majority of Rocky Mountain delegates agreed that some tax had to be imposed.(20) The delegates disagreed, however, on the form and extent of the tax.

Agreeing on the taxability of mines, delegates pondered the proper taxable event on which to impose the burden. The delegates were aware of the various developmental steps of the mining industry. First, delegates approached the mining claim, although a legitimate subject of taxation, with caution for fear that a burdensome levy would crush the claim in the cradle. Excessive taxes could also frighten away capital needed to develop the infant claim. Even when a mine existed, its productivity was uncertain, and adverse taxation could nip a potential local boom in the bud. When "profitable," whatever that meant, the mining company had considerable capital invested and could bear the tax burden. So most delegates reasoned. But how heavy the burden should be and when a mine was profitable remained unsettled questions.

Nevada's convention delegates used a variety of arguments in debating the problem. The issue in Nevada was, of course, most immediate and dramatic because of the rejection of the 1863 document on this exact point. The miners accepted the proposition that a tax had to be levied for political reasons, but they wanted to minimize the burden. J. S. Crosman outlined the moderate pro-mining position, stating that although he was "opposed to taxing the mines indiscriminately," yet he was "in favor of taxing those which [were] yielding a revenue." J. H. Warwick, a Lander County lawyer, joined Crosman, asserting that the mining interests did not want to escape taxation, but needed time to "sprout and grow." It was only "just and right," he continued, to tax "to the extent to which the mines pay" because "this mining interest...[needed] encouragement." This moderate position was undercut by radicals like Samuel A. Chapin, a Storey County miner, who exacerbated the miner-farmer cleavage with his rhetoric. He agreed that the mines needed encouragement, but "would sooner levy a tax upon the people and property of [the] State to offer a bounty for the prospecting, discovery, and development of our mines."(21)

The opposition vehemently blasted mining contentions on all points. John A. Collins admitted that many ingenious arguments had been conjured up against taxing "a hole in the ground, and bed-rock tunnels, and all that, and about legislating against the poor miner," but he asserted "that 'poor miner' was a humbug and a myth." The men who claimed to represent the "poor miner," Collins charged, were trying to fatten San Francisco wallets. George A. Nourse, a Washoe County lawyer, joined Collins and remarked that the mining interest "never would feel it [the tax burden] at all."(22) Many delegates felt that placing the tax burden on net proceeds would be a meaningless gesture and would yield little revenue, so much needed in a new state.

The other 19th-century conventions all developed the pattern of miner versus farmer and rancher over the time and burden of a mining tax. The issues were generally the same, but several delegates contributed their oratorical talents in unusual ways. William A. Clark, infamous copper baron of Montana, warned that adverse taxation would "endanger the greatest industry...in Montana" and argued that the only just basis for taxation was on net proceeds for revenue purposes to "protect those men, those brave pioneers who have come out here and have made the wilderness blossom as the rose." Clarence Clark, a Wyoming lawyer, warned his convention against building "a Chinese wall around Wyoming."

But aside from occasional stirring words, delegates agreed that mining was a unique industry, had to be protected in its infancy, and had to be taxed.(23) With factional battle lines drawn and the issues fully debated, the stage was set for the parliamentary maneuvers and vote counting which determined the text of the constitutions.

The Nevada delegates had the most protracted debates on the mining tax, but the tactics developed were common in the other Rocky Mountain conventions. Nevada delegates recognized the issue as crucial to the constitution, but the resulting deadlock was so devastating that final resolution of the conflict remained for future legislatures. The 1863 section specifically included "mines and mining property" within its provision for a "uniform and equal rate of assessment and taxation." The convention procedure brought the section to the floor, and it was immediately hacked apart with amendment. The miners proposed to strike "including mines and mining property" and add "provided, that in the taxation of mines, the proceeds only shall be taxed" and "the improvements thereon will be taxed as other property."(24) The latter part was a concession to the cow-county delegates because it allowed equipment to be taxed; hence, the miners would be paying at least token taxes. James A. Banks, sponsor of the preceding amendment, explained that he wanted the question of whether net or gross proceeds were to be taxed left to the legislature.(25) The miners wanted to avoid a final convention settlement because they were confident of a favorable state legislature. The rejection of the 1863 constitution gave them not only confidence in their constituency, but a powerful weapon to force compromise solutions, if needed.

The cow-county delegates wanted immediate solutions to force the miners to pay something. To stave off cow-county objections, the miners offered compromise sections from the outset. Charles E. DeLong, a Storey County lawyer, proposed that "net proceeds" be taxed. This, he maintained to soothe the opposition, would eliminate dissension in the legislature.(26) Thomas Fitch, representing "a mining constituency," suggested that leaving the problem to the legislature would avoid deadlock and receive popular support.(27) Both sides of the same coin were offered, but the opposition would have none of it.

The cow-county delegates deluged the convention with amendments similar to the one which defeated the 1863 constitution, but the miners persisted in compromise. In an effort to pass an innocuous section, the miners proposed a bare-bones section without the "including mines and mining property" clause. This gave complete discretion to the legislature; again their efforts lost.(28) As division deepened, the voices of compromise became more apparent. Cornelius M. Brosnan, a Storey County lawyer, called for "a spirit of conciliation," but debate continued unabated. Delegates repeated previous stands; as the furor of debate subsided, Charles W. Tozer's amendment to strike "including mines and mining property" passed. The cow-county delegates continued their amendment fight.(29) The reaction of a majority of delegates to the apparent deadlock produced enough votes to initiate action, but dissidents continued their tactics of disruption.

The growing polarity of opinion in the convention forced delegates to abdicate the decision-making process to the legislature in order to produce a constitution. William Wetherill's statement, late in the debates, was indicative of delegate sentiment. Himself a miner, Wetherill refused to introduce a proposition to restrict the legislature from taxing the mines "one dime." He did so because of "the contrariety of sentiment prevailing" in the convention and contented himself with a general statement favoring abdication to the legislature.(30) The delegates, seeing deadlock and wanting to pursue other business, called for future decisions based on the "will of the people" and the "wisdom of future legislatures." This growing desire to proceed killed radical amendments as soon as they were proposed.(31)

Both sides resorted to procedural devices to delay decision, but this too met strong resistance. George A. Nourse's attempt to have debate cut was branded "an outrage" and "gag law." The chair ruled one delegate after another out of order. Delegates offered amendments and withdrew them. James A. Banks, a leading miner, submitted that the mining interests had sought "by every honorable means which [their] ingenuity could invent to join...in support of all the compromises proposed," but they had "not been met in a like spirit."(32) The cow-county delegates, indeed, did not show a like spirit. They continued to offer amendments that even some of their number thought "absurd."(33)

By the barest of margins, delegates secured final consideration. Charles E. DeLong, in the belief that there was "an object and design to prevent a final vote until members [were] absent from [the] hall," moved the previous question and was sustained by only three votes.(34) The article which excepted "mines and mining claims, the proceeds of which alone shall be taxed" then passed. John A. Collins, leader of the moderate miners, commented that "under the circumstances it [was] the best thing...that [could] be done, and...[he was] compelled to vote" for it.(35) J. G. McClinton, an Esmeralda County newspaper man, expressed a similar thought.(36) The half-a-loaf solution was the only one left to both sides due to the relatively equal strength of the factions. The group of men which allowed the convention to reach a decision was composed of delegates who favored the development of mines, but equally wanted equitable taxes paid.(37) These men first voiced compromise and were able to temper the caustic proposals of the radicals on both sides. Because of the size and intensity of opposing factions, they played an important role in finalizing constitutional provision. In later Rocky Mountain conventions, analogous moderate factions likewise tempered the ire of opposing economic interests. The radicals, of course, helped to defeat their own purpose by advocating the extreme which alienated many delegates. In most conventions, however, miners outnumbered farmers and the industry was made safe for exploitation.

The Colorado convention, following Nevada's in time, entrenched the mines in their tax haven by exempting them from taxation for ten years. Complete exemption was only prevented by agrarian opposition, and the Colorado provision became the goal of miners in later conventions. Montana and Utah delegates adopted similar provisions which taxed mines on their minimum value and net proceeds. Both conventions repeated the outline of debate presented by Nevada's proceedings. Delegates questioned the revenue realizable from mines, debated encouragement, and resolved the issue in favor of minimum taxation.(38) Both conventions rejected the Colorado provision, but the net proceeds sections gave added credence to miners' contentions for protection.

The Colorado convention's section exempting mines from taxation for ten years demonstrated the power of the mining bloc and provided other miners with an example to follow. The Colorado miners were successful because of their voting strength and the depressed economic conditions of the times. Encouragement was a necessity to get the state moving. But other conventions met under different conditions and with different convention delegations. Their use of the Colorado precedent demonstrated the acceptance of a regional experience, illustrating the changing attitudes on mining as conventions repeatedly rejected the exemption.

The Wyoming and Idaho conventions illustrated the divergent paths westerners were taking in the late 19th century. Mining in Wyoming was synonymous with the Union Pacific (U.P.), and in 1889 that company was in political trouble. Westerners in general reacted to railroad abuses with new restrictions, railroad commissions, and the like.(39) Wyoming delegates came to the convention to do something about the U.P., and its coal lands were only part of that effort. Idaho's delegates, on the other hand, were pro-mining and already had written extreme measures like eminent domain into their constitution. Only the unexpected could prevent a tax exemption. Delegates waved the Colorado section before their delegations, but the atmosphere of each convention determined the course of debate.

Wyoming delegates maintained a hard line on mining property taxation throughout the debates due to a concern for adequate revenues, economic stability, and their desire to deal with the Union Pacific. The territorial press urged delegates to be courageous, unselfish men and blasted the inequity of the territorial mining tax that did not pay even the salary of the mine inspector.(40) Henry G. Hay, a Cheyenne banker, led the pro-mining attack. He introduced a substitute for the revenue committee article "taken almost word for word from the Colorado constitution." This measure provided for a ten-year tax exemption and minimal taxation thereafter. Hay used Colorado's "phenomenal" growth in mining as an illustration of what an exemption could do and maintained that Wyoming's condition was not "very different."(41) Melville C. Brown, president of the convention, was not swayed by the argument and pointed out that Colorado's mines had not put "five cents" in that state's coffers since 1876. He did not want Wyoming to be so afflicted and debt-ridden.(42) But Hay persisted with his oratorical offensive, urging the distinction between revenue and general economic prosperity. Tax incentives that yielded little revenue from one source, he maintained, would increase revenues from others.(43) Thus, the conceptual lines were drawn with an equitable concept of deriving tax dollars from mines in competition with the idea that exemptions benefited the whole state.

The attack upon the tax exemption scheme was vehement, and, as division grew more ominous, delegates started to introduce compromise solutions that would give discretion to the legislature. Frederick H. Harvey, a Douglas lawyer, offered the "proceeds alone being taxed" provision of the Nevada constitution, but Brown continued his assaults, arguing that a static tax had to be imposed to prevent state legislative jobbery. He suggested a two-cent-per-ton tax, and this prevailed as the Hay and Harvey sections lost.(44) The Cheyenne Daily Sun editorially supported this tax on actual output, and it received increasing support in the convention.(45) With this additional backing, the Brown forces moved to put specific tax provisions in the constitution. They proposed a minimum tax on output, but this provoked other delegates to call on the convention to leave it to the legislature. Anthony C. Campbell, U.S. Attorney for Wyoming, added his support to moderation by branding the proceeds tax as a speculators' tool that allowed them to sit on their holdings without paying any tax.(46) Campbell's objections found fruition in section two of the article, and although Brown's substitute was lost, its spirit won. Wyoming delegates levied a tax on dormant coal lands, surface improvements, and the gross product of the mines.(47) The tax on the gross product was in lieu of taxes on land, and the taxation of the gross proceeds by value rather than tonnage avoided the specificity the Brown forces advocated.

This compromise solution went far beyond Nevada's in taxing gross proceeds but did not entrench the extreme, Colorado's exemption policy. The Wyoming taxation scheme was harsher than those in other Rocky Mountain states, but the object of taxation, the Union Pacific, was very visible and vulnerable. Only the overconfident efforts of a few delegates prevented a tax policy whose static nature could have crippled the mining industry. The final solution, at least allowed the burden of taxation to fluctuate with the value of coal and the economy in general.

The Idaho convention never seriously deviated from territorial practice in formulating its provisions. Exemptions had been public policy and mining delegates took full advantage of traditional practice. When a general ad valorem section reached the floor, the miners immediately proposed that the legislature be allowed to exempt "a limited amount of improvements upon land."(48) Then the floodgate opened and numerous other interests splashed exemption schemes onto the convention floor.(49) In the exuberant cascade of exemptions, Charles M. Hays, a miner and editor of the Owyhee Avalanche, offered an omnibus provision modeled on Colorado's.(50) Finally one delegate even wanted to exempt "net proceeds," and the convention returned to an orderly discussion of the issues.(51) The exemption provision created a group reaction to overt-interest legislating; with most members moving to exempt something, others wondered who would ultimately pay the state's bills.

The extreme brought delegates back to a consideration of principles. Exempting net proceeds went too far for some, as "exempting a lot of little things from taxation" seemed equally inappropriate to others.(52) Lycurgus Vineyard, a Boise lawyer and Confederate war veteran, thought the convention had missed the point of minimal mining property taxation. It was "the indirect sources of taxation that [grew] out of...mining enterprises" that yielded revenue beyond any net proceeds provision, he maintained.(53) Picking up this argument and not wanting to lose control for their faction, the miners rallied behind the Colorado scheme.(54) Again, as in the Wyoming convention, miners saw the Colorado experience as analogous, lauding it as a work of constitutional genius, while the agrarian delegates damned it as an inequitable farce.

Riding the crest of their own oratory, the pro-mining delegates miscalculated their strength and, in advocating the extreme, alienated the majority. Judge W. H. Claggett, leading exponent of protection, set off the reaction when he offered an ironclad definition of net proceeds favorable to the miners.(55) The proposal contained a slush fund clause that obviously amounted to exempting mines from all taxes. Thereafter, one exemption amendment after another fell before the disgruntled majority.(56) Finally, only a general statement of tax uniformity remained. Delegates then followed the middle path allowing the legislature to exempt property and keeping territorial exemptions in force.(57) The impropriety of multitudinous exemptions and the excesses of the miners turned a majority of delegates to a comfortable resolution of the conflict. That resolution turned discretion over to the legislature which could best vary taxation with need and the ability to pay. It was not by choice, but rather through parliamentary maneuver and interest deadlock that a static solution was not enshrined in Idaho's constitution.

The Rocky Mountain conventions of the 19th century produced tax schemes that directed the taxing power of government away from certain interests. The tax exemption delimited the scope of government discretion, but convention delegates also sought to delimit legislative power that they distrusted. The tax exemption as an incentive to the private sector of the territorial economy was a common feature of life in the 19th century. As the favored industry prospered, the reason for the rule disappeared. Certain industries no longer needed encouragement. The forces of tradition, inertia, and interest group politics argued for continued favoritism. The constitutional convention was only another forum, and a peculiarly powerful one, for this continuing battle. The closer the respective conventions were to economic dependency on mining, the more credible pro-mining arguments seemed. This parochial view of economics overcame constitutional arguments like legislating in fundamental law and drew diverse factions together at times. When mining delegates advocated the extreme as constitutional law, only a handful of radicals followed. Agrarian radicalism also helped to polarize convention debate and opened the way for compromise. When compromise was available, it tempered the radical but continued the familiar. The territorial experience was made fundamental law in many instances. Exemption was the best example. Leaving the matter to future legislatures frequently was no more than allowing previous practice to continue. The overriding feature of the tax debates and provisions was their deep concern with the particular. Taxation was object-oriented; interests fought desperately to get favors for their particular object. Equity and adequate state revenues were secondary matters in the 19th century, and delegates dealt with such concerns with equalization schemes.

New Mexico's convention delegates reflected the same concerns, but political opposition was impossible. New Mexico's legislation and territorial constitutions had always contained tax provisions which favored the landed interests and the Santa Fe Ring. For example, the 1889 constitution placed a limitation of one percent on taxable property at its assessed value. It was obvious to many that, with the Ring controlling the assessment machinery, the landed wealth would pay little.(58) When the 1910 convention met, the Commercial Clubs of New Mexico advocated the same scheme to lower their taxes.(59) The Ring dominated the convention, wrote the taxation article, and suppressed opposition with their overwhelming voting strength. When the article reached the convention floor, Republicans immediately tabled opposition amendments and made the article part of the constitution.(60)

The taxation article was typically 19th-century in orientation. Taxes were to be "equal and uniform," but special interest legislation abounded. Real estate, irrigation, mining, and cattle interests won specific treatment in verbose sections.(610 The defeated Democrats immediately branded the article as a millstone for the poor people and a gang-made refuge for the rich.(62) Nevertheless, the constitution won ratification from the people, more to gain statehood than as a popular affirmation of its contents. The past century became carefully entrenched in constitutional law to assure continued dominance of the political group that ruled.

The Arizona convention, in contrast, more clearly reflected the concerns of the 20th century. The Progressives who captured the 1910 convention were pledged to the "stamping out of graft and corruption, [and] the eradication of all special favors including bounties, subsidies and a tariff for any purpose than revenue."(63) This general proposition of taxation for revenue only failed to question the reason for the locus of the burden, but the Progressives pointed directly to the territorial experience to give substance to their program. If equality and uniformity were the goal, they reasoned, the burden of taxation had to be based on the ability to pay and had to reflect the relative benefit received from the state. They argued that the institutional authority for determining these relative factors was a tax commission. The object of these reforms was the reversal of the territorial situation of the railroads and mines bearing the smallest burden and benefiting the most from the system.(64) The

Progressives wrote a tax article which gave extremely broad discretion to the legislature and rejected specificity when dealing with mining or other interests.(65) These men conceded that the interests had controlled the machinery of government in the past; emboldened by electoral victories and confident of a progressive legislature, they vested power in a new state legislature. Overriding this confidence in the legislature was their initiative, referendum, and recall package that they believed would remedy any legislative indiscretions.

The orientation of the Arizona grant of power distinguished it from the rest of the Rocky Mountain conventions. Although other conventions had prescribed uniformity, tax commissions, and the like, conjunctively they had granted major concessions to interest legislation by taxing the mines specifically. The 19th-century conventions debated the merits of taxation in terms of economic ends. Taxation was primarily a means of stimulation for one economic sector at the expense of another. Whereas the spending power was a concern only in terms of the institutional overhead of the new state, the Arizona convention with its progressive dominance looked to popular control of, and benefit from, government. Tax burdens in those terms were best determined by the people and spent for their benefit. The nemesis of frightened capital carried little weight when mines and railroads were established and flourishing. The Progressives concentrated on taxing and spending for the social overhead of their state and left the determination of relative tax burdens to the beneficiaries, the people.

The constitutional conventions imposed their conceptions of power and propriety upon their respective states in their taxation articles. The delegates of the 19th-century conventions distrusted future state legislatures as they saw them as analogous to those of their immediate past. Some conventions did allow legislative discretion. Nevada's delegates allowed future legislatures to decide whether net or gross proceeds would be taxed. They did so, not out of confidence in the institution, but because of their own irresolution. Similarly, in Idaho, when decision could not be made, the delegates left the issue to future lawmakers. Elsewhere, delegates readily accepted the opportunity to legislate specifically in fundamental law. The conventions were unified in their willingness to use their constitutions as devices to remedy immediate wrongs, as they saw them, for all time. Arizona was, of course, the obvious exception. There the dominance of a political philosophy dictated the delegation of power to the legislature and the people. But political dominance also produced opposite results. New Mexico's Republicans used their convention, as others had, to entrench their interests in fundamental law. They also ensured this victory by making amendment difficult and the referendum relatively meaningless.

Convention delegates also were faced with an institutional dilemma when dealing with taxation. Although they displayed at least some confidence in their judiciaries, few delegates thought legislatures trustworthy. With a matter as crucial as mining taxation, delegates found it even harder to delegate power to their legislatures. The judiciary was a vehicle of enforcement and the legislature one of imposition; therefore, with choice limited, delegates often took the legislative function of tax imposition upon themselves. This assumption of power indicated a concept that blended constitution making with lawmaking. The verbose and detailed nature of 19th-century constitutions was only a product of this role usurpation.

Specificity in Rocky Mountain constitutions was a function of interest voting power. When the miners had not only the territorial experience with legislatures to point to but also the votes to push their programs, favorable tax advantages were obtained. Colorado's miners thus succeeded, but they also were aided by an economic situation that made mining appear crucial to economic growth. Wyoming's delegates, on the other hand, were assembled to penalize the interest that had gouged them for decades. The Union Pacific was an available and vulnerable target and, with its mines, an obvious subject for taxation. Wyoming delegates also pointed to the inequities of their past system and worked for equalization of the burden. This strain of argument was dominant in Arizona and found fruition in their constitution. The spirit of convention debates and constitutional law changed from taxation as a tool of capital enhancement and attraction to one of sorting out the relative equities of the system. The social consequences of taxation, rather than the economic impact, became the dominant concern of progressives in the Rocky Mountain states and the country in the 20th century.

# 6

# Water

The issue of water in the Rocky Mountain constitutional conventions illustrated the impact of the territorial experience, interest politics, and convention maneuver. The results of these factors were conservative, but the convention battles demonstrated the growing dissatisfaction with vested rights and corporate abuses.

The territories developed water rights law and irrigation systems before the conventions met. Under these systems economic interest groups acquired vested rights and came to the conventions to protect them. Subsequent economic developments created newer water users who took their water subject to prior appropriators. They, too, came to the conventions to seek an adjustment of the priorities.

Where territorial water systems were abused, delegates worked to reform their systems. The model of reform was the Wyoming distributive administration system. Efforts at reform faced vested rights arguments and voting power. In many cases, the result was the failure of progressive suggestions to gain inclusion in the constitutions.

The economic interest groups were well represented in the conventions. Farmers, ranchers, and miners combatted each other for advantage while corporate irrigation interests worked for entrenchment in the conventions. This interest cleavage often resulted in the irrigation debate merging into other related issues such as taxation. This interest conflict varied with time and convention but was ever present when water rights reached convention floors.

In debating water rights, the delegates looked to their territorial experience first and then to regional devices for guidance in their deliberations. The territorial experience provided examples both of dynamic legal process and of abuses of the system. Dramatic confrontations over water rights provided as substantial a precedent for change as did Wyoming's system for the status quo there. The plight of the Greeley, Colorado, pioneers was one such confrontation that delegates remembered.

The regional experience provided a variety of alternatives. The Colorado system of prior appropriation maintained the traditional concepts of marketplace functions. It allowed the contractual relationship to operate within the system with the judiciary overseeing the operation. The Wyoming system of distributive administration intruded the coercion of government into the marketplace. Its administrative system provided for the maintenance of the general welfare through the flexible determination of relative priorities to water. A territorial engineer made this determination based on needs and environmental conditions. The other territories developed a variety of systems generally based on the prior appropriation system.

The constitutional convention presented the delegates with a unique forum for the resolution of the issues. The document could be a device for dynamic change or for interest entrenchment. For that reason the delegates fought vociferously for their particular interest goals. Both sides of the issue desired favorable treatment, but reformists faced the forces of inertia and vested interests. This was a problem because prior appropriators had had favorable treatment in the territorial period. These problems frequently resulted in convention deadlock that generally found resolution in favor of continuing territorial practice.

The interest contests over water rights were predicated on beliefs iterated about mining taxation. Both sides wanted economic advantage, to be sure, but equally they desired certainty in marketplace functions. Delegates wanted to end the abuses of the legal system so that they could be assured of a seasonally constant supply of water. This attitude was conservative of legal institutions and process. As a result changes in the territorial system were additionally hard to secure unless alternatives suggested a more equitable and stable system.

The operation of these forces and attitudes in the conventions demonstrated the impact of interests, bloc voting, and parliamentary maneuver. Delegates had to resolve issues within the institutional atmosphere of the convention. This forced political and parliamentary strategy into view and illustrated the conservative nature of the delegates on the issue.

The Nevada convention delegates did not involve themselves in the water question and left it to the legislature to decide. The Nevada statutory law already governed the use of water, and the schism of farmer-miner over water had not materially developed by 1864. As a result the delegates only debated the procurement of water by municipalities, and that issue involved indebtedness rather than water rights. The newness of the situation and the delegates' preoccupation with other issues allowed water rights law to be deferred to the legislature.(1)

The Colorado delegates met in 1875 amid the gloom of the Panic of 1873, a severe locust plague, and the growing public revulsion with monopoly capitalism in the form of water corporations. The

Colorado Grange offered the convention a resolution that prohibited the legislature from ever giving away, selling, bonding, or granting charters to corporations for the use or control of water in the state. The Grangers wanted incorporation only of "actual settlers" upon whose land the water was to be used.(2) The Greeley Tribune reminded the delegates that "nothing [could] be more out of place than for lawyers to undertake to legislate on a subject of which they [could] have but a general idea."(3) The Colorado Transcript (Golden) feared that the Republican majority was not reliable to "effectually guard against water and land grabs."(4) The Denver Daily Tribune urged that the waters of Colorado be declared public property and that the state regulate them for the benefit of the people.(5) The public urgency was apparent; the battle lines were drawn. The first and all-important question was public ownership. Without it, all else failed.

The issue was joined with others when public ownership resolutions hit the floor of the convention. Byron L. Carr, a one-armed Civil War veteran and Longmont lawyer, offered a resolution vesting ownership in the state, instructing the legislature to act equitably in distributing water, and authorizing the legislature to pass irrigation incorporation laws.(6) S. J. Plumb, a farmer-stockman and chairman of the irrigation committee, then offered a similar public ownership section. But the committee version also contained specific reference to prior appropriation, eminent domain, price fixing by a Board of County Commissioners, a taxation provision, and a fence law.(7) Willard B. Felton, a Lake City probate judge, attacked the committee verson and proposed a substitute that limited public ownership to unappropriated water.(8) Felton's substitute then became the basis for a compromise which left appropriated water as private property and the remainder in state hands.(9) This half-a-loaf solution gained constitutional sanction.

The convention then adopted the familiar features of territorial law. Over the protests of a few, delegates gave prior appropriation constitutional sanction. The Greeley Tribune pointed to a particular difficulty. In some counties prior appropriation was not environmentally applicable; therefore, the question needed study and was best left to the legislature.(10) The protest was minimal, and the territorial law became part of the constitution. Similarly, a section authorizing the county commissioners to set water rates became constitutional law. The same provision had been on the books since 1861 and stimulated little debate. Only H. P. H. Bromwell, the Granger leader, suggested substantive alterations, but the familiar was retained.(11)

With the increased usage of water in the intervening 15 years, territorial lawmakers wrestled with the problem of devising an environmentally workable system. Wyoming took the first dynamic step toward a productive and equitable system in 1888. The territorial law established the office of territorial engineer who was vested with the discretionary power to distribute water on the basis of beneficial use. The power was derived from a declaration that all water was public property and subject to government regulation. This Wyoming system enabled the territorial engineer to apply water economically and environmentally without private property rights imposing their restraints.(12)

Elwood Mead was the instigator of the Wyoming system, became its first territorial engineer, and was its chief lobbyist in the constitutional convention. Mead's arguments were splashed across the pages of the Cheyenne papers, and his letters were introduced on the convention floor.(13) Mead worked directly with the irrigation committee chairman, J. A. Johnston, a Laramie County agriculturist. Charles A. Burritt, a Johnson County lawyer, worked constantly with Mead on the text of the article and was its floor leader in the convention.(14)

Opposition to the Mead plan developed immediately. Melville C. Brown, the convention president and Laramie lawyer, offered an amendment that cut the heart out of the plan. Brown's amendment declared all water to be public property "subject, however, to prior or future appropriations for beneficial use." Private appropriations, under the Brown amendment, could put the state out of the water business. Clarence D. Clark, a Uinta County lawyer, immediately realized the "subterfuge" and moved to strike "future."(15) Territorial supreme court justice Asbury B. Conaway then reminded the convention of the riparian rights doctrine and asked for more discussion of the new system's wisdom. Charles N. Potter, later a justice of the Wyoming supreme court and nationally recognized water law authority, rebutted Conaway on the facts of legal history. He noted that "in some of the western states that rule [riparian rights] had been changed by decisions of the courts." The new law of the arid West was prior appropriation. It was the common law of the territorial courts, Potter intimated, and was based on the same environmental necessity that existed in Wyoming.(16) On legal grounds, the Mead system was only the logical extension of what the territorial courts had developed over several decades.

The legal arguments used by the abler members of the convention validated as conservative what some feared to be an innovation. The concept of state regulation was acceptable to the majority, but some delegates wanted to clarify the terms of the constitution. Former territorial governor George W. Baxter wondered aloud what constituted appropriation. There then ensued a flurry of definitional amendments until Charles Burritt called a halt to the deluge. The article was 25 years ahead of its time, he claimed, and did not need to be loaded down with definitions. Others joined his plea, warning against passing legislation or legal dictionaries as a constitution.(17) The constitution had to be elastic so that "the courts in applying the law...[would] give this word such meaning as [would] insure the best interests of the people."(18) So said Melville Brown; and, with the last opposition defeated, the Mead plan became part of the constitution.

The Wyoming delegates demonstrated the faith of many conventions in the work of their courts, past and future. The acknowledgment of territorial court opinion on water law was general. It was not only good law, but also environmentally suited the country. The willingness to allow the courts to define the terms of the constitution to fit the situation was a similar acknowledgment. Moreover, on this crucial issue the delegates refrained from overt legislation. This was extraordinary given the growing verbosity of 19th-century constitutions, and it affirmed the delegates' faith in their judicial system.

The Wyoming system, with the Colorado system its nearest rival, provided a working model for the rest of the Rocky Mountain conventions to deliberate. The Wyoming convention gave the state a system Harold Ickes later termed "revolutionary in the field of water law."(19) As such it ran afoul of the conservative nature of many of the delegates
of other conventions. Just as Wyoming had enacted her territorial albeit revolutionary law, other conventions looked first to their own experience and tended to cling to it.

When the Montana convention met in 1889, the urgency of doing something about irrigation was as great as in Wyoming. The Montana Society of Civil Engineers recommended that a state irrigation engineer be provided for in the constitution. This was essentially the Wyoming schematics.(20) The *Butte Semi-Weekly Miner* ran a lengthy feature on the correlation of famine and irrigation. After its long dissertation on the disasters of India, China, Italy, and Spain, the *Miner* turned to the convention delegates. Montana, it stated, had "grounds for fearing that laws [would] be made which [should] so bear on the agrarian rights of the people as to result in disaster."(21) Other papers called upon the convention to insure future prosperity by having the state construct irrigation works. The *Jefferson County Sentinel* (Boulder) called such a state system "a blessing to the people at large...[which] would mark an era of unexpected prosperity."(22) The public clamor for action was loud, and the expectations were great.

When the convention considered irrigation, it turned first to the Colorado system, became deadlocked on the issues, and resolved the problem by doing nothing. Again, the territorial system prevailed, but not as constitutional law in Montana. The committee on irrigation reported a verbatim copy of the Colorado section to the convention.(23) The provision was innocuous enough, but several delegates got the irrigation issue involved in the taxation controversy. This in turn raised the question of corporate monopolies of water. Martin Maginnis, longtime delegate to Congress, noted the plight of the Greeley pioneers under the worst system of "landlordism and rack-rent" in the world.(24) Great Falls banker Timothy Collins, sporting a bit of his Irish, castigated the corporations as he observed that the best way to eliminate the abuse was to eliminate the source. He called on his fellow delegates to "unite together to bring that water out, and have it brought out by the state."(25) Thus were united the issues that caused the maelstrom of debate.

The delegates debated the wisdom of the Colorado system, but continually digressed to discuss the taxation of irrigation ditches. Several members wanted a definition of "prior appropriation" attached. Others were concerned with rents for water. Llewellyn A. Luce, former Crow Indian commissioner and Bozeman lawyer, tried to suppress the rent question by reminding the convention that territorial law already covered the subject.(26) The irrigation issue remained tied conceptually to taxation and rents. The urgent question became tax exemption rather than water regulation.(27) As with the mining tax, the issue became deadlocked, and the cry of "legislation" or "leave it to the legislature" became more frequent.(28) The taxation measure lost on a close vote; another omnibus measure hit the floor, and delegates renewed the debate. A coalition of miners and interests favoring government action on irrigation applied the tactics of attrition.(29)

The convention was given time for pause by an address by Senator William M. Stewart of Nevada. Stewart was accompanied by members of a Senate committee on irrigation, and all encouraged the delegates to act positively on irrigation.(30) When the convention resumed proceedings, delegates again debated the Colorado system. Collins wanted the section to read "all waters within the state are declared to be public property." But Llewellyn Luce would have none of it. He appealed to emotion and basic property rights declaring that "we would not own the water in our own wells." Others quickly joined Luce, astonished at the "annihilation" of property rights. Collins was forced to retreat, and several delegates tried to soothe tempers by retreating to the "leave it to the legislature" slogan.(31) Hiram Knowles, a Butte lawyer, verbalized the frustration of many by suggesting that the convention "memorialize Congress and ask for this water."(32) The delegates then stampeded to do nothing. They tabled the section and let the territorial law stand for future legislatures to alter.

The Montana convention did nothing because of an almost even division of votes on the irrigation issue. The result of allowing territorial law to stand despite the urgency came from an inability of floor leaders to separate irrigation from the bitterly disputed taxation issue. Delegates became frustrated by their inability to act, but both sides of the issue had solid voting strength. William Clark and Martin Maginnis led a bloc that was offset by Llewellyn Luce's vested rights arguments backed by Conrad Kohr's cattlemen's bloc. Montana failed to act, not out of deference to her legislature, but out of irresolution in the parliamentary atmosphere of convention oratory, procedure, and voting.

The Idaho convention was swamped by regional plans for irrigation and resolved the issue by specifically allotting priorities on an economic district basis. The Idaho press presented delegates with numerous regional plans for deliberation, but the convention resolved itself into a farmer-versus-miner posture.(33) The bone of contention was a Colorado model section that both sides wanted to mold to suit their own interests. The question of setting priorities most detained the delegates, but the agrarian voting strength overwhelmed the radical miners. The final provision was a compromise in which the state was economically divided into farming and mining districts and priority was given in each district to its dominant interest. The constitution also guaranteed the "sage brush" farmers the continuation of their leased water supply. The Idaho irrigation section was a long and detailed essay largely borrowed from Colorado, with particular attention paid to peculiar environmental needs in specific terms.(34)

When the Utah convention met, delegates had a sophisticated district system to channel deliberations. The Deseret Evening News gave a great deal of space to the issue. It termed the Wyoming system a "revolution" and "an exceedingly dangerous experiment." The News called for an irrigation article with "simple and concise language" and suggested a Colorado system article.(35) In the convention the Wyoming and the Colorado systems became items for consideration. The argument against the Wyoming system was fourfold. Most agreed that a territorial engineer was expensive, and the cost to a fledgling state was prohibitive. A few thought that the whole scheme was revolutionary. This view was well received by a conservative convention whose main concern was avoiding experimentation. The system also violated traditional property rights concepts which could also antagonize Congress. One of the most persuasive arguments was that the Wyoming system was only a minor improvement on the district system that Utah already had. Besides, many argued, declaring water to be public property would interfere with business as usual.(36)

The Colorado system proposal drew similar treatment. One delegate charged that Colorado had copied Utah's territorial system and had "made a plumb muddle of it."(37) Hence, if there were no substantive difference, why not maintain the territorial system? A majority of delegates agreed, and the convention passed an innocuous declaration confirming a half century of Mormon practice. The delegates who supported the Wyoming system tried to convince others that uses were becoming more complicated, but the Mormon majority had a vested interest not only in confirming their rights to water, but also in retaining control of the system in the state legislature. Thus, the constitution confirmed the territorial practice.

The Arizona constitutional convention was the last battleground for the Wyoming and Colorado systems. The Arizona delegates considered the full spectrum of 19th-century alternatives. The most conservative proposal abolished the riparian rights doctrine, confirmed existing rights based on beneficial use, and declared running water to be public property.(38) Thomas Feeney, a Cochise County machinist, then asked the convention, "What is meant by the 'common-law doctrine of riparian rights?'"(39) This minority ignorance of Arizona's long irrigation history was cleared up quickly, but it pointed up what the Greeley Tribune had printed a quarter century before: convention delegates did not have the requisite expertise to prescribe comprehensive irrigation articles. In the convention that was not at issue. The fortification of economic interests in constitutional bastions was at issue, and the delegates pushed hard for interest recognition. The Wyoming system would negate this interest objective, and a coalition of Democratic merchants, Republicans, and constitutional conservatives used this as a red herring.(40)

To offset the conservative attack, the agricultural interests conducted an informational campaign and rallied behind a compromise measure. John P. Orme led the floor fight for the agriculturalists. Orme was one of Arizona's great pioneers. He was a University of Missouri graduate in civil engineering and pioneered the irrigation system for the Salt River Valley. When irrigators formed the Salt River Valley Water Users Association, Orme served on its board of governors. He was its president from 1910 until 1918. Orme also served three terms in the Arizona legislature representing over 4,000 farmers in the irrigation project. With this background, his opinion carried a great deal of weight in the convention.(41) Orme led the offensive on the floor parrying thrusts like those of M. G. Cunniff, a mine operator, who claimed the territorial law was sufficient. "The reported cases left the matter of water rights in Arizona in an excellent situation," he claimed, and the convention need not alter them.(42) But Orme replied that specificity was needed. "Give the farmers a little chance," he implored, "let us know our rights."(43) Those rights Orme outlined in a substitute measure that he offered to the convention.(44) The Orme substitute consolidated some of the conservative positions, but specifically enumerated preferred priorities in time of drought.

The opposition immediately attacked the Orme substitute as legislation. A. F. Parsons, a Cochise County lawyer, termed it pure legislation.(45) Orme replied to this attack with a total denial. "The legislature has never passed a law," he claimed. "All the laws in the territory are purely judicial, and this ratifies and confirms all of the judicial rulings heretofore," he stated. Orme's explanation put his substitute in the most conservative framework possible. Fred T. Colter, a stockman and strong Orme supporter, joined the argument, extolling the benefits of certainty in constitutional provision.(46) The Orme forces then resorted to reintroducing the measure section by section. This tactic succeeded in drawing more and more votes. Confusion spread across the convention floor. Voice votes became so close that they were called for again and again. Finally, the delegates adjourned so that both sides could consolidate for the final accounting.

Then the irrigation article came before the convention for the last time. As one delegate observed, "We have tried to get something here that would suit everybody, but somebody brings in something that we do not want."(47) The injection of countless amendments and objections to the general proposition wore down delegate endurance. Cunniff then confidently called for a vote, and delegates indefinitely postponed and buried the matter.(48) The convention simply abolished riparian rights and confirmed existing beneficial rights in water. The forces of change that progressive leader George W. P. Hunt supported with his votes lost decisively to the Goldwater Democrats and the Republicans.(49) Again, the net product was an affirmation of territorial law and an open-ended invitation to the legislature to continue.

The Rocky Mountain constitutional conventions enacted the familiar when dealing with irrigation and water rights. The most familiar was, of course, their own territorial system.(50) Many conventions had a long territorial history of irrigation; where it had worked well, the delegates confirmed it in the constitution. Not all delegations elevated territorial practice to constitution law because of their reverence for tradition. Many constitutional as well as legal schemes for water rights found their way into the delegate files with Colorado and Wyoming provisions the most frequently cited in debates. Delegates were reluctant to experiment with the "revolutionary," such as Wyoming system, or to adopt something relatively unsure, such as Colorado system. Instead, they turned inward, seeing the deficiencies of their own systems, but hesitant to change. The inertia of legal tradition was extremely burdensome because irrigation was so crucial. Some delegations did inject their interest concerns into constitutional law. Others tried and failed. All delegations wanted to achieve some measure of interest recognition in their sections on water rights, but the realities of procedure and voting power often prevented success.

The conventions were not receptive to the Wyoming system of irrigation control. The handling of the system again pointed to the basic conservatism of the delegations. Although physiographic neighbors, all delegations were reluctant to embark upon such a revolutionary course. Later in the twentieth century, the Wyoming system did receive wide acceptance by state legislatures largely due to the conventions' inability to entrench some other system in fundamental law.

# 7

# Fellow Servants: Labor and Corporation Articles

Corporations and labor grievances were closely related issues for Rocky Mountain constitutional convention delegates. The problems of labor stemmed from the corporate working conditions of the mines and the railroads. Corporate abuses extended beyond their employees to producers and consumers, who singled the corporations out as convention targets. Although delegates often united on corporation articles to deal with economic grievances, delegate expertise, the inertia of previous precedent, and the desire to foster economic expansion frequently retarded meaningful regulation.

The problems of labor included working conditions on the job and compensation for industrial accidents within the legal system. The territorial law had taken the first steps toward destroying common-law barriers to compensation. The conventions provided another forum for labor to argue its case and attempt to secure equity in the legal system.

The delegate response to labor's grievances was conservative. Delegates maintained the traditional conduits of the marketplace by utilizing the judicial system, but several conventions did attack aspects of the common-law bars labor faced. This revision of the law included wrongful death provisions, unlimited damages, and the abolition of some common-law defenses to employer liability. This eventually led to workmen's compensation, but only Arizona took this progressive step in convention. The delegates conserved the institutional process of seeking a remedy, and they liberalized the terms of settlement in labor's favor.

Delegates took several steps to improve working conditions. They authorized the creation of regulatory commissions, but this solution was not overly popular until the Progressives used it. They did, however, authorize mine inspectors and encouraged future legislatures to follow their lead. Many of these provisions were more advisory than substantive.

The delegates faced several problems in acting on corporations and labor. One was the considerable apprehension about adverse regulation of corporations as many delegates feared the economic consequences. Moreover, delegates often lacked the expertise to deal with some issues. There also was political and economic interest opposition to acting on corporations. But most delegates saw the need to act and did so in a variety of ways. The problems of labor posed similar difficulties. Technology was lacking on some working-conditions problems. Delegate expertise was occasionally absent, and they often deferred to experts where politically feasible. Labor also suffered extensively from a lack of able representation in the conventions. These factors led to conservative responses in most conventions.

The Comstock Lode graphically illustrated the problems of quartz mining in the Rockies. With the end of placer mining and the rise of extensive quartz mining, the individual miner lost much of his previous independence as he joined a work crew for a mining corporation. Down in the mine, he faced new environmental difficulties: heat and water. Although the best equipment available operated the air shafts, ventilation was never adequate. The temperature of the air increased about three degrees with every 100 feet of depth; when the shafts finally reached 3,000 feet, late in the life of the Comstock, the miners encountered water at 170° degrees Fahrenheit.(1) These were technological problems with which management tried to cope; in conjunction with grievances generated by working conditions, mining labor also had wage difficulties. To meet the challenge, the miners organized unions and had some success in defending themselves against corporate abuses. When hard times came and ad hoc bargaining procedures failed, strikes and violence often became a fact of life. This phenomena was not isolated to Nevada, mining, or any particular industry. It was a problem of national scope with which Rocky Mountain constitutional convention delegates were familiar.

Another labor problem centered on the railroads. Labor had grievances generated by working conditions and wage disputes, and labor leaders saw an archaic set of legal rules denying them recovery when they were injured on the job. These rules became their target. The fellow servant rule, contributory negligence, the assumption of risk rule, and the like all were hated bars to what the laborer felt to be his just claim against the industry. The territorial law had reacted to this growing problem by limiting the operation of the rules or abolishing some of them when applied to railroads.(2) In the conventions, labor pushed for total abolition and a workmen's compensation scheme.

Nevada's 1864 convention was not presented with the adversity of the Comstock or the problem of the railroad, as neither was present at the time. Colorado, on the other hand, had seen labor strikes, the tragedy of industrial accidents, and the increased power of corporations. But Colorado delegates were apprehensive. They feared that a strong regulatory measure would frighten away the capital improvements they so desperately wanted. This was particularly true of the railroads because little over 700 miles of track had been laid. If "communistic ideas" were incorporated into the constitution, some charged, "not another mile of railroad [would] be built in Colorado."(3) But the Grangers, led by Henry P. H. Bromwell, offered a regulatory scheme that gave original jurisdiction to the supreme court in railroad controversies.(4) Part of the scheme was, of course, railroad rates. The Bromwell faction offered numerous "just and reasonable rate" resolutions and amendments that uniformly failed to pass.

The issues of rates was coupled to a section that forebade contracts releasing corporations for liability for negligence. The two issues split the convention wide open, giving the minority Democrats a significant role in the final passage of the article. Failing to achieve rate regulation through his supreme court jurisdiction scheme, Byron L. Carr, one of Bromwell's ardent supporters, offered an amendment to the equal rights in transportation facilities section of the corporation article. The amendment proposed that equal rights to transportation facilities be "at just and reasonable rates." The Carr proposal sparked a strong reaction, and the measure lost by a two-to-one margin.(5) The vote was indicative of the fight that developed over labor contracts.

The spirit of the Granger attack carried over into the debates on labor contracts. The committee version of the section voided contracts that released the employer from injury due to negligence. As drafted, the section was conservative as it only dealt with an extremely limited area of labor grievances. But George G. White, a Jefferson County lawyer and one of the most forceful speakers at the convention, moved to reconsider the article. White received bipartisan support, and his motion prevailed by a single vote. He then offered a radical measure that gave the legislature a broad mandate to strike down all "unreasonable or unjust contracts, or contracts...contrary to public policy." Although this section was quickly abandoned, White's success in getting the measure before the convention spurred bipartisan support for the expansion of the existing section. George Pease, leader of the Democrats, offered an amendment that expanded the section's coverage, and Byron L. Carr, Bromwell's lieutenant, immediately joined Pease to further expand the article. The convention then passed the section with the Pease and Carr amendments. White's assault on conservatism was too radical even for the Grangers, but it served the purpose of expanding coverage.(6) The Colorado Grangers were primarily interested in railroad rates and secondarily in railroad workers. When confronted with a radical proposal to vest vast regulatory powers in the legislature, which they and others distrusted, the Grangers balked. Their labor program was limited to economic problems rather than the pervasive social tragedies.

The Grangers evidenced a similar attitude in dealing with mine labor and safety. Bromwell offered resolutions that the mines be well ventilated and safety devices provided but left penalty provisions to the imagination of future generations.(7) The conventions empowered the legislature to create a commissioner of mines and to pass adequate ventilation, safety, and drainage laws. The Colorado convention took the middle ground on most issues partially out of fear of alienating capital and partially from lack of experience and expertise in the respective areas. The corporation and mining articles of the constitution were less a code of laws than other sections were.(8) The fact that there were only 700 miles of railroad track in the state and that mining technology was largely undeveloped best explains the terse language.

The Grangers' failure to support more radical labor demands also illustrated the gulf that separated farmer-labor groups in their fight for similar constitutional relief. The delegates were concerned with their own economic interests, and laborites were unable to generate enough support based on those interests. Farmers were interested in regulating railroad rate structures, but not in destroying the basic functional approach of the marketplace society. Delegates similarly attacked abuses without altering the institutional operations of the marketplace. They simply altered the balance of the contractual relationships to meet new realities. Labor's pleas for equity in compensation schemes violated the conceptualization of society that most delegates held.

In the intervening 15 years, events in the Rocky Mountain territories made delegates more aware of the need to act. Labor violence in strikes against the railroads and the mines became more frequent. From this unrest came corporation devices to suppress labor. Pinkerton detectives and Chinese laborers became favored devices to break strikes. Blacklisting, yellow-dog contracts, and the like blistered labor's feelings and enflamed its membership. At the same time, railroads were having rate wars, consolidation was a new means of suppressing competition, and railroad stock became a means of manipulation. Litigation and a flurry of injunctions stopped mining production in some areas and put men out of work. These conditions varied from territory to territory, but delegates were aware of the need to do something.

The Montana delegates passed a conservative corporations article largely out of fear of an adverse affect on investment capital. The delegates forbade any corporation to combine to form a trust, fix prices or regulate production, but this was the essence of the English common law that Congress had adopted in the Sherman Anti-Trust Act. The article followed the general pattern of delimiting corporate organization and activities.

When challenged to go beyond the traditional, the delegates balked. Joseph K. Toole, later Montana's first governor, proposed to make stockholders and corporation directors jointly liable for corporate debts. His proposal met a storm of protest. It would "not only drive all foreign capital invested in the state away," William Clark protested, "but would prevent any further inquires." Others agreed, charging that the measure would "ruin half the corporations in this territory." Several delegates tried to soothe tempers on both sides by pointing out that territorial law covered the issue. The convention then voted to give the proposal a quiet burial.(9) The measure was revived this time extending liability only to "their laborers, servants and apprentices." This met a similar fate, and the labor issue was permanently imbedded in the structure of corporate enterprise.(10)

Montana's delegates displayed a similar conservatism on the labor article. The committee of rules had not even included a labor committee in its report, but one was provided for by amendment. Peter Breen, an Irish laborer and itinerant miner and smelter worker, was made chairman of the committee. When the labor committee's report reached the floor, the delegates hacked it apart with amendments. The delegates appended the committee's recommended bureau of labor to the agriculture bureau. The prohibition of convict labor won approval, but the child labor section was rejected. Breen protested the convention's opposition to the child labor section, citing mines and sweatshops as the leading killers of children in the territory. The delegates listened to the opposition who pointed out that territorial law already covered the matter. Here, the evocation of territorial law was a convenient tool of the opposition. It was basically conservative as it offered no changes. Moreover, it assumed that no convention action was needed and, perhaps, that this particular form of overt legislation did not belong in a constitution. This opposition tactic was popular in several conventions and was conclusive except where a determined majority forced convention action.

The opposition forces also used the rhetoric of subterfuge in branding Breen's section as legislation.(11) Characterizing sections as legislation was indeed another common tactic. It was particularly effective if delegates were looking for an excuse not to act or if many found overt legislation repulsive.

The convention dealt other labor measures death blows. The delegates gave the eight-hour day similar treatment.(12) The labor faction failed to achieve any significant constitutional provisions in Montana due to its minority position in the convention, failure to convey any sense of urgency, and the tactic of requiring a specific article rather than incorporating labor clauses in the corporations article. The labor report gave the opposition a specific target, and the voting patterns of the delegates were oriented against anything identified with Breen.(13)

The Idaho convention adopted a similarly conservative corporation article, but their delegates adopted a labor article with promises for labor. Idaho was much more involved with labor disputes because of the antics of the Coeur d'Alene miners. The corporation article granted regulatory power to the state and specifically delimited the operations of the corporations. The convention took the article in great part from Montana, Wyoming, and Colorado constitutions.(14) This borrowing demonstrated the delegates' tendency to look to the regional experience rather than to another source of law.

Proposals that went beyond the traditional were met by violent rebuffs. One delegate charged that radicals were "acting upon the theory that [it was] time to keep railroads from coming here."(15) The delegates were conservative not only of legal and institutional forms, but also of previous territorial policy. The early territorial experience had been one of capital deprivation, and the territorial law had been used to encourage maximum participation in the marketplace. One aspect of that policy was the encouragement of railroads. Many delegates saw railroads as absolutely necessary and were apprehensive of regulation lest it discourage further construction.

The labor article was modest in its goals. The convention empowered the labor commissioner to collect statistics and the legislature to create boards of arbitration. The convention also required the legislature to pass state mechanics' lien laws, although they were already on the books. The convention made the eight-hour day law on state and municipal jobs and prohibited contract prison labor. They also excluded aliens from public works jobs and failed to act on corporate liability or labor contracts.(16) The exclusion of aliens was a particularly abrasive issue because of antagonisms with Chinese and Mormons. The delegates excluded both groups from the polls and attacked them here by excluding them from the public payroll. The Idaho delegates, like their Montana counterparts, feared that any harsh regulatory scheme or overtly favorable labor provisions would frighten the capital they needed to expand their economic potential. The labor provisions won adoption as much to satisfy labor demands as to assure the continuity of a labor supply.

The atmosphere in the Wyoming convention was markedly different from that of Montana or Idaho, and labor provisions reflected an anti-Union Pacific bias. As with the mining tax provisions, the Wyoming delegates were determined to regulate rampant capitalism in the form of the U.P. The provisions crossed traditional constitutional lines, as the U.P. was not only a corporation with railroad employees, but also a holder of vast mineral wealth. The delegates required the legislature to establish an inspector of mines and provide for proper ventilation and drainage of mines. The delegates outlawed child and female labor in the mines and passed a wrongful death act for those killed in mine accidents due to conditions contrary to the law. This wrongful death act remedied the common-law deficiency of a cause of action dying with the victim. The mining article was definitely written as a remedy for wrongs done in the depths of U.P. coal mines.

Similarly, the corporations article contained remedies for wrongs perpetrated in the territorial period. Section four forebade the legislature from passing any limitation on damages in personal injury or death actions. Thomas R. Reid, a U.P. employee from Cheyenne, explained that section four was "to protect the poor man. So far as law [was] concerned," he continued, "I don't care what law is, I have heard so much about law...that I am disgusted with it." It was justice he wanted, "and mercy with justice."(17) The usual arguments of frightening away capital came back at Reid, but others cited the frequent railroad accidents and deaths, and the inadequate settlements.(18) The majority saw unlimited damages as a compensatory remedy for future injury to Wyoming's citizens and as a proper device to punish the U.P. The delegates coupled the damages provision with one taken from the Colorado constitution forbidding labor contracts that released corporations from liability.(19)

The delegates adopted an eight-hour-day provision for public works and also extended the limitation to the mines. The eight-hour day for miners was introduced "at the request of the miners of Uinta" County and received support from a variety of sources. Several delegates admitted that they knew nothing about mine conditions but deferred to the judgment of the miners in passing the section.(20) The delegates also forebade the importation of private armies (Pinkertons).(21)

Wyoming delegates tried to incorporate arbitration machinery into the constitution. An early proposal required the legislature to establish boards of arbitration with the power to hear and determine all controversies, but opposition to this broad proposal was strong.(22) Delegate Reid explained that the measure was aimed at railroad labor disputes, and he was supported by Melville Brown, the president of the convention. Others objected. They saw the convention taking an unwise step in creating a quasi-judicial institution that had no guarantee of success. The best means of settling labor disputes was as yet unclear, they maintained, and the matter was best left to future legislative action. This latter argument won, and the convention merely delegated the power to the legislature to create such boards. The Cheyenne Daily Sun lauded "the most progressive and enlightened provisions," but in practice the lack of constitutional coercion produced legislative apathy as many delegates had suspected.(23)

The territorial experience with personal injuries resulting from railroad and mine accidents was tangible, and delegates acted to remedy old wrongs. The settlement of labor disputes was difficult to fathom. Uncertainty, combined with the desire to provide at least a vehicle, led the delegates to pass judgment on to the legislature.

Utah's convention delegates passed a traditionally worded corporation article but debated the board of arbitration idea at length. In passing the corporation article, the Mormon majority aimed its regulatory schemes at foreign corporations. The convention delegated rate regulation to the legislature and generally delimited the structure and operation of corporations. Among the limitations was the bringing of private armies into Zion.

The delegates were careful not to be "destructive of home institutions." The Mormon economy had been based on self-sufficient home industry from the beginning. Even in the late 19th century, many Mormons still relied on the small local businesses as the lubricants for economic progress in their market society. The Deseret Evening News kept reminding the delegates that it was "foreign" trusts, not local ones, that had to be regulated.(24) Even with these warnings of domestic repercussions, the Mormon majority was confident of controlling the regulatory machinery when statehood arrived.

The Utah delegates had a wide variety of regulatory schemes to choose from, but they resolved the question by granting power to the legislature. Several delegates proposed boards of arbitration as mediating devices. These same men prescribed the composition of the boards in numbers and politics.(25) The labor committee reported a verbose article that many attacked as mere legislation. Brigham Roberts, a leading Mormon and later Utah's first (but rejected) U.S. Congressman, suggested that the convention could empower the legislature to establish such a board. Dennis C. Eichnor, one of the Gentile lawyers in the convention, objected to the whole line of argument. "Yesterday we legislated nearly all afternoon," he protested. He admitted that this was legislation "to a certain extent" and thought that "it [could] bring no harm to any one and it [showed] a good spirit."(26) The nature of the proposal, not its appropriateness in constitutional law, was the central issue.

Eichnor was joined by other delegates who found precedent for action "in these new western states." The delegates looked to their regional experience for guidance. The newness of statehood in the region encouraged action, and the direction of the law emboldened delegates to push for positive response. However, others used the same precedents to defeat the advocates of specificity.(27)

David Evans, a Gentile attorney, finally proposed a directive to the legislature to form a board.(28) Some delegates, reminded of the violence of the Pullman Strike, wanted positive terms and broad powers for the board. If left to the legislature, they argued, the board would not be appointed "until some great strike has overtaken the state." The delegates feared that the traditional legislative inertia previously experienced would lead to disaster. This territorial experience produced a distaste for the delegation of power to the legislature and promoted the propensity to legislate in the constitution. With equal conviction, others thought that a board without specific powers would "only be an irritant instead of the poultice that [was] intended."(29)

Evans used a constitutional argument to quiet dissent. "The constitutional restrictions," he contended, were "only put in for the purpose of averting or preventing some existing evil." Future evils were the province of the legislature. Others wanted to push the argument to its logical end to deny all power to regulate wages and labor practices. Only legislative power extended that far, they said.(30) All arguments were mooted by the overwhelming defeat of the Evans substitute. Only a small minority voted for the Evans proposal as the huge Mormon majority and some Gentiles, who for constitutional reasons voted with them, resoundingly defeated it.(31) A hierarchy-sponsored measure became law.

The convention then went on to pass numerous labor provisions. The eight-hour day on state projects became part of the labor article. The delegates also included directives to the legislature to regulate health and safety conditions in factories, smelters, and mines. Child labor in mines, the contracting of convict labor, blacklising, the "political or commercial control of employees"--all were prohibited. The delegates also inserted a wrongful death and an unlimited damages provision. In all the debates that involved these matters, delegates expressed a desire to secure equity for the working man. They defined that equity in economic terms, but they were ever mindful of the social repercussions. For example, Hubert G. Button, a Salt Lake contractor and union member, in rebutting warnings not to go too far with pro-labor schemes, commented that he "never saw a riot over eight hours a day work."(32) The basis of constitutional action was still the maintenance of a balance of power in a contract society. The delegates were merely tampering with some of the clauses of that contract.

New Mexico passed conservative provisions for corporations and labor as expected. The Republican majority believed that the state needed to attract more investment capital; therefore, everything was done to encourage corporations in their activities. The convention established a weak corporations commission that could fix and regulate railroad, express, and telegraph rates, but could not regulate utility rates. This regulatory power was, in fact, endorsed by the railroads who saw the obvious opportunity to become the policemen of their own industry.(33) The delegates also provided for an inspector of mines with unspecified powers and directed the legislature to regulate mine ventilation, safety, and child labor.(34) The eight-hour day on public works also became law.(35) The corporation and labor provisions were consistent with the whole of the New Mexico document, conservative and cautious.

New Mexico delegates did remove some of the common-law bars to recovery for industrial injury and death. The minority report on corporations included a suggested abrogation of the fellow-servant doctrine. The majority understandably rejected it, but they did grant a limited concession in the miscellaneous article. The delegates passed a section that gave the victim of a railroad accident or his family a cause of action for the failure to supply a safe place to work. The section also extended the right to accidents caused by fellow employees.(36) As it stood, the section was an advanced concession to employee recovery; but the whole system was based on negligence, and it did not remove the defenses available to the employers. Harvey B. Fergusson, a progressive Democrat and minority leader in the convention, branded the corporation and labor provisions as a singular pro-business scheme.(37)

The Arizona convention revolved around the issues of corporations and labor. From the time of the delegate elections, the issue of corporation influence drove the Progressives on to capture the convention. The Republicans who won election were joined across the aisle by "corporation Democrats." This polarity existed in territorial politics and in the convention.(38) The Progressives offered broad proposals for corporations and a corporations commission. The Republicans and their Democratic allies attacked the proposals as ruinous to "the industrial prosperity of Arizona" and apt to "put every small corporation in Arizona out of business."(39) They countered with radical proposals to embarrass the progressives and then offered conservative articles in an attempt to draw compromise votes to status quo measures.(40) When they proposed to strike the corporation commission from the constitution, they lost by eight votes. The progressives, aided by Goldwater conservatives, were then able to pass their regulatory programs that delimited corporate structure and activity and allowed the state an active part in regulation. When challenged on so basic an issue, conservative Democrats voted to push the progressive program over the top.(41)

The Goldwater conservatives similarly played an important role in passing the labor program. Labor had been trying unsuccessfully to get an employer's liability act for 25 years, according to Thomas Feeney, a floor leader for the labor program. Opponents of the liability act immediately branded the proposal as unconstitutional legislation. Feeney replied that the convention was the best vehicle for securing legislative passage and wondered where "the line of demarcation" between legislation and constitution should properly go.(42) The circumstances dictated action, but the convention was far from unanimous in this sentiment. A motion by W. T. Webb, a Graham County stockman, to strike employer's liability resulted in a tie vote. The progressives regrouped, however, and passed the measure with the support of conservative Democrats.(43)

The Arizona labor article swept away many of labor's grievances. The eight-hour day on public works became law. Delegates passed a broad child labor law that restricted not only the places of employment but also the hours.(44) The convention abrogated the common-law doctrine of fellow servant, enshrined the proposition that personal injury actions could never be abrogated or limited, and forebade contracts limiting employer liability (provisions similar to Wyoming's).(45) The defenses of contributory negligence and assumption of risk became questions of fact for the jury to decide. The capstone of the article was a workmen's compensation law that fulfilled the promise of the progressives to do something about industrial accidents.(46) The Arizona convention provision was the culmination of labor demands for the Rocky Mountain conventions. It included many of the elements previously attained, but it gave power to state regulatory bodies and removed the bars to equitable compensation for injured laborers.

The Arizona convention was a marked contrast to its predecessors. The 19th-century conventions had been hypersensitive about alienating capital. The territories were, of course, underdeveloped at the time, and labor was not a strong political force. The provisions that did pass were at least marginally favorable to labor and came more from a sense of maintaining a working economic system than from a concern for the social system. The Arizona progressives inherited the concerns on both sides of the issue but were primarily motivated by a desire to act to improve the social overhead of their society. Poverty was a dominant theme of the labor advocates as they saw it as a derivative of corporate abuses. The removal of common-law impediments eliminated one of the causes. Corporate regulation removed another. Even with the social concern, the Arizona delegates continued to work within a contractual frame of reference with traditional institutional devices initiating change. These were the fundamental principles that delegates had recurrence to after 125 years of constitutional development.

# 8

# Women's Suffrage

Women gained the vote first in the West. As the Rocky Mountain territories approached statehood, women's suffrage became a constitutional question. The way constitutional convention delegates answered that question depended more upon the peculiar economic and political heritage of the territories than upon any other factor. Delegates expressed answers to the question with their votes. Debate and historical events provide the context for analysis of the fundamental principles at stake. Further, the context for debate, as well as the ideas expressed, reveals the transformation of an issue and the domestication of politics in a region credited with liberating women from the bonds of eastern legal traditions.

The issue of women's suffrage in the Rocky Mountain constitutional conventions turned on the respective territorial experiences, the degree of penetration by women into economic life, and the weight of Mormonism in political affairs. The Rocky Mountain territories were among the first to grant women equality at the polls. Wyoming and Utah led the nation in breaking down traditional barriers. Equally significant for women's suffrage, the territories also abrogated the economic disabilities imposed by the English common law. Feme sole and sole traders statutes frequented the territorial statute books, and the territorial courts aided the process. Thus women were allowed to participate as equals in the contract society of the 19th century. But Mormonism as a political and social system was perceived as standing in the way of continued progress. Congress, in its efforts to crush the theocracy, withdrew Utah female suffrage in 1887.(1) Anti-Mormonism was a fact of political life in Idaho and resulted in Mormon disfranchisement.(2) Mormons lost their right to vote through test oaths and coercion at the polls.(3) Women's suffrage suffered from a Gentile assumption that a Mormon's vote would be multiplied by the number of wives he had secreted away. The test oath and a denial of equal suffrage often resulted. The Rocky Mountain constitutional conventions looked first to their territorial experience and either extended the franchise or made such extension possible in the future.

The territorial experience undercut vested interests and promoted equality in the marketplace society. The territorial law allowed women dynamic participation in economic affairs through the enactment of feme sole legislation. At common law, women had no right to conduct business independently of their husbands, but changing economic and social circumstances tied to the declining significance of real property undercut the tradition. The territorial legislatures and courts expanded women's rights very rapidly.(4) This willingness to enable women to participate in the marketplace eroded vested rights attitudes and enhanced women's social status as equals. Women as business operatives and taxpayers were thus in an identical position economically and asked only a similar position politically.

Nevada held its constitutional convention in a wartime atmosphere and before the major thrust of women's rights legislation swept the country. Nevada delegates all considered themselves unionists and sought a means of excluding disunion. They passed a suffrage article which excluded Confederates from the ballot box, but failed to pass a test oath. The nominally sectional alignment of the convention, buoyed by the fact that two-thirds of the delegates voting against the oath had voted against Lincoln in 1860, prevented passage.(5) When a women's rights proposal reached the floor, a similar voting pattern emerged, but the experience of the individual delegates played an important part. Most of the delegates were from California, which had had an extremely bad experience with a sole traders law.(6) But several delegates were originally from New York, the innovator in expanding women's economic rights in the 1840s. This experience, of course, put New Yorkers on both sides of the issue. Those who voted Democratic in 1860 opposed expanded women's rights, as did merchants and Californians who feared the competition. These men were bound together by concepts of male superiority, chivalry, and economic self-interest.

The forces that defeated conservatism were rural and liberal. Charles E. DeLong, a former New Yorker and Storey County lawyer, led the fight for women's rights. His advocacy split the mining bloc of Storey County, allowing the rural delegates to gain enough strength to defeat the conservatives.(7) DeLong's appeal was to the Nevada territorial experience rather than to the national trend. He used this device to allay fears of abuse as seen in the California experience. The ability of women and their need to unshackle themselves from the archaic legal barriers were clear. These arguments were all tied to a need for justice and equity for women struggling in a frontier environment. DeLong's oratory was persuasive, and a pro-women's separate property section rather than a prohibition was passed.(8) But the delegates never seriously considered the issue of female suffrage.(9) The time was not ripe.

The Colorado constitutional convention delegates met with immediate women's rights changes in territorial law, amid pressure from local and national women's rights organizations and with ardent supporters in the convention. Women had been active in litigating their economic rights in Colorado. In 1872 they dramatized their grievance in Holladay v. Dailey when the court pointed out that Colorado law extended only to contracts respecting a married woman's business and estates. Beyond these limits, her contracts were governed by common law and were void. This revelation combined with pressure from local women's clubs and church groups resulted in the passage of a feme sole statute in 1874.(10) The women's suffrage debate in Colorado had been before the public in 1870, when women petitioned the territorial legislature for the vote and the newspapers kept the issue before the public. When the constitutional convention delegates met, Colorado had an organized women's suffrage association, a petition campaign, and some newspaper support. Suffragists deluged the convention with petitions, held mass rallies in Denver, and addressed the convention.(11) On the floor, the Granger fraction led by Henry P.H. Bromwell and Byron Carr continued the agitation for convention action.(12)

The debates of the press and the convention mapped the contours of argument that would be followed for the remainder of the century. The advocates of women's suffrage asked only for an end to the "inequality of law and the tyranny of trousers."(13) Male superiority was repressive. Most abrasive of all was the no-taxation-without-representation argument.(14) The familiar slogan hit responsive chords because women were part of the economic community that filled the public coffers. Feme sole and sole traders statutes had made that possible. Their position was strong enough to stimulate press reactions terming universal suffrage "inevitable."(15) But in the convention the suffragists simply did not have enough votes to pass their program.

Without the political strength to achieve a total victory, the Grangers sought half a loaf. Unable to secure support for female suffrage due to convention politics and a minority condemnation of their efforts as sponsored by outside agitators,(16) Bromwell and Carr attempted to obtain the vote in school elections. This, they said, was a compromise which did not affront male ego or upset local politics.(17) Opposition developed charging that such an "ultra doctrine" could defeat the whole constitution. Advocates then turned to their last resort: leaving it to the legislature, or alternatively, submitting it separately to the people. The convention chose the legislative path with a mandatory directive to that body to do something.(18) Although suffragists failed in the convention, they kept the issue alive and before the public.(19)

When the Wyoming convention met in 1889, female suffrage had been the territorial law for 20 years. The first session of the territorial legislature passed a women's suffrage act, and it remained on the statute books despite a repeal measure that was vetoed by the governor a year later.(20) That same legislature that granted women political rights had also extended marketplace rights to them.(21) Wyoming's women participated as equals in both the political and economic spheres of territorial life. This long experience was a central topic of debate in the convention and, combined with the sense of the equity and justice involved, was determinative of delegate behavior.

A majority of the delegates viewed the territorial suffrage experience as successful and voted to have it continue. Led by Melville Brown, president of the convention, the female suffrage advocates rebuffed an attack on the territorial experience and countered with claims of its success and justice.(22) A brief effort to limit female suffrage to school elections generated only complacency.(23) The suffragists were confident of their strength and their arguments. The political arena was not chaotic due to female votes, and equity was on the side of women taxpayers. In the last analysis, as the Laramie Boomerang observed, "it would [have been] an easier matter to level the mountains in Wyoming than to prevent them from providing...the vote [to] women."(24) The territorial experience was conclusive proof to the delegates that female suffrage was not only right, but also workable politically.

Montana's convention met in 1889, and its territorial experience with expanded women's rights also was extensive. The territorial legislature had extended sole trader rights to women in 1874. The territorial supreme court construed the statute liberally, holding that it relieved women of common-law disabilities and allowed them to own separate property, contract in relation to it, and accrue debts. A woman also could convert her separate property without joinder with her husband.(25) Montana's women had participated in marketplace affairs for 15 years. The delegates also had to consider the abortive 1884 Montana constitution. That constitution had allowed women to vote in school elections and hold school offices, the same provision that existed in territorial law.(26) The political pressure had escalated as women's associations expanded, and suffragists sounded a louder voice in territorial affairs.

In the convention several delegates tried to have the economic rights of territorial law incorporated in fundamental law. Delegates introduced separate property and sole propositions, but some branded them as unconstitutional legislation. B. Platt Carpenter, a Helena lawyer, expressed the feelings of many when he termed a separate property proposition as "clearly legislation." But he was "in favor of their having equal rights with men in every respect in regard to the transaction of business." The constitution was just not appropriate as it could "be safely left to the legislature." The measure had, in fact, "been on the statute books for 20 years."(27) Despite the statutory provisions, advocates raised the issue repeatedly. Each time, their proposition was met with the "leave it to the legislature" argument and tabled.(28) But Walter A. Burleigh, former Dakota Territory delegate to Congress, offered a proposition which specifically linked political and property rights. Burleigh's efforts failed as his measure was narrowly tabled, but the link was irrevocably forged.(29)

Before the final suffrage section passed, a whole panoply of propositions reached the convention. The various roll calls outlined the blocs that molded Montana's suffrage provisions. Hiram Knowles and Walter A. Burleigh led about 20 liberals in the debates with William A. Clark adding his voting and rhetorical support.(30) The liberals opposed a literacy test and worked for universal suffrage. Some of their number hedged on the literacy test issue, but all favored women's suffrage. These men were joined by a faction led by Peter Breen, the laborite. These delegates favored a literacy test and female suffrage. Many of them saw a literacy test as a device to maintain the purity of the ballot. This was tinged with nativism and coupled to the economic self-interest of certainty in the labor market and the stability of wages.(31) The Breen faction was small, but necessary to the movement for expanded women's rights.

Martin Maginnis and Conrad Kohrs led conservatives in the convention. Maginnis was formerly delegate to the U.S. Congress, and in the convention he argued strenuously that the "primary element behind all government [was] force" and that women were physically incapable of participation. They did not want the ballot, he contended, and if they did obtain it, they would be "guided by the preachers and the ministers."(32) Kohrs was one of Montana's most powerful cattlemen and led his own faction without resort to rhetoric. Most of the conservatives favored some kind of limitation on suffrage and the restriction of female suffrage to school elections. These men followed personalities as well as issues, and Maginnis' forceful personality helped maintain a semblance of cohesiveness.(33)

Two to three dozen delegates who desired to maintain discretion with the legislature occupied the middle ground. They realized that the polarity of opinion had to be broken to initiate anything positive. The devices that they chose were conservative. Either a reenactment of territorial law or the abdication of decision to the legislature best satisfied their political and constitutional scruples. They did not want to foreclose change with "ironclad enactments," but most saw change as best left to future legislatures.(34) The convention was basically conservative on this issue due to the support of this middle group, but never reactionary. These moderates refused to look backwards to male suffrage or to suppression of the suffrage movement. Change had to be conservative, and this attitude won fulfillment in the final constitutional enactment.

Opposition to female suffrage developed early in the Montana convention and was conservative and parochial. An application of the secretary of the American Women's Suffrage Association to address the convention met outside- agitation accusations. But Hiram Knowles, former justice of the territorial supreme court, quieted opposition and the application gained approval.(35) The conservatives then offered a literacy test proposal that sparked a spirited debate. The test was designed to exclude alien anarchists, the criminal element, and the illiterate from the polls, but put more plainly it was aimed at "crazy idiot[s] from across the ocean." The liberals branded the proposal as blatant nativism and forced a compromise that used citizenship as the criterion.(36) In this atmosphere the suffragists offered their program.

The advocates of female suffrage looked both to their territorial experience and to Wyoming's long history of universal suffrage for precedent. Perry W. McAdow, a Montana miner for 25 years, opened the debate by referring first to Wyoming's experience. He noted that "from the best testimony that [they had] from the judges on the bench in that territory, from the Governor, from prominent citizens, it has been a grand success." In addition, he continued, they had a right because they were taxed, were due equal protection of the law, and were people within a governmental system.(37) A Butte paper printed an account of the Kansas experience with female suffrage, and the editorial pages were filled daily with various pleas for expanded suffrage.(38) Several delegates reminded the convention of their own territorial experience.(39) Both public and delegate opinion favored some expansion of the present system.

A majority of the convention denied universal suffrage, but conservatives were unable to prohibit it. With the rhetorical battle lines drawn, moderate delegates tried to construct compromise solutions. With both extremes of the issue denied victory, many delegates proposed that the legislature be allowed to act. William R. Ramsdell, an Egan merchant and cattleman, thought that the constitution was not the place for "ironclad enactments...that [precluded] the possibility of change." He expressed this sentiment despite his present opposition to universal suffrage. The constitution had to be a dynamic instrument, Ramsdell contended.(40) Others agreed for practical reasons. Allan R. Joy, who had previously sponsored the literacy test section, suggested that the question be put to the people every four years. William A. Clark, Montana copper baron, and Walter M. Bickford, a Missoula lawyer, added their voices to the growing chorus of abdication. Joseph K. Toole, a Helena lawyer and the first state governor, made a strong plea for allowing the legislature to extend the suffrage to women. The speech recognized "the logic of history, the progress of general enlightenment, the rightful sources of strength and power," according to the Helena Daily Herald. Interestingly, the Herald saw the acceptance of universal suffrage as inevitable, but wanted to wait until "the fullness of time had come." The abdication and separate submission to the people doctrines were convenient arguments for the delegates if convention deadlock seemed imminent. They provided rallying points for moderates as either resolved the dispute by doing nothing. The majority would not leave it to the legislature. They wanted some specific statement of rights.(41)

Compromise in the minds of the majority was specific. Leaving the matter to the legislature denied delegate prerogative to act, and the majority refused to abdicate that authority. The terms of compromise then became the center of contention. First, the territorial law was proposed in an advisory section for future action by the legislature. But William Mayger, a Marysville mining superintendent, wanted the section to be compulsory. This amendment lost, first because it only reenacted territorial law, and many delegates wanted something stronger.(42) Second, the territorial law was expanded to include women's suffrage and office holding in municipalities. This suggestion proved to be too extreme because it contemplated municipal conflict over temperance.(43) With compromise thus delimited, its terms had to be defined. B. Platt Carpenter put it into words. On questions submitted to the vote of taxpayers, women who were taxpayers and who were otherwise qualified could vote.(44) This measure passed and became constitutional law.

The Montana convention reflected many of the dominant features of Rocky Mountain constitution making. The delegates were reluctant to enact radical doctrines on either side of an issue. Many were willing to legislate for the sake of a cause. The desire of the majority of delegates to do something positive rather than to abdicate decision to the legislature was evidenced. Experience with territorial legislatures had soured many minds on the latter.

Power was theirs to use, and they used it irrespective of propriety. The document was specific and wordy as a result. Many commentators called this legislation, but convention delegates thought it merely expedient. Most important for future generations, the delegates wrote a constitution that invited dynamic change rather than one filled with "ironclad enactments." This was due to the relative closeness of votes on the issue rather than any sense of constitutionalism. Specificity and legislation did, in fact, characterize 19th-century constitutions. Female suffrage was specific in its provisions, but not its prohibitions. The territorial experience shaped the contours of the suffrage article that offered both the familiar and the proven. Delegates clung to this precedent, as neither the liberal nor the conservative propositions were realizable. In the resolution of issues, delegate voting behavior provided the portrait of the constitution-making process in action.

Idaho's constitutional convention delegates wrote the territorial law concerning women's suffrage into their constitution but devoted days to the discussion of Mormonism in the body politic. The Idaho delegates were determined to disfranchise the Mormons and politically isolate them. This behavior was inspired not only by local problems, but also by Congress' pervasive attack upon the saints. The Edmunds-Tucker Act had abolished women's suffrage in Utah and prescribed a comprehensive test oath to eliminate polygamists from politics.(45) That was 1887. When the Idaho delegates met in 1889, they enacted a strong test oath and did all else possible to eliminate the Mormon menace.(46) Women retained their voting rights as they existed in territorial law. They did so because delegates so encumbered Mormons with suffrage restrictions that the plural vote issue was moot. The delegates desired to retain the level of political freedom women had won in the territorial period and not to run the risk of legislative repeal.

The territorial law had provided women expanded property rights first and then expanded political rights. The fourth session (1867) of the Idaho territorial legislature provided for expanded property rights regarding a woman's separate property and real property conveyances.(47) The territorial supreme court greeted this legislative activity as part of "the spirit of a more enlightened age."(48) These expanded property rights were followed by extending the suffrage to unmarried female taxpayers in school tax elections in 1879. In 1885 the legislature abolished sex qualifications in school elections and officers.(49) A majority focused upon these statutes and accepted them over the persistent dissent of liberals who wanted universal suffrage.(50) Idaho delegates chose the familiar and tested devices of their own making rather than alien schemes, refusing to trust the entire matter to the legislature. They were more sure to "fix that [territorial law] in the constitution and have it understood," James Wesley Reid, a Lewiston lawyer, contended, than "to have it the creature and subject of the legislature."(51) A majority also were unwilling to expand suffrage beyond territorial law. Efforts to strike "male" from the section met consistent three-to-two defeats.(52) The conservative nature of the majority saw the status quo as concession enough.

Every aspect of suffrage was tinged with anti-Mormonism. When discussing bill of rights provisions prohibiting property qualifications for voting, James Reid offered an amendment to prohibit educational tests. John Lewis, an anti-Mormon Republican from Malad, virulently attacked the section as favoring the saints. "It [was] a well known fact," Lewis ranted, "that in the Mormon church a very large percentage of the members of that church" were unable "to read or write." This ignorance, he contended, was "the source of their strength" as "in their ignorance they [had] absolute control of all their material affairs." Lewis' appeal was successful, albeit his facts were tenuous, and the educational test prohibition was stricken.(53) The delegates were almost unanimous in their determination to outlaw Mormonism, as the Idaho Daily Statesman observed, but they were divided on the means.(54) Lewis' appeal was coupled with a nativist reaction to foreigners generally. The liberals thought a reactionary constitution would permanently damage the state.

The liberals in the convention attempted to delimit the restrictive nature of the suffrage article. George Ainslie, a Boise lawyer and former delegate to Congress, and James Reid led the liberal floor fight. They were supported by a majority of the Democrats and a handful of Republicans. The majority Republicans were well organized and had high- percent agreements on the suffrage issue.(55) The liberals tried to limit Republican voting strength with appeals to democratic principles of government and the probable consequences of reactionary constitutionalism. Aaron Foster Parker, a prominent newspaperman and real estate promoter, verbalized the liberal argument in attacking Republican prejudice. "In the making of constitution law, we hasten to impose political disabilities upon those of our fellow citizens who do not believe as we do," he charged. Depriving Mormons of their political rights "to convince [them] that they [were] wrong" about religion, was an improper means, Parker contended. That matter of conscience was only amenable to moral suasion, not political deprivation. Ainslie argued that overly restrictive provisions could be applied to "some of the secret societies, Masons and Odd Fellows, and...Catholics." He proposed that they "confine it particularly to that class of people which it was intended for originally."(56) The liberals argued that they too wanted to "close every avenue against these tricky Mormons,"(57) but did not want reactionary provisions permanently cemented in constitutional law.

The liberal problem was that their heavily Democratic membership drew heavy fire from the majority Republicans. The Republicans used the caucus in maintaining a consistent voting advantage. The Democrats were able to deny them a quorum by failing to vote, but this tactic gained little for either side.(58) The delegates indulged in lengthy partisan debates that ranged far from the suffrage issue. Members on both sides of the aisle periodically called for the convention to act positively on the issue rather than to continue with polarized debate.(59) The extensiveness of debates and the urgency to act due to the pressing nature of other issues finally pushed delegates to vote.

The Republicans achieved acceptance of extremely broad anti-Mormon provisions in adopting the final draft of the suffrage article. Liberal efforts to limit legislative discretion on suffrage to "the classes of persons referred to in the...section" failed. Ainslie branded the Republican provision as "one of the most infamous declarations that was ever put into a constitution." It left suffrage qualifications "to the whims and caprices of a biennial mob of adventurers." Parker scoffed at Republican motives, as he saw disfranchisement as a means of limiting Democratic electoral strength. But the Republicans had their way because, as Ainslie put it, the convention delegates had "this thing of Mormonism on the brain."(60) What was even more frightening than unlimited legislative discretion was, first, that the legislature could "never annul the provision in [the] article" and, second, that the provisions were extremely broad. Not only were polygamists disfranchised, but also anyone who taught, advised, counseled, aided, or encouraged such or similar conduct lost his vote. Members of any group that so taught were similarly subject. Mormons or people who aided them in any way were politically isolated. Interestingly, those who taught that there was a higher law than the Idaho rules of civil conduct were disfranchised. Chinese and persons of Mongolian descent, along with Indians not taxed, got similar treatment.(61) In the fever pitch of anti-Mormonism, Idaho delegates disfranchised their suspected political enemies, entrenched that decision in constitutional law, and made further repression possible in the future. The whims and caprice that Ainslie feared in legislatures were just as present in constitutional conventions. The political wind that originated in the territorial experience swept anti-Mormons into the convention and blew liberalism away.

Utah's territorial experience with women's rights and suffrage had been extensive. Mormon religious doctrine recognized that women were not basically inferior to men.(62) This religious attitude was part of territorial law. Women were allowed participation in the marketplace and the political arena. Mormon legislators removed many of the common-law limitations on married women's commercial rights and extended the franchise in 1870.(63) Congress abolished women's suffrage in 1887 as part of its effort to remove church influence from secular affairs.(64) This legislation did not remove the economic rights nor the societal assumptions that produced them.

This attitude was quite evident in convention debates. For example, when the miscellaneous article was being debated and each section voted on, a women's separate property section came up. Previously, only a homestead section had survived the convention's cleaver. One proposal after another had been chopped from the article, but not so with women's rights. David Evans, an Ogden lawyer and Gentile, immediately rose to its defense. He feared that the section would be defeated because the convention did not realize its significance. Evans then explained that it was an abrogation of common law and was "in keeping with all the advance of recent years." Charles S. Varian, another Gentile and former U.S. Attorney for Utah, supported Evans and reminded his Mormon colleagues that the section did no more than validify their own handiwork of territorial law. The convention agreed to the section and continued "working hard to give women equal rights with men," as William Howard, a Mormon blacksmith, put it.(65)

Women's suffrage received broad support in and out of convention. The Salt Lake City Daily Tribune reported that a majority of the delegates favored women's suffrage before they entered the convention halls. (66) Various women's organizations bombarded the delegates with petitions and memorials. They also spread their arguments across the press. The arguments of equal rights and taxation without representation were not new, but the quantity and variety of their publicity campaign was persuasive. The Deseret Evening News reported "tumultuous demonstrations" in and out of convention floors.(67) The debates in the convention reflected many of the activities and arguments afoot in the public at large.

The female vote was not a partisan issue in Utah as both parties pledged support for its passage. In the convention the Republican majority split on the issue and those opposed were joined by Brigham Roberts' faction from across the aisle. The resultant impasse forced the convention to go through "hell," as Edward Snow, a Mormon school teacher, put it.(68) The deadlock that prolonged the debate was caused by the political defections. Brigham Roberts led a handful of Democrats away from the fold. Roberts' key contribution to the anti-universal suffrage cause was his stirring oratory and high church position. Richard Mackintosh, a son of Erin and prominent Salt Lake City businessman and miner, led the Republican assault on female suffrage. When the votes were recorded, this coalition controlled a third of the convention.(69)

The delegates who honored their pledges controlled 46 votes, 8 votes short of an absolute majority. This bloc consisted of 30

Democrats and 16 Republicans who voted in complete accord on every issue.(70) This key bloc of votes included four Gentiles, three Republicans and one Democrat. The votes needed for a majority were supplied by David Evans. Together the regular party members and the Evans faction carried the day for women's suffrage in Utah. This suffragist group defended against tactics of delay and irresolution; realizing the unique opportunity to place women's suffrage in fundamental law, they fought vigorously for its inclusion.

Opposition tactics consisted of using old arguments and generating traditional Utah apprehensions. The minority report on suffrage revealed part of the campaign. It reminded delegates that Congress had previously withdrawn women's suffrage "to place this Territory in harmony with the Union." A restoration of women's suffrage "would destroy the present equality of parties," they contended, and restore Mormon tyranny by resuming "their sway by working upon the generous impulses and religious instincts of women." This, they implied, would result in social chaos, political disorder, business depression, and lost statehood. Congress was the final arbiter and could reject the constitution based on this single slip of the pen.(71) These were typical Gentile arguments, but Brigham Roberts also came to the aid of the minority. He chastised the Mormons for their "scant courtesy" and warned them not to stigmatize the report "with improper motives." The issues were important and had to be discussed, he maintained.(72)

With the minority report introduced, Roberts launched his assault on women's suffrage. He noted that the Republicans had already caucused and "almost solidly concluded to support the proposition." This unthinking partisan position was dangerous, he concluded, because statehood could be lost as a result. Opposition to the constitution was developing because of higher taxes, a fear of prohibition being enacted, the political position of the Democrats, and women's suffrage, Roberts said. Women's suffrage was the most dangerous because it would destroy the American political party system. He based this conclusion on the Wyoming experience that he likened to "going to a relief society meeting" on election day. More important, female suffrage generated a fear of "the dominant church organization in this Territory." This probable return of Mormon tyranny would result in problems with Washington. "It [was] not yet accepted abroad that the people of Utah [were] acting in good faith in this movement," Roberts warned. The mere suspicion of a Mormon conspiracy could "arouse a sentiment that shall demand the postponement of statehood for Utah." It would be tragic, given the past failures to gain statehood and the present effort being the first with an enabling act, to miss "the golden opportunity. If this good time [should] pass, if our efforts [should] now be defeated," he cautioned, "God only [knew] when the opportunity [would] come again." Statehood was first and women's suffrage secondary.(73) Past experience and present fears were powerful arguments for immediate reflection on the expediency of action in 1895. The golden opportunity for Roberts was statehood at all costs.

Roberts' arguments received amplification in the territorial press. The Ogden Standard referred to the speech and warned of an adverse reaction in Washington. The Salt Lake Argus saw a popular fear of a scheming clergy working to defeat the constitution and an apprehensive public fearing a return of Mormon tyranny. The Salt Lake Tribune thought that the inclusion of women's suffrage could defeat the whole constitution. Reports from the hustings also revealed a growing popular opposition. Roberts presented "a bundle of letters and dispatches from all parts of the Territory" opposing women's suffrage.(74) Thus, Roberts presented the challenge to the suffragists in the convention.

They replied with shotgun tactics, scattering their arguments across the field. Proponents operated without a single dominant spokesman or cohesive argument. Abel Evans, a Mormon farmer, cited favorable opinions of governors from Kansas, Colorado, and Wyoming. He tried to respond to the relief-society-atmosphere charge of Roberts, but the level of his argument missed the mark. Edward H. Snow, son of a Mormon pioneer and a St. George school teacher, argued that women were becoming an industrial class and that a denial of suffrage was a degradation of class. For social reasons, he contended, female suffrage was just and inevitable. John F. Chidester, the Garfield County clerk, called on the delegates to follow their party pledges and vote for female suffrage. Andrew S. Anderson, a Beaver County civil engineer, advocated women's suffrage because "the principles of justice [demanded] it." Suffrage embraced "the principles of human rights and liberties and the great fundamental principle...[of] no taxation without representation." In addition, Anderson maintained, women purified politics. He pointed to Utah's territorial experience and Wyoming's record as evidence. Anderson then noted that the federal government had extended suffrage to "millions of ignorant slaves." In the same spirit, Utah should extend the vote to women to present a civil libertarian constitution to Congress and the world, he concluded. Samuel Thurman, a Provo lawyer and member of two previous Utah constitutional conventions, joined Anderson in advocating justice rather than expediency. He expressed confidence that the Mormon church would "let political parties alone." Franklin S. Richards, a Salt Lake lawyer, blasted the no-statehood scare as imaginary and lauded the territorial experience. "The women of Utah exercised the privileges of electors for seventeen years, and I have yet to learn of a single instance...[of] abuse," he said.(75) The suffragists attacked opposition arguments piecemeal, but they consistently denied a Mormon conspiracy, doubted congressional adversity, and praised the territorial experience.(76)

Delegates wanted the issues fully debated, but the exuberance of several delegates and the tactics of rhetorical attrition started to fray tempers. Both sides continued their exchanges. Roberts took the floor intermittently and discussed poetry, philosophy, and history. Orson F. Whitney, a Salt Lake newspaperman, countered with a discourse on Milton's Paradise Lost and the guiding hand of "Providence."(77) Increasingly, suggestions of leaving it to the legislature and separate submission to the people echoed in the halls. Many thought both impossible. Elias Morris, a Salt Lake brick manufacturer, warned the delegates against missing the "golden opportunity." "Now is the time," he pleaded. "Leave it to the Legislature, leave it to the voters, and it will not be done. We have learned a lesson in regard to this." Then he strenuously argued that the convention had "a power to-day to place it there [in the constitution], and no man living [could] prevent it." The constitutional convention was a unique forum for the resolution of social issues because its power could cut through the popular and legislative inertia that prevented reform.(78)

The resolution to act in the constitution was met by continued delay, but it strengthened the suffragists' determination to act. Karl G. Maeser, president of Brigham Young University, likened the proceedings to a party convention or caucus. He implored the delegates to stop acting like politicians and "try to be statesmen, and execute the highest workmanship of statesmanship." John Henry Smith, a Mormon Apostle, maintained that delay could not destroy the triumph of women's suffrage and encouraged the delegates to act. Christian P. Larsen, a Manti Republican and justice of the peace, blasted all of the "dodging and straddling and sidetracking" evident in the proceedings. Edward Partridge, a Provo merchant and first- generation Mormon pioneer, tried to flush delegates out, protesting the delay and opening of old wounds by the Gentiles. This protest did not quiet Brigham Roberts who attacked his adversaries personally, argued issues out of context, and used ridicule to amuse the convention.(79)

This debate of attrition gave currency to the movement to have the question submitted separately. The supporters of separate submission included both suffragists and their opponents. Dennis Eichnor, a Salt Lake attorney and Gentile, offered a proposal that section one be submitted to the people separately. Others followed with a host of amendments which put the text of the separate provision in the context of the previous debate. The heated arguments that followed indicated to suffragists that separate submission would not resolve convention deadlock.(80) They then joined to defeat motions for adjournment and recommitment of the article to force a vote. That vote was lopsided, as would be expected on final consideration, but the maneuvers that enabled the vote succeeded by small margins.(81) The Evans faction, which favored separate submission as a means of obtaining female suffrage, joined with other suffragists to include women's suffrage in the constitution.

The Utah convention's handling of the suffrage issue reflected many of the characteristics of other 19th-century constitutional conventions. The delegates came to the convention with party pledges; many forgot them on the floor. All realized that the convention was a unique forum for the resolution of outstanding grievances. They also recognized Congress' prerogative of rejection. The delegates saw their golden opportunity for action limited to both what they could attain in convention and what

Congress and the President would reasonably accept. Their willingness to take advantage of the golden opportunity said much of their role conceptions. Each was elected to write a constitution for the new state, but delegates disagreed on the composition. Suffragists or advocates of positive action generally viewed the constitution as a vehicle for reform. They had the power and sought to use it. Others saw the constitution as a series of prohibitions that were static. Since female suffrage was relatively new, they thought it best to at least defer to the legislature.

The suffrage article evidenced the growing tendency of 19th-century conventions to legislate. Rather than deferring to legislative wisdom on suffrage and allowing future generations to determine qualifications, delegates set them in constitutional law. They did so because a majority in the convention was politically able to act, and they distrusted both popular and legislative ability. The constitution was a dynamic instrument in the hands of reformers, but even they made their judgment static by failing to allow legislative discretion.(82)

The territorial experience played a significant role in convention debates. The previous record of female suffrage convinced many delegates that its revival in statehood was sound. Delegates also saw Utah in a regional context that allowed suffragists to draw on the Wyoming and Colorado experiences. Having a territorial precedent also allowed the suffragists to play upon the conservative nature of their program. They did no more than enliven previous statute when they made women's separate property and suffrage constitutional law. When all was said and done, Utah's long experience was better than all the theoretical arguments for sustaining its inclusion in the constitution.(83) The territorial law provided the bedrock of legal experience upon which delegates built suffrage and other constitutional provisions.

The tactics involved in the debates and the parliamentary maneuvers used influenced the course of convention action. The delegates did not use new arguments, but Utah did have a unique history. Women had participated not only in the marketplace, but also in the polling place in territorial Utah. The division of Mormon versus Gentile had been operative for generations; political party division was a recent invention. Delegates used these experiences in adding a Utah flavor to suffrage arguments. Opposition tactics included reference to the same domestic experience, as well as attempts to defeat suffragists through attrition. Extended debate on controversial issues in 19th-century constitutional conventions was often only a strategy of opposition. It was countered by suffragist maneuvers to exhaust alternative solutions and to force the convention to a final vote. These parliamentary devices revealed the division of delegate sentiment which was far from unanimous. When the delegates voted on issues, the composition of both points of view was revealed.

In the New Mexico convention, delegates used logrolling to obtain limited female suffrage. In return for guarantees for Spanish-speaking voting and educational rights, the Hispanic bloc led by Solomon Luna agreed to limited female suffrage.(84) The Hisplanic bloc generally opposed women's suffrage, and the Republicans were reluctant to support complete equality.(85) But the Hispanic desire to prevent Anglo discrimination was strong. Reuben Heflin, a Democrat from Farmington, introduced the limited-to-school-election bill, and it received support from Luna.(86) Although widely discussed in the convention, this limited concession was all that could be hoped for because of the cultural heritage of the territory. Women had traditionally played minor roles in commercial and social affairs. As the Women's Club of Albuquerque said to the convention, they "heartily endorsed" the limited suffrage.(87) They could ask for no more.

Female suffrage lost in the Arizona convention, but became law in statehood. In 1903 a women's suffrage bill had passed both houses of the territorial legislature only to fall under the executive veto. Although losing in the constitutional convention, women won their vote through the initiative process provided by the constitution.(88) This process again illustrated the territorial struggles within the legal system and the desire to act with constitutional means against the forces of conservatism.

The opposition to female suffrage was strong and vocal. The Arizona Gazette (Phoenix) simply argued that votes for women were bad. D. L. Cunningham, a Chochise County lawyer and Hunt supporter, argued that the delegate elections confirmed his belief that the people did not want equal suffrage at this time. Even more telling was the link between the suffragists and the prohibition issue. Outside the convention, women presented prohibition petitions while pleading for the vote. This joinder of issues caused a split in the Democratic party with both Progressives and conservatives joining the opposition.(89)

However, suffragists in the convention had enough strength to get the issue to the committee on separate submission. Fred Colter maintained that equal suffrage was a right and received enough support to get the measure before the committee. However, Thomas N. Wills, the chairman of the committee, opposed both female suffrage and prohibition. This position again emphasized the split in Democratic ranks, as Wills was also a Hunt supporter. The net result of the convention movement for female suffrage was defeat. The prohibition and suffrage issues came to a vote at the same time and were buried effectively.(90) The Progressives and suffragists generally could afford the split, because they had carefully provided an alternative route to legal fruition, the initiative.

Female suffrage confronted convention delegates with a legal tradition, changing social values, and individually peculiar institutional problems. The territorial experience with expanded female contract rights was eminently crucial to each convention's consideration of female suffrage. This underlay all the traditional rhetoric. Equally important, the extension of the vote proposed a change in social values. Delegates saw women as a stabilizing factor in the frontier situation. This attitudinal context was only a part of the machinery that resolved the issues. Each convention presented an individual setting for delegate deliberations. Female suffrage was only one of many issues confronting delegates, and it was the larger context that exerted additional pressures upon delegates. Hence, each convention presented a very individual portrait of lawmaking, and female suffrage was only a single tile in the larger mural.

Although constitutional conventions did present separate and distinct data, a pattern of behavior can be discerned. Contrary to Alan P. Grimes' thesis that economic factors did not appear significant in the western women's suffrage movement,(91) delegate deference to the concepts of a contract social structure were significant in determining the fate of female suffrage. There was a small percentage of women gainfully employed outside the home, as Grimes observed. Delegates focused much of their attention upon this minority in dealing with economic rights. As early as Nevada's convention and as late as Utah's, delegates fought for and won economic rights for women struggling in the frontier marketplace. This, of course, was tied to their belief that contractual powers in the marketplace were primary rights for all. Once conceding them to women, it was a simple conceptual step to take in female suffrage.

However the influence of the marketplace environment molded delegate behavior, there was an obvious obverse to the coin. Convention voting-bloc structure and the macro-context of issues influenced events. Archconservative on most issues, the New Mexico delegates made token concessions to female suffrage and progressivism alike. Arizona Progressives, on the other hand, passed sweeping progressive reforms, but left female suffrage to the people. As an issue tied to a potentially dangerous threat from anti-prohibition forces, Hunt's Progressives wrote a popular constitution without the female ballot to secure statehood and to allow the people to expand the franchise. Constitutional conventions were, after all, institutions of potential for sweeping change or for the maintenance of the status quo and the attainment of statehood by the most expedient route.

Suffragists used constitutional conventions as another forum for the domestication of politics. This process was varied, but clearly western women were politically astute in pursuing their goals. Suffrage and equality were attributes of fundamental law worth struggling for in frontier politics, legislation, or constitutional provision.

# 9

# A Recurrence to Fundamental Principles

Although each constitutional convention functioned according to the internal dynamics of constitution making, the delegates collectively responded to three basic external factors. The arid environment had impact upon the bulk of constitutional topics. As an adjunct of environmental impact, the territorial law played an important part in deliberations. As precedent, it established a regional legal pattern delegates knew; and, as an evidence of socio-legal attitudes, it provided a specific reference for argument and, oftentimes, compromise. Territorial law gave delegates an authoritative guide to deal with complex policy questions. Whether as pattern, attitude, or authority, territorial law was a constant reference for deliberations. The third major factor was the territorial experience itself. The federal system of appointive officials and congressional veto of legislation were factors that stimulated delegates first to escape the status and second to remedy the weaknesses of the system. These three broad factors working within the peculiar context of each convention had impact in specific areas of constitution making.

The impact of the environment was pervasive. Civil jury reform relating to a regional need for the speedy litigation of rights to resources was a delegate response to a policy of maintaining a continuous release of energy of these resources. This response was to the needs of irrigation and mining, and delegates also remedied a grievance of the territorial period. Grand jury reform related to a frontier attitude that found technical errors and secrecy repugnant to concepts of substantial justice. Again, responding to an environmentally derived attitude, delegates saw a need to remedy the abuses of the past. The impact of the environment was tied closely to territorial problems.

When mining and irrigation were involved, the environmental impact on law was more profound. Delegates molded the law of eminent domain to aid economic resource use in an environmental context. The delegation of the sovereign power to the individual for specific public uses in mining and irrigation responded directly to an environmental need. The taxation of mineral wealth was based on the arguments of environmental uniqueness and conformity with economic necessities. Finally, regional water law was in marked contrast with common-law tradition. It was an intimate part of the response to environmental needs and was part of a general territorial law experience.

The arid environment of the region influenced territorial lawmaking that, in turn, molded much of delegate deliberations. Eminent domain for mining and irrigation, although a direct response to environmental considerations in the conventions, was part of territorial law. The territorial experience verified the need for such a right in delegates' minds. It was good precedent. The taxation of mines also was a pattern of legislation deeply embedded in territorial law. Delegates argued economic policy and past experience. Mines were taxed, in the final analysis, at the minimal rates of the territorial period. Territorial law contributed patterns of legal attitude that had impact. Attitudes toward labor, notably in fellow-servant litigation, were closely related to general marketplace attitudes and corporation law development. However, labor gained if it had had a solid territorial law record. Mine safety legislation came directly from territorial law. It established precedent and gave delegates points for argument in convention. Finally, territorial law also reflected more subtle attitudes about the marketplace that had impact in constitutions. The role of women in a contract-oriented marketplace, coupled with a favorable territorial experience, gave impetus to expanded political participation.

The period of territorial status had impact in several significant areas. That status led to the development of an attitude favoring statehood at all costs. This attitude produced multiple constitutional conventions, hastily drawn fundamental law, and public policy compromises designed to obtain statehood. The territorial period fostered the political parties, interest groupings, and men that filled convention halls. Although delegates retained traditional government institutions, they demanded an independent supreme judiciary to remedy the old wrongs of the territorial period. More specifically, Nevada's delegates responded to a contemporary territorial problem by writing a judicial removal section. Finally, territorial status meant that the congressional ban on special charters forced the territories to use general incorporation statutes. The generally long experience that followed provided the policy background for the delegates. Here, both environmental factors and territorial status had specific impact on Rocky Mountain constitution making.

Whither the fundamental principles of our Founding Fathers? Rocky Mountain constitutional convention delegates spent more time on the issues of their day than they did on certain fundamental principles. This lack of debate was a consensus of silence on certain of America's fundamental principles. Particularly in debates on bills of rights, delegates accepted the rights set out in the federal Bill of Rights. When debating government institutions, delegates expressed faith in the judiciary, fear of the "biennial mob of adventurers" in legislatures in some states, and confidence in the office of governor. The delegates did not doubt the separation-of-powers scheme established in 1787. Their doubts about institutions were doubts about people, not structures. Initiative, referendum, and recall reserved to the people the power to deal with people and institutional inertia. The clearest test of fundamental principle came over suffrage as equality. Although it took an amendment to the United States Constitution to grant the vote, Rocky Mountain delegates found enough substance in fundamental principles and experience to extend the ballot to women. Although a halting and uneven process in the Rocky Mountain conventions, the recurrence to fundamental principles confirmed the faith of Founding Fathers in the state-making process.

The delegate suspicion of the legislature was part of the constitutionalism that was pessimistic about human nature and democratic political processes. In forms ranging from a rabid desire to put legislation into the constitution to demands for the initiative and referendum, delegates expressed the aspect of constitutionalism that concerned itself with the human drive to act selfishly. Fundamental rights needed protection against the shifting bargains of the legislative process. Simply stated, there were certain fundamental rights of individuals that government could not trample no matter how great the legislative majority. This concern for rights was a fundamental principle of the founding period in the late 19th century that received far-ranging specificity and elaboration in the constitutions of the Rocky Mountain states.(1)

# Notes

INTRODUCTION

1. A. E. Dick Howard, "A Frequent Recurrence to Fundamental Principles: The Courts and Constitutional Change," This Constitution, No. 3, 11 (Summer 1984).

2. The actions of the Founding Fathers have been a general continuing historical interest. Arnold A. Rogow, "The Federal Convention: Madison and Yates," 60 American Historical Review 323-35 (January 1955); Charles W. Roll, Jr., "We, Some of the People: Apportionment in the Thirteen State Conventions Ratifying the Constitution," 56 Journal of American History 21-40 (June 1969); Charles Warren, "Elbridge Gerry, James Warren, Mercy Warren, and the Ratification of the Federal Constitution in Massachusetts," 64 Proceedings of the Massachusetts Historical Society 143-64 (1932); Douglass Adair, "The Tenth Federalist Revisited," 8 William and Mary Quarterly 48-67 (January 1951); Douglass Adair, "'That Politics May be Reduced to a Science': David Hume, James Madison, and the Tenth Federalist," 20 Huntington Library Quarterly 343-60 (August 1957); William A. Benton, "Pennsylvania Revolutionary Officers and the Federal Constitution," 31 Pennsylvania History 419-35 (October 1964); Steven R. Boyd, "Antifederalists and the Acceptance of the Constitution: Pennsylvania, 1787-1792," 9 Publius 123-37 (Spring 1979); Robin Brooks, "Alexander Hamilton, Melancton Smith, and the Ratification of the Constitution in New York," 24 William and Mary Quarterly 339-58 (July 1967); Jacob E. Cooke, "Alexander Hamilton's Authorship of the 'Caesar' Letters," 17 William and Mary Quarterly 78-85 (January 1960); William W. Crosskey, "The ExPost Facto and Contracts Clauses in the Federal Convention: A Note on the Editorial Ingenuity of James Madison," 35 University of Chicago Law Review 248-54 (1968); Max Farrand, "The Federal Constitution and the Defects of the Confederation," 2 American Political Science Review 532-44 (November 1908); Robert A. Feer,

"Shays' Rebellion and the Constitution: A Study of Causation," 42 *New England Quarterly* 388-410 (September 1969); E. James Ferguson, "The Nationalists of 1781-1783 and the Economic Interpretation of the Constitution," 56 *Journal of American History* 241-61 (September 1969); William W. Freehling, "The Founding Fathers and Slavery," 77 *American Historical Review* 81-93 (February 1972); Larry R. Gerlach, "'Toward a More Perfect Union': Connecticut, the Continental Congress, and the Constitutional Convention," 34 *Connecticut Historical Society Bulletin* 65-78 (July 1969); Richard Hofstadter, "Beard and the Constitution: The History of an Idea," 2 *American Quarterly* 195-213 (Fall 1950); Merrill Jensen, "The Articles of Confederation: A Re-Interpretation," 6 *Pacific Historical Review* 120-42 (June 1937); Calvin Jillson and Thornton Anderson, "Realignments in the Convention of 1787: The Slave Trade Compromise," 39 *Journal of Politics* 712-29 (August 1977); Ceceilia M. Kenyon, "Men of Little Faith: The Anti-Federalists on the Nature of Representative Government," 12 *William and Mary Quarterly* 3-43 (January 1955); Staughton Lynd, "Abraham Yates' History of the Movement for the United States Constitution," 20 *William and Mary Quarterly* 233-45 (April 1963); Staughton Lynd, "The Compromise of 1787," 81 *Political Science Quarterly* 225-50 (June 1966); Forrest McDonald, "The Anti-Federalists, 1781-1789," 156 *Wisconsin Magazine of History* 206-14 (Spring 1963); Alpheus T. Mason, "The Federalist--A Split Personality," 57 *American Historical Review* 625-43 (April 1952); Albert R. Newsome, "North Carolina's Ratification of the Federal Constitution," 17 *North Carolina Historical Review* 287-301 (October 1940); John P. Roche, "The Founding Fathers: A Reform Caucus in Action," 55 *American Political Science Review* 799-816 (December 1961). Finally, Gordon S. Wood's *The Creation of the American Republic, 1776-1787* (New York, 1969) stands as a necessary ingredient of constitutional study. Also see Jack P. Greene, "The Pursuit of Happiness," *This Constitution*, No. 8, 40-42 (Fall 1985). *The National Forum*, Vol. 64, No. 4 (Fall 1984), contains a series of brief essays on our constitutional heritage.

3. Interest in regional politics has been of long standing. See Ira Sharkansky, *Regionalism in American Politics* (Indianapolis, 1970). The regional development has received recent treatment. See Gordon Bakken, *Development of Law on the Rocky Mountain Frontier* (Westport, Conn., 1983); Peter Harris, "Ecology and Culture in the Communicaton of Precedent Among State Supreme Courts, 1870-1970," 19 *Law and Society Review* 449-86 (1985).

CHAPTER 1

1. Jack Ericson Eblen, *The First and Second United States Empires, Governors and Territorial Government, 1784-1912* (Pittsburgh, Pa., 1968), p. 225. Also see Peter S. Onuf,

The Origins of the Federal Republic (Philadelphia, 1983), pp. 169-71; Arthur Bestor, "Constitutionalism and the Settlement of the West," in John Porter Bloom, ed., The American Territorial System (Athens, Ohio, 1973), pp. 13-44; Robert Berkhofer, "The Northwest Ordinance and the Principle of Territorial Evolution," in Bloom, ed., Territorial System,
pp. 45-55.

2. Eblen, First and Second U.S. Empires, p. 227. Colorado's early statehood movements see Harry E. Kelsey, Jr., Frontier Capitalist: The Life of John Evans (Denver, 1969), pp. 155-60. On Utah's statehood movement see Edward Leo Lyman, Political Deliverance: The Mormon Quest for Utah Statehood (Urbana, Illinois, 1986).

3. See the Boise, Idaho, Daily Statesman, March 27, 1889 for a representative editorial comment.

4. See Howard Roberts Lamar, Dakota Territory (New Haven, Conn., 1956), pp. 222-34, 244, for the Dakota experience. Montana, New Mexico, and Arizona secured enabling acts, but statehood was delayed for the latter two due to their reluctance to join the union as one and Arizona's recall of judges provision. On Utah see Edward Leo Lyman, "Isaac Trumbo and the Politics of Utah Statehood, 41 Utah Historical Quarterly 128-49 (Spring 1973); Joan Ray Harrow, "Joseph L. Rawlins, Father of Utah Statehood," 44 Utah Historical Society 59-75 (Winter 1976); and Howard R. Lamar, "Statehood for Utah: A Different Path," 39 Utah Historical Quarterly 307-27 (Fall 1971). Also see on Utah's 1862 constitution T. Earl Pardoe, Lorin Farr Pioneer (Provo, 1953).

5. Howard Roberts Lamar, The Far Southwest, 1846-1912 (New Haven, Conn. 1966), p. 319.

6. Martin Berkeley Hickman, "Utah Constitutional Law" (Ph.D. dissertation, University of Utah, 1954), pp. 41-42. Thomas F. O'Dea, The Mormons (Chicago, 1957), pp. 97-98.

7. Lamar, Far Southwest, p. 74. Sister Mary Loyola, The American Occupation of New Mexico, 1821-1852 (Albuquerque, 1939), pp. 110-11. Loomis Morton Ganaway, "New Mexico and the Sectional Controversy," 18 New Mexico Historical Review 215 (No. 3, July 1943). See Ralph Emerson Twitchell, The History of the Military Occupation of the Territory of New Mexico from 1846 to 1851 (Denver, 1909), pp. 381-94.

8. See Hubert Howe Bancroft, History of Arizona and New Mexico, 1530-1888 (Albuquerque, 1962), pp. 426-49. Lamar, Far Southwest, pp. 75-77.

9. See Constitution of the State of New Mexico, 1850 (Santa Fe, 1968). L. Bradford Prince, New Mexico's Struggle for Statehood (Santa Fe, 1910), pp. 17-23. On collateral and subsequent developments see Malcolm Ebright, "The San Joaquin Grant: Who Owned the Common Lands? A Historical-Legal Puzzle," 57 New Mexico Historical Review 5-26 (January 1982); William de Buys, "Fractions of Justice: A Legal and Social History of the Las Trampas Land Grant, New Mexico," 56 New Mexico Historical Review 71-97 (January 1981); Iris Wilson Engstrand, "Land Grant Problems in the Southwest: The Spanish and Mexican Heritage," 53 New Mexico Historical Review 317-36 (October 1978); Calvin A.

Roberts, "H. B. Fergusson, 1848-1915: New Mexico Spokesman for Political Reform, 57 New Mexico Historical Review 237-55 (July 1982); Richard Griswold Del Castillo, La Familia: Chicano Families in the Urban Southwest 1848 to the Present (Notre Dame, 1984), pp. 12-14.

10. Constitution...New Mexico, 1850, Art. I, sec. 1.

11. Lamar, Far Southwest, p. 77.

12. Ibid., p. 80. Ganaway, "New Mexico," p. 221.

13. R. H. Weightman, "Communication of R. H. Weightman, September 12, 1850," New Mexico Historical Society, Santa Fe. Weightman as U.S. senator-elect was in Washington immediately after his election and served as territorial delegate when New Mexico territory was created. Bancroft, Arizona and New Mexico, pp. 458, 633.

14. Kent David Richards, "Growth and Development of Government in the Far West: The Oregon Provisional Government, Jefferson Territory, Provisional and Territorial Nevada" (Ph.D. dissertation, University of Wisconsin, Madison, 1966), pp. 145-46. Also see Lynn E. Williamson, "The Bullion-Tax Controversy," 15 Nevada Historical Society Quarterly 3-21 (Winter 1972); Michael J. Brodhead, "Accepting the Verdict: National Supremacy as Expressed in State Constitutions, 1861-1912," 13 Nevada Historical Society Quarterly 3-16 (Summer 1970); Eric N. Moody, "Tom Fitch's 'Sage Brush Sketches': Sidelights on the Legal Profession in Frontier Nevada," 20 Nevada Historical Society Quarterly 265-73 (Winter 1977); James E. Woodin, "Thomas Fitch: The Restless Orator," 4 Arizona 37-41 (Spring 1963).

15. Lorenzo Dow, "Letter to President Millard Fillmore, December 15, 1951," MSS, Bancroft Library, University of California, Berkeley.

16. Thompson and West Publishers, History of Nevada, 1881 (Berkeley, California, 1958), p. 63.

17. Richards, "Growth and Development," p. 161. A copy of the constitution may be found in the July 30, 1850, issue of the Carson Valley Territorial Enterprise (Genoa) or in Thompson and West, Nevada, pp. 69-72.

18. Thompson and West, Nevada, p. 71.

19. Richards, "Growth and Development," p. 162.

20. Lamar, Far Southwest, p. 213.

21. Ibid., p. 214. Wilber F. Stone , ed., History of Colorado, Vol. 1 (Chicago, 1918), p. 170.

22. See Lamar, Far Southwest, pp. 214-15. Stone, Colorado, pp. 170-71. Richards, "Growth and Development," pp. 232-33.

23. Bancroft, Arizona and New Mexico, pp. 504-05. Also see Lamar, "Statehood for Utah," 313-23; Margery H. Brown, "Metamorphosis and Revision: Writing Montana's Constitution," 20 Montana 2-17 (October 1970); Earl S. Pomeroy, "Running a Territory: They Had Their Troubles," 14 Idaho Yesterdays 10-13 (Fall 1970); Ronald A. Limbaugh, "Some Idaho Carpetbaggers and the Moulton War," 14 Idaho Yesterdays 13-20 (Fall 1970); Thomas G. Alexander, "Mason Brayman and the Boise Ring," 14 Idaho Yesterdays 21-27 (Fall 1970); Marjorie Hornbein, "Denver's Struggle for Home Rule," 48 Colorado Magazine 337-54 (Fall 1971); Robert E. Smith,

"Senator T. M. Patterson, The Colorado Supreme Court, and Freedom of the Press," 54 Colorado Magazine 58-71 (Winter 1977); Robert E. Smith, "Thomas M. Patterson, Colorado Statehood, and the Presidential Election of 1876," 53 Colorado Magazine 153-62 (Spring 1976); Stanley R. Davison, "1871: Montana's Year of Political Fusion," 21 Montana 44-55 (April 1971); James D. Allen, "The Unusual Jurisdiction of County Probate Courts in the Territory of Utah," 36 Utah Historical Quarterly 132-42 (Spring 1969); Elizabeth D. Gee, "Justice for All or the Elect? The Utah County Probate Court, 1855-72," 48 Utah Historical Quarterly 129-47 (Spring 1980).

24. Lamar, Far Southwest, pp. 478-79. Montana wrote two constitutions before the 1889 document. The first in an April 9-14, 1866, convention in Helena was copied from California's. The second was written in 1884 in Helena.

25. Richards, "Growth and Development," p. 232.

26. Ibid.

27. The Nevada miners did attempt to give their local mining law constitutional status, but failed in the convention by a vote of 13 to 31. Thompson and West, Nevada, p. 72.

28. Hickman, "Utah Constitutional Law," pp. 45-46.

29. Deseret News, February 28, 1872. Also see Leo E. Lyman, The Mormon Quest for Utah Statehood (Ph.D. dissertation, University of California, Riverside, 1981).

30. Hickman, "Utah Constitutional Law," pp. 56-61. Deseret News, July 6, 1887.

31. Bancroft, Arizona and New Mexico, pp. 720-21. Lamar, Far Southwest, p. 144. Prince, New Mexico's Struggle, pp. 25-28.

32. Prince, New Mexico's Struggle, p. 56.

33. Lamar, Far Southwest, pp. 478-79. For New Mexico's experience see Joan M. Jensen, "Disfranchisement is a Disgrace: Women and Politics in New Mexico, 1900-1940," 56 New Mexico Historical Review 5-35 (January 1981).

## CHAPTER 2

1. See Gilman M. Ostrander, Nevada, The Great Rotten Borough (New York, 1966), pp. 17-34. Hubert Howe Bancroft, History of Nevada, Colorado, and Wyoming (San Francisco, 1890), pp. 159, 161, 172-74. Thomas Wren, A History of the State of Nevada (Chicago, 1904), p. 66. Effie Mona Mack, Nevada (Glendale, Calif., 1936), p. 248. Rodman Paul, Mining Frontiers of the Far West (New York, 1963), pp. 172-73. Mathew Josephson, The Politicos (New York, 1938), pp. 533, 536, 663, 681. Stewart was continually involved in statehood schemes that would allow Nevada to annex some part of a neighboring territory. See the Daily Statesman (Boise, Idaho), January 25, 1889. William Stewart Papers, MSS, Nevada Historical Society, Reno. Of particular interest was Stewart's scheme to annex part of Utah. He wanted the territory and the revenue, but

not the Mormons. To remove the objectionable saints, Stewart proposed a test oath similar to Idaho's. Ibid., Letter number 194 to Mayhugh, number 200 to Goodwin, number 186 to Smith on annexing Idaho. See Ronald Hadley Limbaugh, "The Idaho Spoilsmen: Federal Administrators and Idaho Territorial Politics, 1863-1890," (Ph.D. dissertation, University of Idaho, 1966), p. 202. Kenneth N. Owens, "Patterns and Structure in Western Territorial Politics," 1 *Western Historical Quarterly* 373-92 (October 1970). David A. Johnson, "A Case of Mistaken Identity: William M. Stewart and the Rejection of Nevada's First Constitution." 22 *Nevada Historical Society Quarterly* 186-98 (Fall 1979).

2. See generally Joseph K. Howard, *Montana, High, Wide, and Handsome* (New Haven, Conn., 1959). C. B. Glasscock, *The War of the Copper Kings* (New York, 1935). Josephson, Politicos, pp. 536, 629, 663, 666.

3. *Wyoming Times* (Evanston), November 20, 1930. Marie H. Erwin, *Wyoming Historical Blue Book* (Denver, 1943), p. 1312. Lewis L. Gould, *Wyoming, A Political History, 1868-1896* (New Haven, Conn., 1968), pp. 121, 164, 170, 172-74, 184, 187, 218, 223-28, 233, 237-38. *Twenty-Second Biennial Report of the Idaho State Historical Department* (Boise, 1950), p. 16. *Twenty-Seventh Biennial Report of the Secretary of State of Idaho* (Boise, 1944), p. 67.

4. Hunt file, MSS, Arizona Pioneers' Historical Society, Tucson. "George W. P. Hunt and the Constitution of Arizona," MSS, University of Arizona Library Special Collections, Tucson. Lamar, *Far Southwest*, pp. 501-3. Also see Sharon Faye Kearney, *Arizona Legislature, 1912-1914: A Study of Progressivism* (M.A. thesis, California State University, Fullerton, 1977); Gene R. Hayes, *The First State Legislature of Arizona* (M.A. thesis, Arizona State University, 1954).

5. *Twenty-Second Report...Idaho*, pp. 11-12. *Twenty-Seventh Report...Idaho*, p. 60. *Santa Fe New Mexican*, September 30, October 3, 7, 1910. *Tribune Citizen* (Albuquerque), October 4, 26, 28, 1910. Robert W. Larson, *New Mexico's Quest for Statehood, 1846-1912* (Albuquerque, 1968), pp. 143, 247, 259, 275-77, 282, 300. Lamar, *Far Southwest*, pp. 499-500.

6. *Salt Lake Tribune*, March 4, 1895. Lamar, *Far Southwest*, p. 407.

7. Lamar, *Far Southwest*, p. 407. Leonard Arrington, *The Great Basin Kingdom* (Cambridge, Mass., 1958), p. 404. Thomas F. O'Dea, *The Mormons* (Chicago, 1957), pp. 100, 123, 173, 252, 254. Kimball Young, *Isn't One Wife Enough* (New York, 1954), p. 378. Jean Bickmore White, "The Making of the Convention President: The Political Education of John Henry Smith," 39 *Utah Historical Quarterly* 350-69 (Fall 1971).

8. Erwin, *Wyoming Blue Book*, pp. 643-45. Gould, *Wyoming*, pp. 124, 163-64, 174, 184, 186-87, 191. James Winton Eaton, "The Wyoming Stock Growers Association's Treatment of Nonmember Cattlemen During the 1880's" 58 *Agricultural History* 70-80 (Jan., 1984).

9. "Autobiography of Conrad Kohrs," MSS, Montana Historical Society, Helena. Ernest Staples Osgood, *The Day of the Cattleman*

(Minneapolis, 1929), pp. 55, 122, 161. James U. Sanders, ed., *Society of Montana Pioneers*, Vol. 1 (Akron, Ohio, 1899), pp. 82, 215. Henry Knippenberg, *History of the Society of the Framers of the Constitution of the State of Montana* (Glendale, Mont., 1890), p. 49. James M. Hamilton, *From Wilderness to Statehood* (Portland, Oreg. 1957), pp. 223, 225, 321, 385-86, 388-89, 391, 404, 513, 515, 520-21, 539. Myers and Loud were Kohrs' chief allies. Ibid., p. 539.

10. Hamilton, *From Wilderness to Statehood*, pp. 585-95. Howard, *Montana*, pp. 60-66. Knippenberg, *History...Framers of the Constitution of Montana*, p. 20. Thompson and West, *History of Nevada* (Berkeley, Calif., 1958), p. 86. Ostrander, *Nevada*, pp. 33-39. James G. Scrugham, *Nevada* (Chicago, 1935), pp. 192-95. Bancroft, *History of Nevada*, pp. 180-81. James H. Hawley, *History of Idaho*, 3 vols. (Chicago, 1920), Vol. 1, pp. 187-200. Carl Ubbelohde, *A Colorado History* (Boulder, Colo., 1965), p. 146. Donald Wayne Hensel, "A History of the Colorado Constitution in the Nineteenth Century" (Ph.D. dissertation, University of Colorado, 1957). Lamar, *Far Southwest*, pp. 293-97. Also see Robert A. Murray, "Miner's Delight, Investor's Despair: The Ups and Downs of a Sub-Marginal Mining Camp in Wyoming," 44 *Annals of Wyoming* 25-56 (Spring 1972); H. Lee Scamehorn, "In the Shadow of Cripple Creek: Florence from 1885-1910," 55 *Colorado Magazine* 203-30 (Spring/Summer 1978); Robert L. Spude, "Mineral Frontier in Transition: Copper Mining in Arizona, 1880-1885," 51 *New Mexico Historical Review* 19-34 (January 1976); Chris Aspin, "The Fall of Troy: A Nineteenth-Century Mining Venture in Nevada," 21 *Nevada Historical Society Quarterly* 130-42 (Summer 1978). Steven F. Mehls, "Success on the Mining Frontier: David H. Moffat and Elben Smith: A Case Study," in David Wetzel, ed., *Essays in Colorado History* (Denver, 1983), pp. 91-105; James W. Byrkit, *Forging the Copper Collar: Arizona's Labor-Management War of 1901-1921* (Tucson, 1982). Also see Richard L. Hogan, *Law and Order in Colorado*, 1858-1888 (Ph.D. dissertation, University of Michigan, 1982). Hogan sets out miner interests as those of producers and provides a thought-provoking analysis of constituent politics in Colorado.

11. Hutchinson file, MSS, Arizona Pioneers' Historical Society, Tucson. *Albuquerque Evening Herald*, August 30, 1912. *Santa Fe New Mexican*, September 24, 1910. Larson, *New Mexico's Quest*, pp. 194, 196, 199, 201-2, 227, 245-47, 275, 277, 280. Lamar, *Far Southwest*, pp. 199, 500.

12. *Portrait and Biographical Record of the State of Colorado*, 2 vols. (Chicago, 1899), Vol. 1, pp. 109-10. "Constitutional Convention Members," from the *Denver Tribune* in Colorado Constitutional Convention file, Colorado Historical Society, Denver. Barela was originally from New Mexico. Two of his comrades in the convention were Agipeto Vigil and J. M. Garcia, both formerly of New Mexico. Vigil was a New Mexico legislator, judge, and stockman in Colorado. Garcia came to Colorado in 1865 and held several elective posts before going to the convention. See Lamar, *Far Southwest*, pp. 236-37, 270-71, 291. "The Story of Carlos Jacome" in Jacome file, Arizona Pioneers' Historical

Society, Tucson. For Luna see supra, note 11. There were several other Spanish-American members of the New Mexico convention. Alejandro Sandoval was a member of the territorial council, frequent county official, and stock grower. Santa Fe New Mexican (SFNM), October 4, 1910. J. Frank Romer was a merchant, sheep raiser, and "warm friend of Santa Fe." SFNM, October 27, 1910. Onesimo G. Martinez was also a merchant and sheep raiser. SFNM, November 8, 1910. Antonio A. Sedillo was an Albuquerque lawyer. He was a county Republican leader and ran the Spanish-language propaganda machine for the party. SFNM, October 29, 1910. Venceslao Jaramillo was another successful merchant and stock raiser. He too entered the territorial legislature and held numerous county posts. SFNM, November 1, 1910. Raymundo Harrison was a Guadalupe County merchant and a Democrat. SFNM, November 5, 1910. Juan Navarro was a farmer by vocation and an active politician. He was county sheriff, probate clerk, territorial legislator, and member of the Territorial Board of Penitentiary Commissioners. SFNM, November 11, 1910. George Washington Armijo was a former Rough Rider, successful politician, and chief clerk of the convention. He had the singular honor of having President Theodore Roosevelt stop in Santa Fe to be godfather to his son, Theodore Roosevelt Armijo. SFNM, November 14, 1910. Nepomuceno Segura was from an old Spanish family in Santa Fe. Although poor, Segura received a college education, became a telegrapher, printer, lawyer, and finally an appointed public servant. SFNM, November 15, 1910. Francisco Gauna was a three-term probate judge, Raton City councilman, and postmaster before going to the convention. SFNM, November 16, 1910. Tranquilino Labadie similarly had a long public service career mostly in appointive office. SFNM, November 17, 1910. Isidora ("Sunny Jim") Armijo was a Las Cruces politician and real estate investor. He also edited El Progreso when resident in Trinidad, Colorado. SFNM, November 19, 1910. Anastasio Medina was a merchant, sheep rancher, and "staunch Republican." SFNM, November 23, 1910. Margarito Romero was also a merchant Republican. SFNM, November 26, 1910. E. A. Miera was the last speaker of the territorial assembly. He was a wealthy sheep and cattle grower, bank director, and influential Republican politician. SFNM, September 26, 1910. Aniceto C. Abeytia was also a prominent Republican and longtime office holder. SFNM, October 8, 1910. Another holder of numerous minor offices was Atanasio Roibal, a San Miguel bookkeeper. SFNM, October 21, 1910. Eufracio Gallegos, a Union County rancher, was a territorial legislator. SFNM, September 19, 1910. Nestor Montoya was a powerful Santa Fe real estate owner and legislator and a leader of the Spanish-American delegation. SFNM, September 17, 1910. This brief and incomplete list is representative of the delegates. They were deeply involved in New Mexico's economy and part of the Republican patronage machine. Those political leaders without an economic base were given one in appointive office. See Robert W. Larson, "Territorial Politics and Cultural Impact," 60 New Mexico Historical Review 249-69 (July 1985). G. Emlen Hall, Four Leagues of Pecos: A Legal History of the Pecos Grant, 1800-1933 (Albuquerque, 1984), pp. 72-75, 149-56,

202-203. Michael Miller "Las Gorras Blancas: Night Riders of Las Vegas," 91 El Palacio 16-21 (Winter/Spring, 1986). C.S. Peterson, New Mexico Constitutional Convention Book (Denver, 1910). Francis Lewis Stanley, Ciudad Santa Fe: Territorial Days, 1846-1912 (Pampa, Texas, 1965), pp. 275-87.

13. See "Constitutional Convention Members" from the Denver Tribune in Colorado Constitutional Convention file, Colorado Historical Society, Denver. Portrait...Colorado, Vol. 1, pp. 367-68. H. P. H. Bromwell, "Bromwell's Minority Report on Suffrage 1875-76 and Other Original Documents of the Colorado Constitutional Convention," MSS, Colorado Historical Society, Denver. Lamar, Far Southwest, p. 293. There were 15 lawyers in the Colorado convention.

14. This description is a paraphrase of Allan G. Bogue's in "Bloc and Party in the United States Senate: 1861-1863," Civil War History, Vol. 13, No. 3 (September 1967), pp. 224-25. Also see Lee F. Anderson et al., Legislative Roll-Call Analysis (Evanston, Ill., 1966).

15. The program used was Allen G. Bogue's Boguetab, Social Systems Research Institute, University of Wisconsin. For another statistical technique see Robert A. McGuire and Robert L. Ohsfeldt, "An Economic Model of Voting Behavior over Specific Issues at the Constitutional Convention of 1787," 66 Journal of Economic History, 79-111 (March, 1986). The authors conclude that "The voting patterns indicated by our statistical analysis generally support an economic interpretation of the Constitution because personal and constituent interests affected voting behavior on particular issues primarily when the interests would be significantly advanced by the outcome." p. 110.

16. See Thompson and West, Nevada, p. 86. John H. Kinkead, "In Nevada and Alaska," MSS, Bancroft Library, University of California, Berkeley. The generalization is based on 28 roll call votes covering the issues of aid to the Pacific Railroad, mining taxation, a test oath, treason, a fee system in courts, a franchise ban, and impeachment and removal of constitutional officers. Debates and Proceedings in the Constitutional Convention...Nevada (San Francisco, 1866), pp. 196, 405, 491, 498, 499, 406, 416, 420, 422, 429, 431, 437, 443, 444, 446, 446, 520, 520, 521, 739, 492, 493, 494, 280, 564, 564, 565 (See Table 1). For a complete set of scales and/or cluster blocs, refer to Gordon Morris Bakken, "Rocky Mountain Constitution Making, 1850-1912" (Ph.D. dissertation, University of Wisconsin, 1969), pp. 176-86. Idem, "The Impact of the Colorado State Constitution on Rocky Mountain Constitution Making" 47 Colorado Magazine 152-75 (Spring 1970); "Voting Patterns in the Wyoming Constitutional Convention of 1889" 42 Annals of Wyoming 223-35 (October 1970); "Taxation of Mineral Wealth and the Nevada Constitutional Convention of 1864," 12 Nevada Historical Society Quarterly 5-15 (Winter 1969); "Judicial Removal in Nevada," 18 Rocky Mountain Social Science Journal 109-17 (April 1971); "The Arizona Constitutional Convention of 1910," 1978 Arizona State Law Journal 1-30 (November 1978).

17. See Lamar, Far Southwest, pp. 290-93. Ubbelohde, Colorado

History, pp. 146-48. The Colorado analysis is based on 20 roll calls. Proceedings of the Constitutional Convention...Colorado (Denver, 1907), pp. 86, 206, 206, 206-7, 201-2, 203, 203, 448, 450, 450, 498, 498, 499, 231, 231, 231, 454, 454, 502, 363-64. The roll calls involve the issues of the grand jury, religion, eminent domain, railroad rates, corporations, prohibiting a release of liability in a labor contract, a board of county commissioners, and salaries. On the Head, Barela, Thatcher, Stone relationship, Head voted with Barela 50 percent, Thatcher 56 percent, and Stone 69 percent. Barela voted with Thatcher 53 percent and Stone 50 percent. Thatcher voted with Stone 90 percent. Both Thatcher and Stone were from Pueblo County, but the former was a Republican and the latter a Democrat.

18. See Gould, Wyoming, A Political History, pp. 13, 48, 112-13. The Wyoming analysis is based on 17 roll calls concerning women's suffrage, salaries, labor, constitutional offices, and taxation. Journals and Debates of the Constitutional Convention of the State of Wyoming (Cheyenne, 1893), pp. 51, 51, 69, 69, 70, 79, 87-88, 88, 89, 92, 105, 108, 109, 116, 122, 122.

19. Daily Inter Mountain (Butte), July 8, 1889. Merrill G. Burlingame and K. Ross Toole, A History of Montana, 3 vols. (New York, 1957), Vol. 1, pp. 239-40. Hamilton, Wilderness to Statehood, pp. 483-84, 488, 526, 528, 575, 579-88. The Montana roll calls analyzed involved the location of the capital, salaries, irrigation, taxation, women's suffrage, corporations, the eight-hour day, and the free pass. Proceedings and Debates of the Constitutional Convention...Montana (Helena, 1921), pp. 763, 763, 763-64, 764, 764, 765, 774, 779, 782, 782, 782-83, 783, 790, 795, 796, 797, 799, 799, 800, 827, 857, 858, 724, 245, 445, 446, 647, 568, 570, 571, 680, 901, 321, 322, 587, 80, 449, 459, 462, 466, 855, 915. Also see Thomas A. Clinch, Urban Populism and Free Silver in Montana: A Narrative of Ideology in Political Action (Helena, Montana, 1970).

20. The Guttman scaleogram vividly portrayed the county voting pattern. Washington County, with two Democrats and a Republican, consistently voted with the Morgan Republicans. The 25 roll calls analyzed included ones on women's suffrage, eminent domain, taxation, water rights, salaries, apportionment, the free pass, and the Bible in public schools. Proceedings and Debates of the Constitutional Convention of Idaho (Caldwell, Idaho, 1912), pp. 1051, 1054, 1054-55, 1210, 1210-11, 1261, 1364, 1364, 1419, 1420, 1423, 1423, 1424, 1443, 1449, 1601, 1626, 1629, 1629, 1631, 1673, 1672, 1683, 1684, 1802, 1877, 1892. On Clagett, see Stanley R. Davison, "1871: Montana's Year of Political Fusion," 21 Montana 44, 47 (April 1971). Also see Louis J. Clements (ed) Fred T. Dubois's The Making of a State (Rexburg, Idaho, 1971).

21. See Salt Lake Tribune, March 4, 1895. Lamar, Far Southwest, p. 407. The 19 roll call votes analyzed include ones on labor, salaries, women's suffrage, indebtedness, and anti-corruption measures. Official Report of the Proceedings and Debates of the Convention...Utah (Salt Lake City, 1898), pp. 1167, 1173, 1176, 1179, 1158, 685-86, 703, 732-33, 736-37, 765, 767, 804, 950-51, 956, 957, 972, 1002-3, 1517-18, 1518.

22. Lamar, Far Southwest, pp. 501-3. Morris Goldwater file, Arizona Dictations, Yavapai County, MSS, Bancroft Library, University of California, Berkeley. Goldwater file and W. T. Webb file, MSS, Arizona Pioneers' Historical Society, Tucson. The issues involved in the roll call analysis (27 roll calls) involve water rights, corporations, labor, institutions, and the passage of each article. Minutes of the Constitutional Convention... Arizona (Phoenix, 1910), pp. 134-35, 391, 391, 391, 391, 399, 399-400, 409, 404, 410, 415, 415, 416, 423, 314, 314, 250, 250, 289-90, 219, 325, 324-25, 326, 326, 327.

## CHAPTER 3

1. Journals and Debates...Constitutional Convention...Wyoming (1889), pp. 723-24. Erwin, Wyoming Blue Book, pp. 635, 643, 938. Also see Gould, Wyoming, A Political History, pp. 111-13. Henry J. Peterson, "The Constitutional Convention of Wyoming" 7 University of Wyoming Publications 101-30 (May 1, 1940). T. A. Larson, History of Wyoming (Lincoln, Neb., 1965), pp. 243-56. The same observation can be made for Colorado and the remaining states. Edwin B. Smith, "The Formation of the Constitution of Colorado," MSS, Colorado Historical Society, p. 11.

2. See Dennis L. Thompson, "Religion and the Idaho Constitution," 58 Pacific Northwest Quarterly 169-78 (October 1967). Merle W. Wells, "The Idaho Anti-Mormon Movement, 1872-1908" (Ph.D. dissertation, University of California, Berkeley, 1950). E. Leo Lyman, "A Mormon Transition in Idaho Politics," 20 Idaho Yesterdays 2-11, 24-29 (Winter 1977). Michael E. Christensen, "Footnote to History: Charles W. Nibley and the Idaho Test Oath," 22 Idaho Yesterdays 19-20 (Fall 1978).

3. Idaho Daily Statesman (Boise), January 22, 1889; July 7, 1889; July 11, 1889.

4. Idaho Constitution (1889), Art. I, sec. 4; Art. VI, sec. 3; Art. IX, sec. 6.

5. Proceedings and Debates of the Constitutional Convention of Idaho, 1889, 2 vols. (Caldwell, Idaho, 1912), pp. 684-85.

6. Ibid., p. 702. (A compromise amendment lost here 23 to 25.) See Idaho Daily Statesman, July 24, 1889, for editorial comment.

7. Official Report of the Proceedings and Debates of the Convention Assembled at Salt Lake City on the Fourth Day of March, 1895, to Adopt a Constitution for the State of Utah, 2 vols. (Salt Lake City, 1898), p. 230.

8. Ibid., p. 231.

9. Ibid., p. 239.

10. Ibid., p. 240. Note the Van Horne, Wells, and Kimball (Weber) speeches for the outlining of concepts.

11. See Leonard J. Arrington, Great Basin Kingdom (Cambridge, Mass., 1958), pp. 353-79.

12. See Arizona Constitution, Art. III, sec. 12. Homer R. Wood commented that proposition three on religious toleration offered by W. T. Webb of Graham County was "pretty good for a Mormon." Homer R. Wood, "Book of Propositions and Notes as Kept by Homer R. Wood, Member of Constitutional Convention from Yavapai County," MSS, State of Arizona Department of Library and Archives, Phoenix.

13. The analysis of constitutional convention delegate behavior also fits into the larger current debate on the concepts of constitutional rights. The philosophical debate was set off by the publication of John Rawls' Theory of Justice (Cambridge, Mass., 1971) and given sharper relief by Ronald Dworkin and Rex Martin. Of particular interest here is Dworkin's Taking Rights Seriously (Cambridge, Mass., 1977), pp. 150-183. Dworkin provided useful distinctions on the right of liberty and equality. For the Rocky Mountain constitutional convention delegates the concept of liberty as freedom from government in their economic affairs was important. Also see Dworkin, A Matter of Principle (Cambridge, Mass., 1985), pp. 237-89. Clearly more on point for this chapter and for the concepts debated over women's suffrage is Rex Martin's Rawls and Rights (Lawrence, Kansas, 1985). Martin points out that constitutional convention delegates start with the idea of the rational interests of the representative citizen and find that adequate "only when they combine it with the relevant institutional history of the society whose basic structure they are designing." Rawls and Rights, p. 147. The repeated reference to the national constitutional context as well as the stronger pull and haul of territorial experience makes Martin's observation even more compelling. Clearly, the 19th-century desire for increased liberty had economic as well as civil overtones. The society that they were creating was one both American and western, as was their experience. Nevada Constitution, Art. I, sec. 8.

14. Santa Fe New Mexican, October 31, 1910.

15. Colorado Constitution, Art. II, sec. 23. Proceedings of the Constitutional Convention...of Colorado (Denver, 1908), pp. 60, 70, 91, 144, 216, 378, 489, 523, 527, 666. The convention also allowed criminal process by information. Art. II, sec. 8. Efforts to abolish grand jury indictments failed by two-to-one margins. Proceedings, pp. 202-3. For previous proposals, see Ibid., p. 86.

16. For the interplay of issues in Utah see the Deseret Evening News, March 19, 1895, which warned the convention to allow legislative regulation. The convention responded with a section that allowed both grand jury indictment and proceedings by information. It also set the size of the grand jury at seven and required a verdict of five to sustain an indictment. Utah Constitution, Art. I, sec. 13. This section was a compromise measure on two counts. First, the original section allowed a grand jury of from five to fifteen. This the Evening News found offensive as it was a legislative question. Deseret Evening News, March 19, 1895. The delegates, for reasons of public expense in large measure, fixed the number. Proceedings...Utah, p. 313. Second, the article allowed information concurrently with indictment with a proviso giving district judges discretion in

calling the grand jury. The historical tradition of the institution and the inability of reform elements to exert practical power in the convention produced the compromise. For the Idaho history, see Idaho Constitution, Art. I, sec. 8. Proceedings...Idaho, pp. 260, 1589.

17. Helena Daily Herald, July 19, 1889.

18. Ibid., July 29, 1889.

19. Northwest Tribune (Stevensville, Missoula County), July 5, 1889.

20. Proceedings and Debates of the Constitutional Convention...of Montana (Helena, 1921), pp. 100-1 (Clark and Burleigh speeches).

21. Ibid., p. 101. "Delegate Robinson's [Deer Lodge County] speech was representative of the institutional conservative as it called for compromise and moderation which conserved the institution: 'Fear of political influences, of classes of men, may operate on the minds of time serving district attorneys, who would fail to file information against men where [there] was merit in the case. Through the influences of these men prosecuting attorneys might not at all times do their duty. Then as a check...upon such influences as that, whether or not it would not be wise to retain a grand jury of seven or nine persons, to be called at the discretion of the presiding judge, or to be called once a year, as a check upon the influences that official men, or cliques of men who have large political influence, might exercise over the minds of these prosecuting attorneys, who would not be willing at all times to come up squarely to the mark irrespective of influences that might be brought to bear upon them'."

22. Ibid., pp. 107 (Dixon speech), 109 (Whitehill speech). The compromise measure passed 53 to 10, Ibid., p. 116.

23. Helena Daily Herald, July 20, 1889.

24. "Complete Verbatim Report of the Arizona Constitutional Convention," 4 vols. MSS, Special Collections of the University of Arizona Library, Tucson, Vol. 1, p. 24.

25. Arizona Constitution, Art. II, sec. 30. See David J. Bodenhamer, "Criminal Justice and Democratic Theory in Antebellum America: The Grand Jury Debate in Indiana," 5 Journal of the Early Republic 481-502 (Winter 1985). Bodenhamer's observations are important and provide a useful comparison with my findings. Issues rather than politics motivated institutional change.

26. "Report...Arizona," Vol. 2, afternoon session, November 15, 1910 (no page number).

27. Arizona Constitution, Art. VI, sec. 22.

28. "Report...Arizona," vol. 3, night session, November 25, 1910.

29. See the Colorado Transcript (Golden), December 8, 1875; Idaho Daily Statesman (Boise), July 17, 1889; Helena Daily Herald, July 12, 1889; Jefferson County Sentinel (Boulder, Montana), July 9, 1889; and Salt Lake City Daily Tribune, March 11, 1895, for representative comments on jury reform.

30. Nevada Constitution, Art. I, sec. 3.

31. Official Report of the Debates and Proceedings in the Constitutional Convention of the State of Nevada (San Francisco,

1866), pp. 53-59.

32. Ibid., p. 56 (Chapin speech).

33. For the cow-county delegate argument see Ibid., p. 54 (Fitch and Hawley speeches).

34. Proceedings...Idaho, p. 148. Idaho World, July 26, 1889.

35. See Idaho World, July 19, 1889, for the public comment and Proceedings...Idaho, pp. 146-61, 209-60, for the debates.

36. The Helena Daily Herald, July 12, 1889. Proceedings...Montana, pp. 264-67.

37. Proceedings...Utah, p. 275 (Creer speech).

38. Ibid., p. 261 (Goodwin: "What we want in the framing of the Constitution of this new State, is to do exact justice by the people, if we can, and do it at the least possible expense."). Also see p. 277 (Richards--notes the regional precedents and calls for solidarity "with our sister states around us"), p. 290 (Smith speech emphasizing the burdensome cost to a new state), and Salt Lake City Tribune, March 11, 1895, which called for the adoption of a system that would "secure speedy trials at minimum expense."

39. See Proceedings...Nevada, pp. 60-63, 165. Also see Harry N. Scheiber, "Public Rights and the Rule of Law in American Legal History," 72 California Law Review 217-51 (1984). Harry N. Scheiber and Charles W. McCurdy, "Eminent-Domain Law and Western Agriculture, 1849-1900" 49 Agricultural History 112-30 (Jan., 1975).

40. See Colorado Constitution, Art. II, sec. 14, 15. Proceedings...Colorado, pp. 205-7. Note that the Felton and Rockwell amendments to expand the included exceptions win wide margins. The Stone amendment (p. 207) to insert "needlessly" before "disturbed" in section 15 wins by a much narrower margin, 17 to 10. This Stone amendment was "Granger" in nature, but reasonable in context, and enough "miner" votes swung this minor victory. On final passage, only southwestern delegates and their allies opposed the measure; and this opposition was consistent on most issues related to mining interest. Also see David Wayne Hensel, "A History of the Colorado Constitution in the Nineteenth Century" (Ph.D. dissertation, University of Colorado, 1957), pp. 138-39.

41. Laws...Idaho, 1st session, p. 577. Also see Proceedings...Idaho, pp. 288-313. (Note Claggett speeches for reference to precedent in federal mining law.)

42. Idaho Daily Statesman, July 20, 1889. When the convention completed its work, the paper praised the measure as a positive step toward prosperity. Idaho Daily Statesman, August 2, 1889.

43. See Proceedings...Idaho, p. 299 (Gray), p. 328 (Claggett), p. 1615 (Beatty).

44. Ibid., p. 356 (Batten), pp. 358-61 (Ainslie).

45. Ibid., p. 366.

46. Ibid., p. 1597.

47. Ibid., pp. 1607-9.

48. Ibid., p. 1610.

49. Ibid., pp. 1619-21.

50. See "What Is a Public Use?" in "Idaho Constitutional Convention Journal Proceedings, Book B," MSS, Idaho Historical

Society, Boise.

51. Proceedings...Idaho, p. 1623.

52. See Ibid., p. 1625 (Shoup).

53. See Ibid., p. 1633. Note Morgan's change of attitude as evidenced in his speeches and cutting non-miners off in debate, p. 1612 (taking chair), p. 1619 (allowing Claggett extra time over protests of Mayhew), p. 1624 (cutting Hampton short), and p. 1633 (announcing voice vote). George Ainslie was one of Morgan's chief antagonists and was one of the anti-miner spokesmen. See "Hawley Notes on Idaho Biography," in "James H. Hawley, Private Accounts," Boise, January 1, 1907, MSS, Idaho State Historical Society, Boise.

54. Based on the three above-mentioned roll call votes, the non-miner bloc was composed of Batten, Chaney, Clark, Heyburn, Jewell, Lamoreaux, Mayhew, Pyeatt, Reid, Wineyard, and Pefley (100 percent agreement score). The miners consisted of Allen, Anderson, Armstrong, Beatty, Bevan, Cavanah, Claggett, Coston, Crutcher, Glidden, Hampton, Harris, Hays, King, Lewis, Maxey, McConnell, Melder, Myer, Moss, Sinnott, Underwood, Whitton, Wilson, and Lemp (100 percent agreement). Beane, Morgan, Pinkham, Ainslie, Campbell, Hasbrouck, and Hogan were the delegates who swung their allegiance before the voice vote.

55. Proceedings...Montana, p. 122.

56. Ibid., p. 123 (Maginnis), p. 148 (J. K. Toole).

57. Ibid., note speeches by Marshall, p. 120, and Luce, p. 123, both of which evidence the general displeasure with the term "private use" and the belief that it was unconstitutional.

58. Ibid., p. 148.

59. Ibid., p. 149.

60. Wyoming Constitution, Art. I, sec. 32, 33.

61. Arizona Constitution, Art. II, sec. 17. For the conservative proposition see Homer R. Wood, "Wood Notes," MSS, Lovin proposition number 116, University of Arizona Library, Tucson.

62. See Proceedings...Utah, pp. 326-28, for the early formulation of these issues in debate.

63. Ibid., pp. 329-31 (especially Van Horne speech).

64. Ibid., p. 328 (Eichnor).

65. Ibid., p. 332.

66. Salt Lake City Daily Tribune, March 4, 1895.

67. Proceedings...Utah, pp. 333-34. James specifically attacked the Richards argument on historical grounds, noting that when the matter was left to the legislature and the courts, railroad warfare was the result. Blockades and destruction were the results, all to the detriment of Utah. He then launched into his environmental argument, saying: "You take the state of Montana, the state of Wyoming, the state of Idaho, and the territories of Utah and Arizona, and the state of Colorado, and the state of Nevada, and the territory of New Mexico, and it represents an area in extent equal to a country east of the Mississippi River, or say east of the Missouri River, that contains pretty nearly thirty-seven millions of population. What is the population of these states of this intermountain country that I have just named to you? Less than eleven hundred

thousand. Now, in that sparsely settled community with interests in common with each other, where railroads must extend in order to make them valuable, are you going to put an obstruction in the way of building those roads? You will, my friends, if you adopt the proposition that the lands must be paid for and damages assessed and paid for before the railroad can move, or...you will find instances where they will remain in the courts maybe for two years and prevent an enterprise being carried out which will be of great advantage and great value to the community in which that railroad is constructed." James' argument specifically associated the issue with regional interests and more particularly with urban benefits from the railroad.

68. Ibid., p. 339 (Van Horne), p. 354 (Hart on Idaho section), p. 346 (Eichnor using Wyoming precedent), p. 347 (Creer), p. 348 (Eldredge).

69. Ibid., p. 339. It is important to note that Varian saw the origins of the section he was defending in the Nevada constitution and not the federal model. The appeal of regional precedent was extremely strong in Utah. Ibid., p. 341.

70. Ibid., p. 632 (Thoreson), p. 635 (Howard).

71. Ibid., p. 638.

72. Ibid., pp. 641-47.

73. Ibid., p. 1800. Note the weakness of the response to James' amendment and the force of a word from Varian at this time.

74. This tendency was well illustrated in the long and detailed bills of rights produced, but a study of some of the minor inclusions and exclusions illustrates the breadth of delegate thinking on appropriate measures for inclusion. On the right to unionize in the Arizona convention, see Fred T. Coalter, "Book of Propositions and Notes as Kept by Fred T. Colter, Member Constitutional Convention," MSS, State of Arizona Department of Library and Archives, Phoenix, substitute number 94. Colter often noted that many proposals made "no distinction between laws and the Constitution." On the question of bail in Colorado, Proceedings...Colorado, pp. 144, 209. The proposed section sought to accomplish what the courts were already doing and as such was struck. On prohibition in New Mexico, "Bill of Rights miscellaneous," MSS, New Mexico Archives, Santa Fe. Both the majority and the minority report of the committee on liquor traffic agreed that "the regulation of the Liquor Traffic is a proper subject of legislative regulation under the Police Power of the state and is not a proper matter to be incorporated in the constitution, or considered by this convention." Proceedings...Colorado, majority report. Gordon Morris Bakken, "The Impact of the Colorado State Constitution on Rocky Mountain Constitution Making," 47 Colorado Magazine 152-75 (Spring 1970); Idem, "The Arizona Constitutional Convention of 1910," 1978 Arizona State Law Journal 1-30 (November 1978).

## CHAPTER 4

1. For a sample of the argument see the following. Salt Lake Daily Tribune, November 1, 1895. Tribune Citizen (Albuquerque), October 3 and November 4, 1910, in which the paper accuses the Republicans of getting high salaries for constitutional officers as part of a general pork barrel constitution. This was the obverse of the economy-in-government issue, but New Mexico was an anomaly in this respect. Rocky Mountain Daily News (Denver), January 29, 1876. Also David Wayne Hensel, "A History of the Colorado Constitution in the Nineteenth Century," (Ph.D. dissertation, University of Colorado, 1957), p. 165 on indebtedness. Cheyenne Daily Sun, September 28, 1889. The paper advised the convention to "revise each department and save every dollar to the taxpayer that [was] possible to save." Cheyenne Daily Leader, September 27, 1889. This paper thought unreasoned cutting harmful and advised that salaries be commensurate with the dignity of the offices and not be cut to "clerk hire." Idaho Daily Statesman (Boise), July 10, 1889. Economy was urged by this paper, but not at the expense of the judiciary, saying that "wherever else she may practice economy, let her be liberal with her courts." The Montana papers bombarded the convention with advice on economy in government. See Helena Daily Herald, July 18, 19, 22, 23, 24, and 25, 1889. Jefferson County Sentinel (Boulder, Montana), July 2, 1889. In convention the issue was ever present. For example, the Arizona and New Mexico conventions did not even print records of the conventions for economy reasons. The economy rationale in New Mexico was buoyed by a Republican desire to keep the affair secret. "Verbatim Report, Arizona Constitutional Convention," 4 vols. MSS, Special Collections of the University of Arizona Library, Tucson, Vol. 1, October 15, 1910 (forenoon), p. 11. See Harvey Butler Fergusson letter file, MSS, Coronado Archives of University of New Mexico Library, Albuquerque, Fergusson to Baca, November 29, 1910: "The burden of taxation under the high salaries and the large number of offices created will grind the poor people, besides it leaves the corrupt [Santa Fe] ring to work the state as they have worked the Territory for twenty years past." Santa Fe New Mexican, November 16, 1910, described the ring's methodology in passing on constitutional offices. Caucus and controlled voting enabled the ring to write the constitution.

2. Good examples of this were Francis E. Warren in Wyoming, several of the Dakota territory governors, and, of course, Brigham Young, who had a ready-made political organization when he became territorial governor of Utah. See Lewis Gould, Wyoming, A Political History, 1868-1896 (New Haven, Conn., 1968). Howard R. Lamar, Dakota Territory, 1861-1889 (New Haven, Conn., 1956). Howard R. Lamar, The Far Southwest, 1846-1912 (New Haven, Conn., 1966). But Brigham Young could never be considered a carpetbagger. Jack Erickson Eblen's First and Second United States Empires, Governors and Territorial Government, 1784-1912 (Pittsburg, 1968) provides a broad outline of the activities of

territorial governors. See Kenneth N. Owens, Frontier Governors: A Study of the Territorial Executives in the History of Washington, Idaho, Montana, Wyoming and Dakota Territories (Ann Arbor, 1975).

3. Official Report of the Debates and Proceedings in the Constitutional Convention...Nevada (San Francisco, 1866), pp. 146, 157-62, 247-51, 797-99. The Denver Daily Tribune, Jan. 15, 1876, thought a four-year term best for business because it allowed longer periods of political calm. The convention thought two years better to allow "the people frequent opportunities to correct the administration of affairs." Proceedings of the Constitutional Convention...Colorado (Denver, 1907), p. 724. Also see Hensel, "Colorado Constitution," p. 135. Carl Ubbelohde, A Colorado History (Boulder, Colo., 1965), p. 146. Proceedings and Debates of the Constitutional Convention of Montana (Helena, 1921), pp. 423-24. Proceedings and Debates of the Constitutional Convention of Idaho, 1889, 2 vols. (Caldwell, Idaho, 1912), pp. 1223-26, 1419-28. William Potts to John T. Morgan, July 5, 1889, in "Morgan letters," MSS, Idaho Historical Society, Boise. Morgan was the chief justice of the territorial supreme court. This particular letter urged the restriction of appointive powers in hopes of laying the foundation or a civil service system. Journals and Debates of the Constitutional Convention of the State of Wyoming (1889) (Cheyenne, 1893), pp. 461-66. Official Report of the Proceedings and Debates of the Convention...Utah (1895) (Salt Lake City, 1898), pp. 653-54, 929-33, 1006-31. John R. Murdock, The Constitution of Arizona (Phoenix, 1929), pp. 73-79. Santa Fe New Mexican, November 16, 1910. S. B. Axtell file, MSS, New Mexico Historical Society, Santa Fe.

4. The working alliance was between Albert Fall, later famous for his involvement in Teapot Dome, and the Thomas Benton Catron-Charles A. Spiess group that represented the Santa Fe Ring. Tribune Citizen (Albuquerque), October 4, 1910. Fall had been a New Mexico resident since 1886, a lawyer, and successful politician. He was a territorial supreme court justice from 1893 to 1895, but spent most of his time in the territorial legislature. Santa Fe New Mexican, September 30, 1910. Catron was a Confederate army veteran who came to Santa Fe after the war. He established a law practice there and received subsequent appointments as third judicial district attorney and U.S. attorney. Catron served in the legislature and as territorial delegate. He also was a member of the 1889 constitutional convention. Catron played a key role in the foundation and continuing domination of the Republican party in New Mexico. Ibid., October 7, 1910. Lamar, Far Southwest, pp. 145, 164-65, 192-98, 498-501. Charles A. Spiess had a similarly successful political career and was a strong party boss in the territorial assembly. Santa Fe New Mexican, October 3, 1910. Fall was the key whip who forced insurgents into line, and the Catron-Spiess alliance provided controlled votes. Tribune Citizen, October 16 and 28, 1910. Also see Robert W. Larson, New Mexico's Quest for Statehood 1846-1912 (Albuquerque, 1968), p. 277. Larson notes the

Republican use of procedural rules such as asking the previous question that were used as "gag rules" to cut debate at any time.

5. The Republicans suggested a non-partisan slate of candidates for the convention due to internal party divisions caused by Governor Edward McCook. The Democrats refused, hoping to benefit from the division, but voters elected 24 Republicans and 15 Democrats. The Republicans took advantage of their voting strength to portion out convention offices to the faithful. Rocky Mountain Daily News, December 22, 1875. Colorado Chieftain (Pueblo), January 13, 1876. Colorado Transcript (Golden), December 29, 1875. The Republican use of caucuses and partisanship in portioning out offices angered many Democrats. Denver Daily Times, December 18, 1875. Colorado Chieftain, January 13, 1876. Democratic party leader George Pease maintained a consistent line of non-partisanship for public consumption. Denver Daily Times, December 21 and 22, 1875. Wilbur Stone, a Pueblo County Democrat, also maintained this line. Ibid., December 22, 1875. H. P. H. Bromwell, leader of the Granger faction, reminded the populace of the legislative atmosphere of a convention which implied its partisanship. Ibid., December 22, 1875. Colorado Chieftain, March 1, 1876.

6. Based on one vote to reduce assembly salaries and two on the power of county commissioners, the Guttman scaleogram reveals a pattern that was evident in the convention on other money issues. The Granger faction was composed of H. P. H. Bromwell, an Arapahoe County Republican, William E. Beck, a Boulder County Republican, Byron L. Carr, also a Boulder County Republican, William M. Clark, a Clear Creek County Republican, A. D. Cooper, a Fremont County Republican, LaFayette Head, a Conejos County Republican, William James, a Park and Lake counties Republican, S. J. Plumb, a Weld County Republican, A. K. Yount, a Weld and Larimer counties Republican, William H. Cushman, a Clear Creek County Democrat, W. C. Stover, a Larimer County Democrat, and J. S. Wheeler, a Weld County Democrat. The Democrats voted with Republicans from their home counties. A cluster bloc analysis of these same votes included A. D. Cooper, a Fremont County Republican, W. C. Stover, a Larimer County Democrat, and William Lee, a Jefferson County Democrat. Cooper and Stover voted with fellow county delegates. The Grangers were opposed by regular Democrats led by George Pease and the rest of the Republicans. The votes were recorded in the Proceedings...Colorado, pp. 363-64, 453, 454. The pattern of delegate voting also showed a definite southeastern faction in opposition to the northern or Denver group.

7. The four votes considered may be found at Proceedings... Montana, pp. 445, 446, 321, 322. The first two involve the governor's salary, and the latter judges' salaries. John Ezra Rickards led the high salary advocates, arguing that a high salary would allow even the poorest to aspire to the office. Ibid., p. 427. Martin Maginnis argued for the constitutional conservatives that the constitution should be "ironclad so that the legislature could not raise the salaries." Ibid., p. 426. The lowest salaries for governor were proposed by Lewis H. Hershfield. Ibid., p. 445.

8. This pattern was very evident in the votes on county salaries. The salaries were paid according to county valuation which discriminated against the western counties. For the votes see *Proceedings...Wyoming*, pp. 108, 122. The Guttman scaleogram analysis puts all the Unita County delegation in opposition to the eastern counties of Carbon, Laramie, and Albany. Party affiliation quantitatively was equal for both groups (See Table 2).

9. Alexander Mayhew and Frank Harris led the fight for high salaries. *Proceedings...Idaho*, pp. 1419-23. The Guttman scaleogram analysis of votes on the salaries of the governor, secretary of state, and attorney general designate the following as consistent opponents of high salaries: Peter J. Pefley, J. S. Whitton, Augustine M. Sinnott, James W. Reid, Abel J. Pierce, John H. Myer, Isaac N. Coston, A. S. Chaney, and Frank P. Cavanah. A cluster bloc analysis includes John Lewis of Oneida County and John T. Morgan of Bingham in the opposition group. Both men represented eastern counties. This bloc of delegates was able to deny a raise from $1,800 to $2,000 to the secretary of state and avoided a raise to $2,500 for the attorney general. Ibid., pp. 1420, 1424. They were able to accomplish this by drawing votes from another bloc made up of delegates who were from similarly situated counties, but who were reluctant to pass a bare-bones constitution. William H. Claggett led this group consisting of W. C. B. Allen, J. W. Ballentine, Solomon Hasbrouck, Edward S. Jewell, Thomas Pyeatt, John L. Underwood, and John Lemp (Guttman analysis) (See Table 3).

10. The high salary bloc was led by Hubert Button, a Salt Lake City contractor, Samuel Francis, a Morgan County councilor to the stake president and attorney, Charles H. Hart, a Cache County attorney, and Jeremiah D. Page, a Sanpete County sheep rancher. Of the 36 delegates in this bloc, 17 were from Salt Lake City or County, 4 from Cache County, north of Salt Lake, and 3 from Summit County, abutting Salt Lake County on the east. There were were 25 Republicans and 11 Democrats; 16 delegates were Gentile, and 20 were Mormon. David B. Stover, a Toole County miner, Joel Ricks, a Sevier County railroad agent, and Abel J. Evans, a Utah County farmer, led the opposition. The small county delegates were joined by Utah County (Provo) Democrats. The votes used for analysis were on the pay for the superintendent of public instruction, judicial mileage, and salary. *Proceedings...Utah*, pp. 1158, 1517-18, 1518. The debate and parliamentary maneuvers on the superintendent's pay were most extensive. The judicial salary issue was pushed by Abel Evans in both instances. On mileage and salary the strict economy forces lost, but their votes isolated them most vividly. Some other votes on salaries may be found at Ibid., pp. 1017-21 (governor), pp. 1021-23 (secretary of state), p. 1023 (state auditor), pp. 1023-24 (state treasurer), pp. 1027-28 (attorney general), pp. 1030-31 (superintendent of public instruction).

11. Gilman M. Ostrander, *Nevada, The Great Rotten Borough* (New York, 1966), pp. 33-34. Gordon Morris Bakken, "Taxation of Mineral Wealth and the Nevada Constitutional Convention of 1864," 12 *Nevada Historical Society Quarterly* 5-15 (Winter 1969); Idem,

"Judicial Removal in Nevada," 18 Rocky Mountain Social Science Journal 109-17 (April 1971).

12. Nevada Constitution, Art. 7, sec. 3.

13. Proceedings...Nevada, p. 542 (Nourse).

14. Ibid., p. 542 (Brosnan).

15. A Guttman scaleogram analysis of the four roll calls on Article 7 identifies F. M. Proctor, J. G. McClinton, B. S. Mason, Frank H. Kennedy, Almon Hovey, E. F. Dunn, Charles E. DeLong, Cornelius M. Brosnan, and James A. Banks as the liberal opposition. Proceedings...Nevada, pp. 564-65. The majority contained all of the Washoe and Roop County delegates and three from Ormsby (See Table 4).

16. Proceedings...Nevada, pp. 643-44. DeLong argued that one of the objections to the constitution was expense, and two extra judges only increased tax burdens.

17. Kent David Richards, "Growth and Development of Government in the Far West" (Ph.D. dissertation, University of Wisconsin, 1966), pp. 145-46. See Proceedings...Nevada, p. 231 (Johnson resolution), p. 243 (Johnson).

18. Proceedings...Nevada, pp. 682-84.

19. Ibid., p. 684 (Frizell), pp. 689-700, 725.

20. Rocky Mountain Daily News, December 18, 1875.

21. Proceedings...Colorado, pp. 238, 338, 395, 470, 589, 596, 679. Ubbelohde, A Colorado History, p. 147.

22. Hensel, "Colorado Constitution," pp. 265, 270-76, 280.

23. Lamar, Far Southwest, p. 293. Ubbelohde, Colorado, p. 147. Colin B. Goodykoontz, "Some Controversial Questions Before the Colorado Constitution Convention of 1875," 17 Colorado Magazine 10-12 (January 1940).

24. The Colorado court was accorded the dubious power of issuing advisory opinions. This again evidenced the confidence in judicial authority. See Hensel, "Colorado Constitution," pp. 266-70. William H. Robinson, Jr., "Limitations Upon Legislative Inquiries Under Colorado Advisory Opinion Clause," 4 Rocky Mountain Law Review 237-50 (June 1932). Edwin P. Banks, "The Colorado Advisory Opinion" (M.A. thesis, University of Colorado, 1952). Probate courts were abolished and probate jurisdiction given to county courts.

25. Proceedings...Montana, pp. 151-55, 218-31, 276-329, 377-82. Helena Daily Herald, July 23 and 25, 1889. Jefferson County Sentinel (Boulder), August 2, 1889. The Sentinel voiced the anxiety of the cow counties in commenting that the inclusion of Silver Bow and Beaverhead counties with Jefferson in a judicial district would "put the people of Jefferson county in a much worse fix so far as prompt administration of justice [was] concerned."

26. The "verge of calamity" characterization was Melville Brown's. Brown had a long and distinguished career of public service as a member of the territorial house, mayor of Laramie, U.S. attorney, and president of the constitutional convention. Journals...Wyoming, p. 530. Cheyenne Daily Sun, September 17, 1889. Henry J. Peterson, "The Constitutional Convention of Wyoming," 7 University of Wyoming Publications 115-19 (May 1940).

27. Journals...Wyoming, p. 332 (Conway).

28. Ibid., p. 79.

29. Proceedings...Idaho, pp. 1497-98.

30. Ibid., pp. 1526-40, 1545-57, 1585-88.

31. Idaho World (Idaho City), July 19 and August 9, 1889. The World thought that all public officials should be elected by the people. In convention the judiciary committee split seven to seven on the issue of election or appointment. Proceedings... Idaho, p. 1501. Elwood T. Beatty, a frequent holder of territorial office and probate judge, feared that political conventions would elect judges by presenting a single choice to the people. Ibid., pp. 1504-5. William Claggett, president of the convention, thought appointment the only way of getting the best men, while men like Willis Sweet, Idaho's first congressman, argued that the intelligence and the virtue of the people had to be relied upon by the new state. Ibid., pp. 1514-16. The conservative argument was soundly defeated, 36 to 7, with Beatty and Claggett being joined by Hampton, Harris, Hasbrouck, Maxey, and Pinkham. Ibid., pp. 1519-20. This group represented the conservative element in the Idaho Republican party. H. S. Hampton was a probate judge; Frank Harris was a lawyer but a Democrat; Solomon Hasbrouck was a Washington County merchant; W. C. Maxey was a physician, and A. J. Pinkham a lawyer. Harris joined the Republicans on this issue out of allegiance with Hasbrouck, both coming from Washington County and a conservative bent. Harris voted with Hasbrouck 71 percent of the time, (Boguetab analysis).

32. On procedure see Utah Constitution, Art. 8, sec. 25, 26. The nepotism section is number 15. The Deseret Evening News commented that the convention was using too much detail to create too many courts: "Twelve judgeships at the outset seems to be crowding the judiciary to the front at the expense of equally important interests. The judicial article should be made less elaborate and extravagant." News, April 15, 1895. The Salt Lake City Daily Tribune also thought the system "too top heavy." Tribune, March 10, 1895. This tendency to expand the judicial article had been evidenced in the convention of 1872. Martin B. Hickman, "Utah Constitutional Law" (Ph.D. dissertation, University of Utah, 1954), p. 53.

33. Proceedings...Utah, p. 1318 (Evans).

34. Ibid., pp. 1398-1412.

35. Lamar, Far Southwest, pp. 499-503. John R. Murdock, The Constitution of Arizona (Tempe, Ariz., 1929), pp. 91-92. Edward H. Peplow, History of Arizona (New York, 1958), Vol. 2, pp. 18-25. Larson, New Mexico's Quest pp. 272-82.

36. The judiciary committee was chaired and run by Republicans. Frank W. Parker, a justice of the territorial supreme court and "a staunch Republican," was chairman. Santa Fe New Mexican, September 27, 1910. Tom Catron and Albert Fall were his chief allies and party whips in committee. Republican faithfuls like Malaquias Martinez, periodic appointee to territorial positions, and C. J. Roberts, a territorial legislator who "always voted the Republican ticket from the day of his majority," helped move committee matters along. Ibid., October 26

and September 14, 1910. A minority opinion did appear in convention, but gained approval only on section 16, which made the article consistent in limiting legislative initiative. In general, the minority only tried to delimit majority actions and proposed no revolutions. Proceedings...New Mexico, pp. 135-45.

37. Lamar, Far Southwest, pp. 502-3. Larson, New Mexico's Quest, p. 274. See "George W. P. Hunt Scrapbook," MSS, University of Arizona Library, for representative clippings in September and October 1910.

38. This argument was stated in the convention and in the press. See "Report...Arizona," Vol. 1, morning, November 8, 1910, and Vol. 2, morning, November 10, 1910, for representative debates. The Daily Globe, July 12, 1910, presented the argument at an early stage. Also see "Weinberger Collection, Scrapbook," MSS, University of Arizona Library.

39. Proceedings...Nevada, pp. 128, 138-45, 146-57, 275-90, 301-16, 787-91, 795-97. The Pacific railroad debate was under Article 8, municipal and other corporations.

40. Nevada Constitution, Art. 4, sec. 30, 31. The railroad debate involved the pledging of the credit of the state. This lost, but lesser jurisdictions were allowed to pledge their credit. The original section (Art. 8, sec. 9, p. 166) allowed the state to pledge its credit to educational and charitable organizations and to issue $3 million in bonds to support the Pacific railroad. Pro-railroad men tried to raise the ceiling on the bond issue, while anti-railroad men tried to belittle their efforts with ad absurdum measures. Thomas Fitch proposed raising the issue to $25 million at ten percent. Others like A. J. Lockwood forecast high taxes and poverty as a result. The debate raged for days, but the climax came when Leland Stanford graced the convention to plug his Central Pacific Railroad Company. Stanford made a strategic mistake when he revealed that state aid would not be material for the transcontinental, but would be needed for spurs. This gave Charles E. DeLong the ammunition he needed. Following a question-and-answer period with Stanford, DeLong launched his most massive attack, asserting that "this aid would not help the road a pin, yet he would like it, because it would be an endorsement of the enterprise, that is all." Prodeedings...Nevada, p. 390. The debt of $4 million, he claimed, would be more than the people could bear. J. H. Warwick, a Lander County lawyer and leader of the pro-railroad faction, retorted with fruitful picture of transportation blessings. Josiah Earl, a Storey County lumber dealer, tried to call the delegates to their senses: "Are we to legislate in this instrument, and say that the people shall not do this, and that, and the other thing? I consider that we are here only to establish the landmarks. The Legislatures which are to succeed us can tell better in future times what the necessities of the State require, than we can tell now." Ibid., p. 397. The delegates answered Earl's question affirmatively and continued the debate. But when the votes were counted the pro-railroad men were overwhelmingly defeated. Warwick was joined only by James A. Banks, J. S. Crosman, and Almon Hovey. This group received peripheral support from a

faction led by Earl, Albert T. Hawley, a cow-county delegate, and J. Neely Johnson. This group was an amalgam of miners and farmers who wanted transportation at a minimal cost rather than at any cost. H. B. Bradley, Israel Crawford, G. N. Folsom, J. H. Kinkead, and H. G. Parker joined them. The opposition faction saw no need to raise taxes and thus make fiscal waves when the federal government was underwriting the transcontinental. Led by DeLong and Lockwood, the group included Thomas Fitch, Lloyd Frizell, J. W. Haines, George A. Hudson, Frank H. Kennedy, B. S. Mason, J. G. McClinton, F. M. Proctor, James H. Sturtevant, and Frank Tagliabue. Guttman scaleogram analysis of roll calls, Proceedings...Nevada, p. 405 (Fitch amendment), p. 491 (Kinkead amendment), p. 498 (Crosman amendment), p. 499 (Article 9) (See Table 5).

41. Proceedings...Nevada, pp. 632-38.

42. Proceedings...Colorado, pp. 407-13, 520-21, 560-61, 677-78. Ubbelohde, Colorado, p. 147.

43. Proceedings...Montana, pp. 133-35, 596-626, 644-45. The greatest cynicism was generated over pay. See Ibid., p. 602 (Goddard).

44. Conrad Kohrs, "Autobiography of Conrad Kohrs," MSS, Montana State Historical Society, p. 142. Kohrs was a cow-county delegate to the Montana convention.

45. Butte Daily Intermountain, August 14, 1889. Other papers commented differently depending upon their constituency. See the Avant Courier (Bozeman), August 8, 1889. Helena Daily Herald, July 16, 1889. The economic issues involved were adequately raised by these papers in conjunction with the senate issue.

46. Journals...Wyoming, p. 413 (Teschemacher), p. 417 (Morgan).

47. Ibid., p. 417.

48. Ibid., p. 555 (Brown).

49. Ibid., p. 557 (Elliot). Cheyenne Daily Sun, September 12, 1889.

50. Proceedings...Idaho, pp. 454-63 (King).

51. Ibid., pp. 471-73.

52. Ibid., pp. 487-88. Later attempts at one senator, one representative also failed. Ibid., pp. 1202-11.

53. Proceedings...Utah, p. 203. Deseret Evening News, March 12, 1895.

54. Proceedings...Utah, p. 849 (Eldredge), pp. 849-64.

55. Ibid., p. 841 (Varian).

56. Ibid., p. 846 (Thurman).

57. Ibid., pp. 852-59. The anti-Mormon coalition mustered a maximum of 34 votes against the hierarchy's apportionment. Of those 34, 27 were Republicans, 12 of whom were Gentile, and 7 were Democrats, 2 being Gentile. Sectionally, 18 were from Salt Lake City and County. The total delegation was only 29. Four were from Sanpete County of a seven-man delegation. These delegates joined in opposition primarily because their apportionment was even smaller than that for the constitutional convention. Gentiles feared the use of the one-county provision as a Mormon political tool.

58. Ibid., pp. 869-79 (salaries), pp. 889-928, 938-57.

59. See the Daily Globe, August 2, 1910, Arizona Democrat (Phoenix), July 21, 1910, August 1, 1910, in "George W. P. Hunt Scrapbook," MSS, University of Arizona Library.

60. "Verbatim Report...Arizona," morning, November 4, 1910, pp. 6-17, 20. W. T. Webb, a University of Utah graduate and owner of the most extensive cattle ranch in southern Arizona, was one of the leaders of this movement. Thomas Feeney and M. G. Cunniff gave Webb their support. From their voting records in the convention, they were never consistent supporters of Hunt. Webb agreed 60 percent, Feeney 74 percent, and Cunniff 67 percent of the time. On Webb see Webb file, MSS, Arizona Pioneers' Historical Society, Tucson.

61. Harvey Butler Fergusson file, MSS, New Mexico Historical Society, Santa Fe. Calvin A. Roberts, "H. B. Fergusson, 1848-1915," 57 New Mexico Historical Review 287-55 (July 1982).

62. Santa Fe New Mexican, September 21, 1910, October 17, 1910.

63. Ibid., October 27, 1910.

64. See Fergusson letters, MSS, University of New Mexico Library Archives, Albuquerque. The gold brick phrase was used in Fergusson's letter to E. A. Martin of November 29, 1910. Also see "New Mexico in 1910, Letters and Addresses Relating to the Constitution, by H. B. Fergusson, Frank Springer, and Frank W. Clancy," MSS, University of New Mexico Archives, for the progressive case against the constitution.

65. A good example of this growing awareness was The Grass Range Review's story on the cow-county maneuver in the Montana convention. The article detailed the whole story. Hebard Collection, University of Wyoming Library.

## CHAPTER 5

1. See Kent David Richards, "Growth and Development of Government in the Far West: The Oregon Provisional Government, Jefferson Territory, Provisional and Territorial Nevada" (Ph.D. dissertation, University of Wisconsin, 1966), p. 202. David A. Johnson has provided an important reinterpretation of the role of William Morris Stewart in the constitution ratification campaign of 1863. Johnson convincingly argues that the people rejected the 1863 constitution because they feared and distrusted Stewart. Johnson, "A Case of Mistaken Identity: William M. Stewart and the Rejection of Nevada's First Constitution," 22 Nevada Historical Society Quarterly 186-98 (Fall 1979). Although it is clear that Stewart's role in molding public attitudes was substantial, the mining tax issue also was part of the popular debate and an issue before the electorate that rejected the 1863 constitution.

2. Official Report of the Debates and Proceedings of the Constitutional Convention of the State of Nevada (San Francisco, 1866), p. 222. The original section read, "The Legislature shall provide by law for a uniform and equal rate of assessment and

taxation, and shall prescribe such regulations as shall secure a just valuation for taxation of all property, both real and personal, including mines and mining property; excepting such property only as may be exempted by law for municipal, education, literary, scientific, religious, or charitable purpose."

3. Ibid., p. 224 (Haines), p. 412 (Haines), p. 357 (Lockwood).

4. *Proceedings and Debates of the Constitutional Convention... of Montana (1889)* (Helena, 1921), p. 492. Howard Robert Lamar, *Dakota Territory* (New Haven, Conn., 1956), pp. 96-97, 233. Also see Joseph Kensey Howard, *Montana, High, Wide and Handsome*, (New Haven, Conn., 1959), pp. 62-65. Burleigh was the floor leader for the cow-county delegates in the taxation debates.

5. *Journals and Debates of the Constitutional Convention of the State of Wyoming* (Cheyenne, 1893), p. 684.

6. *Proceedings and Debates of the Constitutional Convention of Idaho (1889)* (Caldwell, Idaho, 1912), p. 1713 (Parker). The Colorado revenue committee reported a section which exempted mines and mining property, but this position was tempered by the agrarian interests to a ten-year exemption. This, at least, put discretion into the hands of the legislature by 1886. *Proceedings of the Constitutional Convention of Colorado* (Denver, 1907), pp. 414, 483, 505-7, 616-17. Also see David W. Hensel, "A History of the Colorado Constitution in the Nineteenth Century" (Ph. D. dissertation, University of Colorado, 1957), pp. 177-78. On related tax matters, especially taxing church property, see the *Rocky Mountain Daily News*, December 30, 1875, January 9, 1876; *Denver Daily Times*, January 8, 1876; *Colorado Chieftain* (Pueblo), January 6, 1876. Also see "Bromwell's Minority Report on Suffrage 1875-6 and Other Original Documents of the Colorado Constitutional Convention," MSS, Colorado Historical Society, Denver, pp. 3-4. The Colorado tax exemption did not extend to net proceeds or surface improvements, but exemption policy did give the mines a de facto exemption as the law was administered. Other conventions concentrated their attention upon exemption as a general policy rather than the particulars of the Colorado model. For the best recent mining town history see Malcolm J. Rohrbough, *Aspen, The History of a Silver-Mining Town, 1879-1893* (New York, 1986). Although the time frame is after the Colorado convention, this book provides an excellent socio-economic analysis.

7. Supra, note 2, for the section being debated. *Debates...Nevada*, p. 353 (Crosman), p. 424 (Murdock), p. 444 (Hawley).

8. *Denver Daily Times*, January 12, 1876. *Colorado Springs Gazette*, January 15, 1876. The *Greeley Tribune*, January 5, 1876, wanted more precise language in the constitution. The *Colorado Chieftain* (Pueblo), February 13, 1876, feared popular rejection if too much objectionable legislation was included. The *Colorado Transcript* (Golden), January 26, 1876, March 1, 1876, saw too much time being consumed on trifles. The *Rocky Mountain Daily News* (Denver), December 19, 1875, January 12, 1876, January 19, 1876, kept a running editorial critique of convention legislation and warned against "all the new fangled notions of the period."

9. *Proceedings...Montana*, pp. 492, 496. The *Jefferson County*

*Sentinel* (Boulder), August 2, 1889, used the Cooley argument. Also see *Daily Inter Mountain* (Butte), August 9, 1889, and *Helena Daily Herald*, July 29, 1889.

10. *Journals...Wyoming*, p. 637. The Colorado constitution provided that "mines and mining claims bearing gold, silver, and other precious metals (except the net proceeds and surface improvements thereof), shall be exempt from taxation for the period of ten years from the date of the adoption of this constitution...." *Colorado Constitution*, Art. 10, sec. 3. The Wyoming provision taxed surface improvements and the gross product. *Journals...Wyoming*, p. 655 (Potter), p. 660, (Campbell), p. 661 (Campbell), p. 661 (Baxter), p. 663 (Harvey), pp. 667-68 (Brown). *Cheyenne Daily Sun*, September 4, 22, 29, 1889. *Cheyenne Daily Leader*, September 4, October 1, 1889. "Scraps," MSS, Hebard Collection, University of Wyoming Library, Laramie. Brown touched on the legislation issue in a 1917 speech: "All power is with the people in the democracy but the Constitution limits what the officers may do. The Constitution legislates just what powers may be delegated by the Constitution, hence, there is usually some legislation in all Constitutions. Some things were supplied in our State Constitution that [the] legislature could control, like the Railroads and other interests. As a matter of fact, the railroad controlled for a number of years Legislature after Legislature." Brown made the correlation of delegate will with popular will, and the duty of delegates to legislate for the general welfare in the constitution as the people could not in their own legislature. "Notes from Judge Brown's Lecture, May 9, 1917," MSS, Hebard Collection, University of Wyoming Library. Also see Henry J. Peterson, "The Constitutional Convention of Wyoming," *University of Wyoming Publications*, Vol. 7, No. 6 (May 1940), pp. 119-123.

11. *Proceedings...Idaho*, p. 1748 (Beatty), p. 1761 (Morgan).

12. *Salt Lake City Daily Tribune*, March 5, 1895, cited Cooley as did the *Idaho Daily Statesman*, Aug. 4, 1889. Also see *Deseret Evening News*, April 22, 1895.

13. *Debates...Nevada*, p. 325.

14. Ibid., p. 337 (Hawley), p. 356 (Lockwood).

15. Voting agreement scores based on 14 roll calls on the mining taxation section show Lockwood voting with Hawley 92 percent, Collins with Hawley 50 percent, Collins with Lockwood 67 percent (Boguetab analysis). The Guttman scaleogram analysis of the same roll calls put Hawley in undisputed leadership of the cow-county delegates, Lockwood closely associated, and Collins voting more with the mine owners. The roll calls may be found at *Proceedings...Nevada*, pp. 406, 416, 420, 422, 429, 431, 437, 443, 444, 446, 446, 520, 520, 521.

16. *Journals...Wyoming*, p. 638 (Brown), p. 652 (Clark), p. 681 (Campbell).

17. *Proceedings...Idaho*, p. 1708 (Morgan), p. 1731 (Heyburn), p. 1739 (Ainslie and Mayhew).

18. *Official Report of the Proceedings and Debates of the Convention...to adopt a Constitution for the State of Utah (1895)*, (Salt Lake City, 1898), pp. 1069-1074 (Cannon and Varian), p. 1075

(Evans), p. 1086 (Ivins), p. 1079 (Cannon statement of origins of section), and Ibid., p. 1083, for the vote.

19. Debates...Nevada, pp. 222-223 (Nourse), p. 224 (DeLong), pp. 224-25 (Banks), p. 225 (Hawley), p. 229 for the text of the ad valorem amendment and p. 323 for the statement on the amendment by J. Neely Johnson, its author, p. 407 (Kennedy).

20. Proceedings...Montana, pp. 475-76 (Clark). Journals...Wyoming, pp. 653-55 (Teschemacher), p. 663 (Brown), p. 685 (Baxter). Proceedings...Idaho, p. 1704 (King), p. 1719 (Batten). Proceedings...Utah, p. 1070 (Varian), p. 1075 (Evans), p. 1081 (Heybourne).

21. Debates...Nevada, p. 228 (Crosman), pp. 332-33 (Warwick), p. 340 (Chapin). Their respective voting records also bear out their role as pro-mining leaders. On the Guttman scaleogram J. S. Crosman has the most extreme voting record. Samuel Chapin's voting record agrees 100 percent with Crosman's. J. H. Warwick agreed with Crosman 85 percent and Chapin 86 percent of the time (Boguetab analysis). For the 14 votes considered in the analysis see note 15, supra.

22. Ibid., p. 325 (Collins), p. 334 (Nourse). George A. Nourse voted with his Washoe and Roop delegates and ranks next to Hawley in the extremity of his voting record. In the Boguetab analysis, Nourse and his fellow county delegates voted as a bloc 100 percent of the time. Hawley voted with this group 79 percent; John A. Collins, 57 percent.

23. For representative statements see: Proceedings...Montana, pp. 475-76 (Clark); Journals...Wyoming, pp. 637, 643 (Hay), pp. 648-49, 672 (Clark); Proceedings...Idaho, pp. 1646, 1704 (King), p. 1708 (Morgan), p. 1718 (Mayhew), pp. 1719-20 (Batten); Proceedings...Utah, p. 1074 (Varian), p. 1078 (Kearns).

24. Debates...Nevada, pp. 222-23.

25. Ibid., p. 223.

26. Ibid.

27. Ibid., p. 226. Fitch amendment: "The Legislature shall provide for a uniform and equal rate of assessment and taxation, and shall prescribe such regulations as shall secure a just valuation for taxation of all property." Thomas Fitch was a member of a voting bloc which represented a pro-mining attitude, but backed off from support for radical proposals. As a center group, it was essential in the compromises made in convention. Its members, based on a minimum 64 percent agreement score, were Thomas Fitch, Storey County lawyer, John A. Collins, Storey County miner, Cornelius M. Brosnan, Storey County lawyer, George A. Hudson, Lyon County mill owner, Frank Kennedy, Lyon County lawyer, H.G. Parker, Lyon County mining superintendent, and Charles E. DeLong, Storey County lawyer.

28. Ibid., p. 229. See the Johnson amendment: "The Legislature shall provide by law for the assessment and collection of taxes by a uniform rule, so that taxes shall be assessed and collected on all property, possessory rights and claims, according to their true value in money." See Ibid., p. 328. See the Mason amendment. Ibid., p. 342 (Collins).

29. Ibid., p. 351 (Brosnan), p. 359 (Banks), pp. 383, 406

(Tozer). Nourse amendment test: "The Legislature shall provide by law for a uniform and equal rate of assessment and taxation of all property, possessions, and possessory rights, excepting such only as may be exempted by law for municipal, educational, literary, scientific, religious, and charitable purposes." The Nourse amendment would have included mines and mining property under "possessions" (personalty and chattels) and "possessory rights" (mining claims). Frank Kennedy also offered an amendment which covered similar ground: "all property, real, personal, and mixed."

30. Ibid., pp. 410-11.

31. Ibid., p. 416 (Kennedy amendment), pp. 416-17 (Chapin amendment introduced and p. 420 lost), p. 420. (Banks amendment: "Provided, that no tax shall be imposed on any mining claim, or possessory right thereto, which, at the time of making the assessment, has a market value in money of less than ____ dollars per foot", p. 420. Chapin's amendment was $25, Kennedy's $5, and Tozer's $15,000. Banks amendment with blank left to legislature lost 9 to 24. p. 422.)

32. Ibid., pp. 423, 424-26 (Murdock). The Murdock amendment lost, p. 431. Ibid., p. 431. Banks amendment: "Provided, that no tax shall be imposed on any mining claim, or possessory right thereto, which, during the year immediately preceding the time of making the assessment, has produced an amount of ore the value of which is less than one thousand dollars." He withdrew the amendment. p. 436.

33. Ibid., pp. 436-37, 442 (Hawley), p. 443. Nourse amendment: "Provided, further, that the rate of taxation upon the annual proceeds of the mines shall be so fixed as to make the burden of taxation upon the owners of mines as nearly as possible equal, in proportion to their property, to that upon the owners of other property." The amendment lost, p. 444.

34. Ibid., p. 443.

35. Ibid., p. 444.

36. Ibid., p. 445. The final vote on the article was 20 to 10. Ibid., p. 521.

37. Supra, note 15. See Table 6.

38. Proceedings...Montana, pp. 467-82, 490-519, 550-71. Proceedings...Utah, p. 1080. Delegate Squires reminded the convention that the normal claim of 22.5 acres would yield only $1.35 per year in taxes if the committee section was passed, but the argument was to no avail. For a debate on foreign capital and mortgages, see Ibid., pp. 1085-113. Also see Deseret Evening News, March 15, 1895.

39. Robert E. Riegel, The Story of the Western Railroads (Lincoln, Neb., 1964), p. 291.

40. The Cheyenne Daily Sun, September 17, 1889, urged the delegates on and equated an equitable tax with statehood itself. The Cheyenne Daily Leader, September 25, 1889, noted the failure of the mining tax revenues to pay the salary of the mine inspector. Also see "Scraps," MSS, Hebard Collection, University of Wyoming Library, Laramie. The Boomerang (Laramie), September 19, 1889, outlined the encouragement argument for the

new tax system.

41. Journals...Wyoming, p. 637.

42. Ibid., pp. 637-38.

43. Ibid., p. 643.

44. Ibid., p. 663 (Harvey), p. 663 (Brown), p. 673 (Hay amendment), pp. 680-81 (Harvey amendment).

45. Ibid., p. 681 (Campbell). Brown substitute: "provided further, that the output of coal mines shall be taxed at not less than one cent per ton for state purposes on each ton of coal mined, and not less than one-half a cent per ton for county purposes on the same product." Ibid., p. 683. Cheyenne Daily Sun, September 22, 1889. Also see Ibid., September 15, 19, 24, 25, and 27, 1889, of continuing editorial comment. In terms of the relative weight of the territorial tax system, the coal mines greatly benefited, paying only 1.5 percent of the total, while livestock owners paid 32 percent. Ibid., September 25, 1889.

46. Journals...Wyoming, pp. 684-697 (Campbell amendment and debates).

47. "Section 2: All coal lands in the state from which coal is not being mined shall be listed for assessment, valued for taxation and assessed according to value. Section 3: All mines and mining claims from which gold, silver and other precious metals, soda, saline, coal, mineral oil, or other valuable deposits, is or may be produced shall be taxed in addition to the surface improvements, and in lieu of taxes on the lands, on the gross product thereof, as may be prescribed by law; provided, that the product of all mines shall be taxed in proportion to the value thereof." Wyoming Constitution, Art. 15.

48. Proceedings...Idaho, p. 1645.

49. Ibid., pp. 1652-53. The Parker amendment survived briefly in convention and became the central point of controversy. "Property, real and personal, of the United States, and property of the state and counties, and property of municipalities and common school properties, cemeteries not owned or used for private or corporate profit, public libraries, growing crops, livestock under six months old, and all mines and mining claims, both placer and rock in place, containing or bearing gold, silver, copper, coal or other valuable mineral deposits, shall be exempt from taxation: Provided, that all machinery used in mining, and all property and surface improvements appurtenant to or upon mining claims, which have a separate and independent value, shall be taxed as provided by law, and all laws exempting from taxation property other than hereinbefore mentioned shall be void."

50. Ibid., pp. 1654-55. Hays substitute: "All taxes shall be uniform upon the same class of subjects within the territorial limits of the authority levying the tax, and shall be levied and collected under general laws, which shall prescribe such regulations as shall secure a just valuation for taxation of all property, real and personal; provided that mines and mining claims bearing gold, silver or other precious metals, except the net proceeds and surface improvements thereof, shall be exempt from taxation for a period of ten years from the date of the adoption of this constitution, and thereafter may be taxed as provided by

law; and provided further that the household goods of every person being the head of a family to the value of $200 shall be exempt from taxation; and ditches, canals and flumes owned and used by individuals or corporations for irrigating land owned by such individuals or corporations, or the individual members thereof, shall not be separately taxed so long as they shall be owned and used exclusively for such purpose; and lots with buildings thereon, if said buildings are used solely for religious worship or for charitable purposes; also cemeteries not used or held for corporate or private profit, shall be exempt from taxation unless otherwise provided by general law. All laws exempting from taxation property other than that herein mentioned shall be void."

51. Ibid., pp. 1703-7 for the other amendments and the Glidden amendment to strike "net proceeds."

52. See Ibid., p. 1708 (Morgan) and p. 1713 (Parker).

53. Ibid., p. 1716.

54. Ibid., pp. 1716-17 for King speech, pp. 1718-27 for the response, also pp. 1722-23 (Ainslie).

55. Ibid., pp. 1729-30. Claggett amendment: "Provided that mines and mining claims bearing gold and silver or other precious metals, and the gross proceeds thereof shall be exempt from taxation; but the surface improvements and net proceeds thereof shall be taxed, and such net proceeds shall consist of the gross proceeds of the mine remaining after deducting all ordinary and proper expenses of conducting the business of the mine, the cost of all permanent improvement made during the fiscal year in which the tax is levied, and any surplus fund accumulated and undivided and held by the owner of the mine for the purpose of making further permanent improvements thereon, or for the working thereof, or meeting any disaster thereto, or unfavorable development therein."

56. Ibid., pp. 1742-59. The Gray amendment struck all the exemption provisions, leaving the general statement. pp. 1758-59.

57. Ibid., p. 1759 (Morgan amendment) and p. 1765 (Claggett amendment). The Morgan amendment passed 33 to 14, and the Claggett amendment passed 41 to 10, indicating a desire to maintain the exempt status of certain properties. Idaho Constitution, Art. 7, sec. 5: "All taxes shall be uniform upon the same class of subjects within the territorial limits, of the authority levying the tax, and shall be levied and collected under general laws, which shall prescribe such regulations as shall secure a just valuation for taxation of all property, real and personal: Provided, that the Legislature may allow such exemptions from taxation from time to time as shall seem necessary and just, and all existing exemptions provided by the laws of the Territory, shall continue until changed by the Legislature of the State: Provided further, that duplicate taxation of property for the same purpose during the same year is hereby prohibited."

58. Robert W. Larson, <u>New Mexico's Quest for Statehood, 1846-1912</u> (Albuquerque, 1968), pp. 165-66. Also see pp. 99, 105, 107, 155, 167, 283 on territorial taxation.

59. <u>Tribune Citizen</u> (Albuquerque), October 7, 1910.

60. <u>Proceedings of the Constitutional Convention...New Mexico</u> (Albuquerque, 1910), pp. 176-82.

61. Ibid., pp. 176-80. Larson, *New Mexico*, p. 283.
62. Larson, *New Mexico*, p. 283; Fergusson Letters, MSS, University of New Mexico Archives, Albuquerque.
63. "Weinberger Scrap Book," MSS, University of Arizona Library, Tucson. The pledge in the scrapbook was from the *Daily Globe*, August 24, 1910.
64. "George W. P. Hunt and the Constitution of Arizona," MSS, University of Arizona Library, Tucson, pp. 15-17. "Complete Verbatim Report of the Arizona Constitutional Convention," 4 vols. MSS, Special Collections of the University of Arizona Library, Tucson, Vol. 2, morning, November 19, 1910, debates on taxation. The mines and railroads paid 40 percent of total tax revenues in 1911. They paid 60 percent under state government in 1913.
65. On mining taxation see debates in "Report...Arizona," Vol. 3, afternoon, November 26, 1910, part 5. *Arizona Constitution*, Art. 9. "Hunt and Constitution," pp. 16-17.

## CHAPTER 6

1. *Debates and Proceedings in the Constitutional Convention of...Nevada* (San Francisco, 1866), pp. 165-66. On agricultural development in Nevada see Thompson and West, *A History of Nevada* (Berkeley, Calif., 1958 reprint of 1881 edition), pp. 76, 134-39. Also see John W. Bird, "The End of the 'Monster' of Riparianism in Nevada," 22 *Nevada Historical Society Quarterly* 271-77 (Winter 1979). Gordon Morris Bakken, "The English Common Law in the Rocky Mountain West," 11 *Arizona and the West* 109-28 (Summer 1969).
2. *Denver Daily Times*, December 20, 1875. Colorado irrigation was fairly extensive by the time the convention met. The Greeley colony started extensive works, but previously "an intelligent class of farmers" and cattlemen had extensive works. For a firsthand description of some of these works, see T. J. Hickman, "Irrigation in Colorado, Colorado Dictations," MSS, Bancroft Library, University of California, Berkeley. George H. Church, "Irrigation in Colorado, Colorado Dictations," MSS, Bancroft Library. Church came to Colorado in 1861, built the first reservoir for irrigation purposes in 1868, introduced the first Herefords, and built a substantial cattle empire, according to him. John S. Routt, "Territory and State," MSS, Bancroft Library. Also see generally Carl Ubbelohde, *A Colorado History* (Boulder, Colo., 1965), pp. 187-95. See Donald J. Pisani, *From the Family Farm to Agribusiness* (Berkeley, Calif., 1984), pp. 30-53. Gordon Morris Bakken, "The Impact of the Colorado State Constitution on Rocky Mountain Constitution Making," 47 *Colorado Magazine* 152-75 (Spring 1970); Idem, "The Development of Law in Colorado, 1861-1912," 58 *Southern California Quarterly* 499-513 (Winter 1976).
3. *Greeley Tribune*, January 12, 1876.

4. *Colorado Transcript* (Golden), November 3, 1875.

5. *Denver Daily Tribune*, December 18, 19, 1875.

6. *Denver Daily Tribune*, February 14, 1876. *Portrait and Biographical Record of the State of Colorado*, 2 vols. (Chicago, 1899), pp. 85-86. *Proceedings of the Constitutional Convention ...Colorado* (Denver, 1907), p. 44.

7. *Denver Daily Tribune*, February 14, 1876. *Proceedings... Colorado*, pp. 296-97.

8. *Proceedings...Colorado*, p. 344.

9. Ibid., pp. 393, 406, 501, 504, 594, 615, 700. Also see David Wayne Hensel, "The Colorado Constitution in the Nineteenth Century" (Ph.D. dissertation, University of Colorado, 1957), pp. 169-71.

10. *Proceedings...Colorado*, pp. 296, 394, 406, 501, 502-504, 594, 615, 616, 700. *Greeley Tribune*, February 2, 1876.

11. *Proceedings...Colorado*, pp. 61, 146, 297, 393, 490, 491, 505, 595, 616, 700-1. Hensel, "Colorado Constitution," p. 173. *Denver Daily Tribune*, January 7, 1876. Even the *Greeley Tribune*, January 12, 1876, criticized Bromwell's proposals. Also see H. P. H. Bromwell, "Bromwell's Minority Report on Suffrage 1875-6 and Other Original Documents of the Colorado Constitutional Convention," MSS, Colorado Historical Society, Denver, p. 2.

12. See in general Moses Lasky, "From Prior Appropriation to Economic Distribution of Water by the State Via Irrigation Administration" 1 *Rocky Mountain Law* 167 (April 1929); 2 *Rocky Mountain Law* 58 (November 1929).

13. *Cheyenne Daily Sun*, September 6, 1889. *Cheyenne Daily Leader*, September 13, 1889. Also see the *Boomerang* (Laramie), September 26, 1889, and the *Boomerang* (weekly), Oct. 3, 1889. The *Daily Leader* kept the water issue before the public to the greater extent. See *Cheyenne Daily Leader*, September 12, 13, 22, 1889. Also see in Hebard Collection, "Light is Thrown on Very Dark Irrigation Laws," MSS, University of Wyoming Library, Laramie.

14. W. E. Chapin, "The Making of the Constitution of Wyoming," MSS, Hebard Collection, University of Wyoming Library, Laramie. "Interview with Mr. W. E. Chapin," MSS, Hebard Collection. Also see *Cheyenne Daily Leader*, September 13, 1889. Henry J. Peterson, "The Constitutional Convention of Wyoming," 7 *University of Wyoming Publications* 126 (May 1940). Gordon Morris Bakken, "Voting Patterns in the Wyoming Constitutional Convention of 1889," *42 Annals of Wyoming* 233-35 (October 1970).

15. *Journals and Debates of the Constitutional Convention...Wyoming* (Cheyenne, 1893), p. 289.

16. Ibid., pp. 291-92 (Conaway), p. 292 (Potter).

17. Ibid., pp. 497-501.

18. Ibid., p. 503.

19. Peterson, "Wyoming," p. 126.

20. James M. Hamilton, *From Wilderness to Statehood* (Portland, Ore., 1957), p. 556.

21. *Butte Semi-Weekly Miner*, July 20, 1889.

22. *Jefferson County Sentinel* (Boulder), July 26, 1889. Also see the *Avant Courier* (Bozeman), August 1, 1889, for similar sentiments. See the *Helena Daily Herald*, July 15, 20, August 2,

9, 1889. Butte Semi-Weekly Miner, July 20, 31, August 3, 1889.

23. Proceedings and Debates of the Constitutional Convention...Montana (Helena, 1921), p. 376.

24. Ibid., p. 472. On Maginnis see Hamilton, Wilderness to Statehood, pp. 202-3, 483-84, 526, 528, 532, 575-88. Henry Knippenberg, History of the Society of the Framers of the Constitution of the State of Montana (Glendale, 1890), p. 63. Daily Inter Mountain (Butte), July 8, 1889.

25. Collins ably observed that "if there is a monopoly on earth that is grinding, it is the monopoly of a great corporation that owns the water of an arid country." The urgency of action was paramount in the call for union. Proceedings...Montana, p. 473. Also see Knippenberg, Montana, p. 19.

26. Proceedings...Montana, p. 473. On the prior appropriation definition see Ibid., p. 533 (Robinson). Robinson's definition was an ironclad vested rights proposition which would have confirmed absolutely the holders of a priority right.

27. See the continuing debate, Ibid., pp. 551-71.

28. Ibid., p. 554 (Stapleton), p. 555 (Knowles), p. 557 (Middleton), p. 558 (Maginnis).

29. For the votes, Ibid., pp. 568, 570, 571. The new omnibus measure was introduced under the taxation article, p. 675. The bloc of miners and activists were led by William A. Clark, Timothy Collins, John C. Robinson, James E. Callaway, and Charles S. Hartman. Others in their number included Peter Breen, Edward Burns, David G. Browne, Simeon Buford, Alexander F. Burns, William T. Field, Paris Gibson, Joseph Hogan, William Mayger, Martin Maginnis, William Parberry, William M. Bullard, Andrew J. Burns, George O. Eaton, Warren C. Gillette, Richard O. Hickman, Allan R. Joy, William Kennedy, Louis Rotwitt, G. J. Reek, Francis E. Sargeant, William H. Watson, Charles S. Warren, and Aaron Witter. Guttman scaleogram. The Boguetab analysis of the same votes revealed 75 percent agreement scores for all the delegates involved, and for the 17 delegates following Clark and Maginnis, a 100 percent agreement score. The five votes involved in the analysis are on Ibid., pp. 568, 570, 571, 680, 901.

30. Ibid., pp. 803-16. Helena Daily Herald, August 9, 1889.

31. Ibid., pp. 895-97.

32. Ibid., p. 900.

33. The Idaho World (Boise), August 2, 1889, noted "the zeal with which the press of Idaho is inspired in forwarding the general plan of irrigation, but more particularly of each and every one of the respective locality in which they reside." Also see the Daily Statesman (Boise), July 13, 30, 1889.

34. For the debates, see Proceedings and Debates of the Constitutional Convention of Idaho (Caldwell, Idaho, 1912), pp. 1115-76, 1305-29, 1333-36, 1340-64. The Guttman scaleogram of the votes involved reveals a miners' coalition built around W. B. Heyburn. Other members included Stephen S. Glidden, John S. Gray, Alexander Mayhew, Abel J. Pierce, James M. Shoup, J. S. Whitton. In the words of Edgar Wilson, the majority felt "the first interests of this arid country [were] agriculture." Ibid., p. 1360 (See Table 7).

35. Deseret Evening News, March 7, 19, 20, April 3, 1895. Also see Leonard J. Arrington and Dean May, "A Different Mode of Life: Irrigation and Society in Nineteenth-Century Utah" 49 Agricultural History 3-20 (Jan., 1975). Eminant Dom.

36. Proceedings and Debates of the Constitutional Convention...Utah (Salt Lake City, 1898), p. 1203 (Chidester: "the engineer and board of control...is an expensive luxury in which we do not, or should not wish to indulge), p. 1203 (Lauritz Larsen: "I am not in favor or creating new and expensive offices in this state"), p. 1208 (Maloney: "You cannot take away vested rights by constitutional amendment or enactment"), p. 1211 (Snow: "We are very jealous of our water rights"). Deseret Evening News, March 7, 1895: "The idea of district systems of irrigation in which land owners are also owners of waters, has shown itself to be well adapted here."

37. Proceedings...Utah, p. 1213 (Hammond).

38. "Homer R. Wood Notes," MSS, University of Arizona Library, Tucson, proposition number 149. Minutes of the Constitutional Convention of the Territory of Arizona (Phoenix, 1910), p. 324. Jacob Weinberger, "Book of Propositions and Notes as Kept by Jacob Weinberger, Member of Constitutional Convention," MSS, State of Arizona, Department of Library and Archives, Phoenix. Gordon Morris Bakken, "The Arizona Constitutional Convention of 1910," 1978 Arizona State Law Journal 1-30 (November 1978).

39. "Complete Verbatim Report of the Arizona Constitutional Convention, 1910," 4 vols. MSS, University of Arizona Library, Tucson, Vol. 3, afternoon, November 26, 1910, p. 1.

40. E. W. Coker, a Pinal County lawyer, consistently voted with the Republicans who also opposed any substantive changes. He offered a Wyoming system plan more to embarrass the agricultural interests than to offer a meaningful alternative. "Wood Notes," proposition number 127. Coker's agreement scores with prominent Republicans on the issue were high: Carlos C. Jacome 100 percent, Samuel L. Kingan 100 percent, William F. Cooper 100 percent, Bracey Curtis 100 percent, and James C. White 100 percent. Boguetab analysis of six roll calls, Minutes...Arizona, pp. 325, 324-25, 325, 326, 326, 327.

41. J. P. Orme file, MSS, Arizona Pioneers' Historical Society, Tucson.

42. "Verbatim Report...Arizona," Vol. 3, afternoon, November 26, 1910, p. 5.

43. Ibid., Vol. 3, afternoon, November 29, 1910, p. 2.

44. Minutes...Arizona, p. 324. Orme substitute: "The common law doctrine of riparian water rights within this state shall not hereafter obtain or be of any force or effect in this state.

The waters of every river, creek or running stream in this State are hereby declared to be public property, subject, however, to the beneficial use of any person or persons, company or corporation under such reasonable restrictions and regulations as the legislative powers may prescribe.

Beneficial use shall be the basis, the measure and the limit of the right to the use of public waters, and priority of appropriation for such use shall give the better right except that in times of scarcity a preference shall be given to the following purposes in the order named, viz: Domestic, stock water, agriculture, mining and manufacturing purposes.

All existing rights to the use of water in this State for beneficial purposes are hereby recognized and confirmed, subject to the limitations herein prescribed in the case of future appropriations and use of water."

45. "Verbatim Report...Arizona," Vol. 3, afternoon, November 29, 1910, p. 3. Parsons also voted with the Republican opposition on this issue. His agreement scores were with Carlos Jacome 100 percent, Samuel Kingan 100 percent, William F. Cooper 100 percent, Bracey Curtis 100 percent, James C. White 100 percent. He also voted 100 percent with E. W. Coker (Boguetab analysis). The Guttman scaleogram also puts Coker and Parsons together against the Orme bloc.

46. "Verbatim Report...Arizona," Vol. 3, afternoon, November 29, 1910, p. 3; part 3, page 1 (Colter).

47. Minutes...Arizona, p. 325.

48. "Verbatim Report...Arizona," Vol. 4, afternoon, December 1, 1910.

49. Hunt's agreement score with all of the Orme forces was 83 percent. Goldwater voted 67 percent to 83 percent of the time with individual members of the Coker-Republican forces. The Goldwater bloc was made up of W. T. Webb, A. M. Tuthill, Mit Simms, John Langdon, and R. B. Sims with a minimum bloc agreement score of 100 percent; Thomas Feeney, John Bolan, Albert M. Jones, Henry Lovin, Homer R. Wood, J. J. Keegan, and C. M. Roberts with a minimum bloc agreement score of 67 percent. George Pusch and Jacob Weinberger voted with Goldwater 83 percent and 80 percent of the time respectively. On the Guttman scaleogram Goldwater occupies a middle position. Hence, his influence was significant in drawing moderates to his side of the issue (See Table 8).

50. New Mexico's convention did the same. See New Mexico Constitution, Art. 16.

## CHAPTER 7

1. Rodman W. Paul, Mining Frontiers of the Far West, 1848-80 (New York, 1963), p. 67; Eliot Lord, Comstock Mining and Miners (Washington, D.C., 1883).

2. See Lawrence M. Friedman and Jack Ladinsky, "Social Change and the Law of Industrial Accidents" 67 Columbia Law Review 50-82 (January 1967).

3. Denver Daily Tribune, February 28, 1876. For subsequent developments see David T. Brundage, The Making of Working-Class Radicalism in the Mountain West: Denver, Colorado, 1880-1903 (Ph.D. dissertation, University of California, Los Angeles, 1982).

4. Howard Roberts Lamar, The Far Southwest (New Haven, Conn., 1966), p. 293. David Wayne Hensel, "The Colorado Constitution in

the Nineteenth Century" (Ph.D. dissertation, University of Colorado, 1957), p. 149. Denver Daily Tribune, February 28, 1876. Carl Ubbelohde, A Colorado History (Boulder, Colo., 1965), pp. 147-49.

5. Proceedings of the Constitutional Convention...Colorado (Denver, 1907), p. 448. Bromwell received support from the following delegates who also voted with him the indicated percentage of the time on corporation issues: William E. Beck 100 percent, Byron L. Carr 67 percent, A. D. Cooper 100 percent, Daniel Hurd 50 percent, S. J. Plumb 100 percent, A. K. Yount 75 percent, William Lee 67 percent, W. C. Stover 100 percent, George G. White 17 percent (the only vote cast with Bromwell), and W. T. Wells 50 percent. The hardcore Grangers were Bromwell, Cooper, Plumb, and Beck. They all had 100 percent agreement scores with each other based on six roll calls. Ibid., p. 448 (Carr amendment), p. 450 (Wheeler motion), p. 450 (Clark motion), p. 498 (Beck motion) p. 498 (White motion), p. 499 (adoption of section 9, finally Article 15, section 15). Lee, Stover, and White were Democrats (See Tables 9 and 10).

6. Proceedings...Colorado, pp. 498-99. The Grangers voted against White's motion to reconsider, and none of them voted against the passage of the section. The key role played by the Democrats was emphasized by their voting record. The Guttman scaleogram reveals a central bloc comprised of William M. Clark, L. C. Ellsworth, C. P. Elder, William James, Alvin Marsh, Henry C. Thatcher, all Republicans, and William H. Cushman, John S. Hough, George Pease, Robert A. Quillian, Wilber Stone, Agepeta Vigil, and J. W. Widderfield, all Democrats. Ellsworth, Thatcher, Quillian, Stone, Widderfield, and Hough had a 100 percent agreement score on all issues. With Elder, Marsh, and Cushman, they formed a bloc with a minimum agreement of 83 percent (Boguetab analysis). On White and the others see Denver Daily Tribune, February 14, 1876.

7. Denver Daily Times, January 7, 1876. Proceedings... Colorado, 57, 58, 70, 212, 278, 385, 387, 500, 700. Also see Thomas Tonge, Colorado Mineral Resources (Denver, 1904).

8. Hensel, "Colorado Constitution," p. 151. Also see Denver Daily Times, January 29, 1876, for an editorial view of the middle way for corporations. Wayne C. Williams, "The Argument for Workmen's Compensation: The Colorado Industrial and Compensation Laws," 22 Case and Comment 304-7 (1915).

9. Proceedings and Debates of the Constitutional Convention...Montana (Helena, 1921), pp. 699-711.

10. Ibid., p. 712 (Field amendment to section 19).

11. Ibid., pp. 65, 210 (note Gibson and Marion amendments and Knowles' reply), p. 210 (Breen defense), p. 211 (Knowles' rebuttal).

12. Ibid., pp. 213, 214, 245. On Chinese labor see pp. 60, 177, 215, 698 (lost 20 to 27).

13. Breen drew consistent support only from William J. Kennedy, B. Platt Carpenter, John C. Robinson, Joseph Hogan, and Thomas Courtney. They all agreed 100 percent of the time with Breen on the corporation article, the eight-hour day, and an anti-free pass section (Boguetab analysis). Ibid., pp. 245, 657, 724. He also

drew occasional support from Thomas F. Courtney and Lewis H. Hershfield. Also see Henry Knippenberg, History of the Society of the Framers of the Constitution of the State of Montana, (Glendale, Mont., 1890). James M. Hamilton, From Wilderness to Statehood (Portland, Oreg., 1957), pp. 555-57.

14. Proceedings and Debates of the Constitutional Convention...Idaho (Caldwell, Idaho, 1912), pp. 877-980.

15. Ibid., p. 884 (Beatty).

16. Ibid., pp. 869-901 (corporations debate), pp. 1372-95 (labor article).

17. Journals and Debates of the Constitutional Convention...Wyoming (Cheyenne, 1893), p. 448.

18. Ibid., pp. 448, 615-21.

19. Ibid., p. 449 (Russell: "This is taken verbatim from the Colorado constitution.").

20. Ibid., pp. 606-11. See p. 610 (Holden on ignorance of conditions) and p. 610 (Russell for miners' side of issue).

21. Wyoming Constitution, Art. 19, sec. Police Powers, Labor Contracts.

22. Journals...Wyoming, p. 588.

23. Ibid., p. 588-93. Cheyenne Daily Sun, September 21, 1889.

24. For the numerous propositions concerning corporations see Proceedings and Debates of the Convention...Utah, (Salt Lake City, 1898), pp. 56, 66, 75, 129, 155, 157, 163, 192, 193, 199, 397, 951, 976, 994, 1050, 1164, 1484, 1547, 1588, 1654, 1809, 1815, 1819, 1872-75. Deseret Evening News, April 25, 1895. Also see Stanley S. Ivins, "A Constitution for Utah," 25 Utah Historical Quarterly 111 (April 1957).

25. Proceedings...Utah, p. 112 (Strevell proposition prescribed a three-member board with no more than two from one political party), p. 156 (Crane proposition, file number p. 46), 202 (Kimball, file number 110).

26. Ibid., p. 1032 (Peters: "purely legislation and wholly unnecessary"), p. 1032 (Cannon: "purely legislative), p. 1033 (Eichnor), p. 1043 (Roberts substitute).

27. Ibid., p. 1033 (Strevell), pp. 1044-45 (Evans of Weber cited the Montana and Wyoming constitutions). The delegates who desired specific provisions did so because they distrusted future legislatures based on their past experience in Utah. See Hubert Button's speech, p. 1038.

28. Evans substitute: "The Legislature shall provide by law for a board of labor arbitration which shall fairly represent the interests of both capital and labor, and it shall be the duty of said board, under such regulations as may be provided by law, to endeavor by mediation and conciliation to effect a settlement of difficulties between employer and employees." Ibid., p. 1050.

29. Ibid., p. 1039 (Squires), p. 1043 (Goodwin), p. 1046 (Partridge).

30. Ibid., p. 1165 (Evans), p. 1165 (Thurman).

31. Joining Evans and voting with him on the eight-hour-day section and the labor article were John S. Boyer, William Creer, Abel J. Evans, Charles H. Hart, William Howard, Joseph A. Hyde, Anthony Ivins, James P. Low, Karl G. Maeser, Ingwald Thoreson,

Orson F. Whitney, Noble Warrum, Jr., Anthony Lund, James N. Kimball, and Andrew Kimball. Brigham Roberts voted for the Evans substitute. Ibid., pp. 1167, 1173, 1176 (Boguetab analysis).

32. Ibid., p. 1172.

33. Proceedings of the Constitutional Convention...New Mexico (Albuquerque, 1910), pp. 165-70. Robert W. Larson, New Mexico's Quest for Statehood (Albuquerque, 1968), p. 281.

34. Proceedings...New Mexico, pp. 153, 240.

35. Ibid., p. 244.

36. Ibid., pp. 170-72 (minority report), p. 240-44 (miscellaneous).

37. H. B. Fergusson, Frank Springer, and Frank W. Clancy, New Mexico in 1910: Letters and Addresses Relating to the Constitution (printed for Frank Clancy, no date), pp. 78-79. For comparative material on social legislation in the Rocky Mountain States see George Cleveland Atteberry, "Social Legislation in New Mexico-A Survey and Analysis" (M.A. thesis, University of Colorado, 1924).

38. Arizona Democrat (Phoenix), July 18, 1910. The Democrat saw a "death blow to the corporation scheme" in Democrat refusal to forward a bipartisan delegate ticket. The Tucson Star, July 21, 1910, warned, on the other hand, that "Arizona [would] receive a severe set back if the impression [were] permitted to go abroad that the new state of Arizona [was] opposed to corporations." Also see Lamar, Far Southwest, p. 501.

39. "Complete Verbatim Report of the Arizona Constitutional Convention," 4 vols. MSS, University of Arizona Library, Tucson, Vol. 3, night, November 23, 1910, p. 5 (Cunniff and Short).

40. See Arizona Gazette (Phoenix), December 29, 1910, on E. E. Ellinwood's opposition to the constitution based on "the corporation regulation measure." "Propositions Presented to the Constitutional Convention, 1910, Arizona; File of H. R. Wood," MSS, State of Arizona Department of Library and Archives, Phoenix, proposition number 29. The Arizona Democrat labeled the proposition the "most drastic ever drawn." Wood commented on others that "there [was] no question but what there [was] a whole lot of stuff in it that should be left to the legislature." Gordon Morris Bakken, "The Arizona Constitutional Convention of 1910," 1978 Arizona State Law Journal 1-30 (November 1978). James W. Byrkit, Forging the Copper Collar (Tucson, 1982), pp. 33-49.

41. Minutes of the Constitutional Convention of the Territory of Arizona (Phoenix, 1910), p. 314. The Lynch amendment to strike the corporation commission lost 20 to 28. The vote on this, the Roberts amendment to expand commission coverage to banks and other financial institutions, and the final passage of the corporation and corporation commission articles revealed the delegate alignments. On the Lynch amendment, the Republicans were joined by Fred T. Colter, D. L. Cunningham, E. A. Tovrea, J. J. Keegan, Lamar Cobb, A. R. Lynch, Mit Simms, A. M. Tuthill, W. T. Webb, A. C. Baker, John P. Orme, Orrin Standage, Henry Lovin, E. E. Ellinwood, and Alfred Franklin. The Hunt Democrats formed a 16-man bloc on these issues with a 75 percent minimum bloc agreement score (Boguetab analysis). The corporation Democrats

and Republicans, on the other hand, had only a 50 percent minimum on all issues. Goldwater's faction voted with the Hunt bloc 75 percent of the time, but agreed among themselves 100 percent of the time. R. B. Sims, Jacob Weinberger, M. G. Cunniff, and A. A. Moore voted with Goldwater (See Tables 11 and 12).

42. "Verbatim Report...Arizona," MSS, University of Arizona, Tucson, Vol. 3, afternoon, November 22, 1910, p. 3; Vol. 4, morning, December 5, 1910, pp. 1-8.

43. Minutes...Arizona, p. 250. The Webb motion to strike resulted in a 23-to-23 vote, but the second vote was 29 to 19. On the labor issues of employer's liability, workmen's compensation, and the labor article as a whole, the Hunt Democrats, numbering 18 strong, voted as a bloc 100 percent of the time. Goldwater's faction included Mulford Winsor, C. M. Roberts, F. A. Jones, and A. C. Baker, all voting together 100 percent and with Hunt 75 percent. The opposition came from the Republicans joined by Lamar Cobb, Alfred Franklin, John P. Orme, Sidney Osborn, and Fred T. Colter who voted with them on half the roll calls (Boguetab analysis).

44. Feeney again led the floor fight for child labor. He pleaded that "society [cried] its eyes out for the widows and orphans, and here [was] an opportunity to act." The opposition used the old saw of unconstitutional legislation but to no avail. "Verbatim Report...Arizona," Vol. 2, afternoon, November 18, 1910, p. 16 (Feeney), p. 19 (Osborn and Winsor).

45. Ibid., Vol. 1, afternoon, November 1, 1910, p. 14 (Parsons: The proposition was taken directly "from the verbatim copy of the constitution of Wyoming.").

46. See Tru Anthony McGinnis, "The Influence of Organized Labor on the Making of the Arizona Constitution" (M.A. thesis, University of Arizona, 1930). An anti-blacklist section was also included in the article. See "Verbatim Report...Arizona," Vol. 4, forenoon, December 2, 1910. Also see Wood file, proposition number 137 and substitute 137. See Table 13 for the voting alignment on labor.

## CHAPTER 8

1. Leonard J. Arrington, Great Basin Kingdon (Cambridge, Mass., 1958), pp. 356-64. Thomas F. O'Dea, The Mormons (Chicago, 1957), pp. 110, 246. Kimball Young, Isn't One Wife Enough (New York, 1954), pp. 354-55, 370-73, 417-18. Also see Salt Lake Tribune Alamanac, 1896 (Salt Lake City, 1896); Norma Basch, "Equity vs. Equality: Emerging Concepts of Women's Political Status in the Age of Jackson," 3 Journal of the Early Republic 297-318 (Fall 1983). The issue of women's suffrage is multi-dimensional as indicated in the text. As Paula Baker has demonstrated, the issue is also one of the domestication of politics in America. This chapter supports many of her observations, particularly the interrelated nature of domestic, economic, and political spheres. Further, the bibliography that

she sets out in her article provides an excellent basis for historiographical context. Paula Baker, "The Domestication of Politics: Women and American Political Society, 1780-1920," 89 American Historical Review 620-47 (June 1984). Interestingly, Baker's article does not credit the women of the West with having much influence upon their suffrage victories. The studies by Billie Barners Jensen and Virginia Scharff, cited below, clearly indicate that the women of Wyoming and Colorado used politics to secure suffrage gains. Female suffrage was a partisan issue with Republicans opposing it in Kansas, Washington and the Dakotas. See Peter H. Argersinger, "Idealogy and Behavior: Legislative Politics and Western Populism" 58 Agricultural History 43-58 (Jan., 1984). Also see on the Pacific Northwest, Ruth Barnes Moynihan, Rebel for Rights (New Haven, 1983).

2. See Merle W. Wells, "The Idaho Anti-Mormon Movement, 1872-1908" (Ph.D. dissertation, University of California, Berkeley, 1950). Dennis L. Thompson, "Religion and the Idaho Constitution" 58 Pacific Northwest Quarterly 169-78 (October 1967). Idaho Daily Statesman (Boise), January 22, 1889; July 7, 11, 1889.

3. Supra, note number 1. William Stewart's congressional schemes to annex part of Idaho to his faultering Nevada always included a test oath. The test oath was a guarantee of the status quo. In an 1887 letter Stewart made this clear: "But whatever is done, the Mormons must not obtain control of our State. If by amending the Nevada Constitution and making a test oath alien enemies can be excluded from the franchise, we can take in some Mormon territory with safety, otherwise not." Stewart to Goodwin, February 8, 1887. "Stewart Letter Books," MSS, Nevada Historical Society, Reno.

4. See Richard B. Morris, Studies in the History of American Law (New York, 1930), pp. 128-35, 171. James F. Mister, "Law of Married Women," 20 American Law Review 356, 359 (May and June 1886). On the territorial law see Laws...Colorado, 1st session, p. 152; 10th session, p. 185. Compiled Laws...Arizona (1871), p. 305. Ibid., ch. 32, containing the Howell Code and the 1871 act amendatory to it. Miller v. Fisher (1875), 1 Ariz. 232. Charauleau v. Woffenden (1876), 1 Ariz. 243. Woffenden v. Charauleau (1876), 1 Ariz. 346. Laws...Montana, 8th session, p. 93. Laws...Wyoming, 1st session, ch. 19; 7th session, p. 154. Manton v. Tyler (1882), 4 Mont. 364. Palmer v. Murray (1886), 6 Mont. 169. Granger v. Lewis Bros. (1880), 2 Wyo. 231. Ray v. Ray (1874), 1 Idaho 566. Laws...Idaho, 4th session, pp. 65, 138; Laws...New Mexico, 2nd session, p. 358; 26th session, p. 44. Martinez v. Lucero (1857), 1 N.M. 208. Compiled Laws of Utah (1888), II, sec. 2528. Warr v. Honeck (1892), 8 Utah 61. Also see Eleanor Flexner, Century of Struggle (Cambridge, Mass., 1959), pp. 159-63. On female suffrage in the region see T. A. Larson, "Woman Suffrage in Western America" 38 Utah Historical Quarterly 8-19 (Winter 1970). Alan P. Grimes, The Puritan Ethic and Woman Suffrage (New York, 1967). Billie Barnes Jensen, "Colorado Woman's Suffrage Campaigns of the 1870's," 12 Journal of the West 254-71 (1973). Thomas G. Alexander, "An Experiment in Progressive

Legislation: The Granting of Women's Suffrage in Utah in 1879" 38 *Utah Historical Quarterly* 20-30 (Winter 1970); Jean Bickmore White, "Woman's Place is in the Constitution: The Struggle for Equal Rights in Utah in 1895," 42 *Utah Historical Quarterly* 344-69 (Fall 1974); Beverley Beeton, "Woman Suffrage in Territorial Utah," 46 *Utah Historical Quarterly* 100-20 (Spring 1978); T. A. Larson, "The Woman's Rights Movement in Idaho," 16 *Idaho Yesterdays* 2-15, 18-19 (Spring 1972); Idem, "Idaho's Role in America's Woman Suffrage Crusade," 18 *Idaho Yesterdays* 2-15 (Spring 1974)' Idem, "Montana Women and the Battle for the Ballot. Woman Suffrage in the Treasure State," 23 *Montana* 24-41 (January 1973); Leslie Wheeler, "Henry B. Blackwell, "Woman Suffrage's Gray-Bearded Champion Comes to Montana, 1889," 31 *Montana* 2-13 (July 1981); Joan M. Jensen, "Disfranchisement is a Disgrace: Women and Politics in New Mexico, 1900-1940," 56 *New Mexico Historical Review* 5-35 (January 1981). Idem, "Pioneers in Politics," 92 El Palacio 12-19 (Summer/Fall 1986). For developments in the East on women's property rights, see Norma Basch, *In the Eyes of the Law* (Ithaca, N.Y., 1982). Richard H. Chused, "Married Women's Property Law: 1800-1850," 71 *Georgetown Law Journal* 1359-1425 (1983).

5. *Official Report of the Debates and Proceedings in the Constitutional Convention of the State of Nevada* (San Francisco, 1866), pp. 243-72, 478-94. The roll calls used were on Crosman's amendment to eliminate the test oath, p. 492, the Article 2 report, p. 493, and the adoption of Article 2, p. 494. The group referred to in the test had a 100 percent agreement score and consisted of 17 members of the convention. Members of this bloc who voted for Lincoln in 1860 included Samuel A. Chapin of Storey County, who moved to recommit the oath to committee to strike it, and J. S. Crosman of Lyon County, who moved to strike it altogether. Forty-eight percent of the bloc favoring a test oath had voted for Lincoln in 1860. Sectionally, the Storey, Lyon, and Esmeralda County delegates opposed the oath and the Washoe and Roop and some Ormsby County delegates favored it. This was the usual miner-versus- agriculturalist split evident in the convention.

6. See Wetherill speech, Ibid., p. 154. In terms of the voting pattern, the consistent opponents of the test oath also opposed allowing women an equal economic position. These men were all 1860 Democrats and easterners.

7. The proposition to forbid the legislature from ever passing a sole traders statute was taken from the 1863 Nevada constitution. In the early debates DeLong took no part, and the section was approved by a narrow margin. A motion to strike lost 11 to 14, and the section was adopted 13 to 10. Ibid., p. 154. When the issue was renewed, DeLong took the floor, favoring the emasculation of the section, and it was approved 24 to 6. Ibid., pp. 276-78.

8. For a sample of DeLong's arguments see Ibid., p. 276.

9. On suffrage see Ibid., pp. 70-73, 80-88, 97-120.

10. 1 Colo. 460. *Laws...Colorado*, 10th session, p. 185.

11. Jensen, "Colorado Woman's Suffrage Campaigns" 256-63. One

thousand persons from Denver petitioned the convention for equal suffrage. The petition was presented by H. P. Bromwell. Denver Daily Times, January 13, 1876. Proceedings of the Constitutional Convention...Colorado (Denver, 1907), p. 165. The suffragists addressed the convention the same day. Rocky Mountain Daily News, January 13, 1876. The group held a mass meeting at the Unity church in Denver on January 11, 1876, to build support. Ibid., January 11, 1876. These meetings were greeted with mixed emotions. The Colorado Chieftain (Pueblo) called them "hen conventions" and went on to condemn the movement. Colorado Chieftain, December 29, 1875.

12. The Denver Daily Times, January 13, 1876, and the Rocky Mountain Daily News, January 23, 1876.

13. Rocky Mountain Daily News, January 16, 1876. H. P. H. Bromwell, "Bromwell's Minority Report on Suffrage 1875-6 and Other Original Documents of the Colorado Constitutional Convention," MSS, Colorado Historical Society, Denver, p. 21.

14. Rocky Mountain Daily News, January 13, 1876. Greeley Tribune, January 5, March 15, 1876. Colorado Transcript (Golden), January 5, 1876. Colorado Springs Gazette, February 26, 1876.

15. Greeley Tribune, January 5, 1876. Colorado Springs Gazette, February 26, 1876.

16. The Colorado Chieftain (Pueblo) kept a running criticism of the suffragists as outside agitators. Some of its editorial attacks were bitter: "The advocates of women's rights...possess two characteristics in common, viz, age and ugliness." It encouraged the convention to "close its doors hereafter against the incursions of carpet bagging female mountebanks and vinegar faced advocates of women's rights. Colorado Chieftain, January 14, 30, 1876.

17. "Bromwell's Report," p. 21. Rocky Mountain Daily News, January 23, 1876.

18. Rocky Mountain Daily News, January 8, 1876. Greeley Tribune, January 5, 1876. Proceedings...Colorado, pp. 265, 322, 429-30, 583 (substitute directing legislature to act adopted).

19. Edwin B. Smith, "The Formation of the Constitution of Colorado," MSS, Colorado Historical Society, Denver, p. 27.

20. See T. A. Larson, History of Wyoming (Lincoln, Neb., 1965), pp. 74-94. Lewis L. Gould, Wyoming, A Political History, 1868-1896 (New Haven, Conn., 1968) pp. 26-27. T. A. Larson, "Wyoming's Contributions to the Regional and National Women's Rights Movement." 52 Annals of Wyoming 2-15 (Spring 1980). Virginia Scharff, "The Case for Domestic Feminism: Woman Suffrage in Wyoming." 56 Annals of Wyoming 29-37 (Fall 1984). Scharff's article provides an evidentiary basis for the revisionist position that Wyoming women were far more active in securing the vote in 1869 than prior opinion had offered. In fact, women used the politics of the period to their advantage.

21. Laws...Wyoming, 1st session, ch. 19; 7th session, p. 154. Granger v. Lewis Bros. (1880), 2 Wyo. 231.

22. Journals and Debates of the Constitutional Convention... Wyoming (Cheyenne, 1893), p. 346 (Campbell termed the territorial law a joke), pp. 352-53 (Brown lauds territorial law), p. 347

(Baxter, who introduced the bill, termed it "right, fair and just"). The Cheyenne Daily Sun, September 7, 1889, noted that the danger apprehended from the adoption of women's suffrage was not as great as had been anticipated. The Daily Boomerang (Laramie), September 9, 1889, noted the 20-year experience had been a success.

23. Cheyenne Daily Leader, September 12, 1889.

24. Daily Boomerang (Laramie), September 9, 1889. In the context of American political freedom, women's suffrage was a burst of liberalism, especially in the 19th century. But it is interesting to note that some of the same delegates that advocated female suffrage favored a literacy test. It also created strange bedfellows. Anthony C. Campbell, who led the opposition to female suffrage, joined George Baxter, who introduced the section in opposition to a literacy test. Campbell associated the right to vote with citizenship alone, although he also talked in terms of a taxpayer's right. Journals...Wyoming, pp. 370-72. Douglas A. Preston, who held the most radical voting record on the issue, branded the literacy test as a disaster to Wyoming economy. Campbell tried to use the absurd to discredit proponents with an amendment requiring that "no person shall be entitled to vote who cannot translate Hamlet's Soliloquy into Pennsylvania Dutch." Ibid., p. 385. But the majority, buoyed by strong anti-immigrant feeling, easily passed a literarcy test. Ibid., pp. 389, 391-95. (Harvey: "It is uniformly agreed that the most serious problem which confronts us is the simple question of the ignorance of the vast hordes that are coming in among us year by year.") The Boomerang feared that some women would also lose the vote under such a literacy test. Boomerang, September 26, 1889. The Guttman analysis of the literacy test and suffrage article roll calls identified 13 liberals. Voting with Campbell, Baxter, and Preston were Henry S. Elliott, John R. Riner, Herman Menough, James A. Casebeer, William C. Irvine, Noyes Baldwin, Elliott S. N. Morgan, Charles N. Potter, Jonathan Jones, and Asbury Conway. John L. Russell, Charles Vagner, and Clarence Clark agreed with William C. Irvine 75 percent of the time and should be included with the Baxter-Campbell faction (Boguetab analysis). In support of the argument that women's property interests and rights were significant in the economic and political background of women's suffrage see Paula M. Bauman, "Single Women Homesteaders in Wyoming, 18880-1930," 58 Annals of Wyoming 39-53 (Spring, 1986). Bauman found that women homesteaders exploited their claims to earn money for their ventures and that in the Homestead Act, they had a peculiar challenge to achieve equal rights. The period studied followed that of the initial suffrage experience, but provides an important context for understanding the woman's struggle for equal rights and responsibilities on the Rocky Mountain frontier.

25. Laws...Montana, 8th session, p. 93. Manton v. Tyler (1882), 4 Montana 364. Palmer v. Murray (1886), 6 Mont. 125. A woman was legally feme sole when her husband deserted her. Palmer v. McMasters (1886), 6 Mont. 169.

26. James M. Hamilton, From Wilderness to Statehood (Portland,

Org., 1957), p. 530. Also see Stephenie Ambrose Tubbs, "Montana Women's Clubs at the Turn of the Century," 36 *Montana: The Magazine of Western History* 26-35 (Winter 1986).

27. *Proceedings and Debates of the Constitutional Convention... Montana* (Helena, 1921), p. 575. On Carpenter see Henry Knippenberg, *History of the Society of the Framers of the Constitution of the State of Montana* (Glendale, Mont., 1890), p. 24.

28. *Proceedings...Montana*, pp. 585-87, 645-47.

29. Ibid., p. 587: "The property rights and political rights of married women shall in all respects be placed upon an equality with the property and political rights of men." Burleigh's proposition lost 38 to 32. Ibid., p. 587. On Burleigh see Knippenberg, *Framers*, p. 10. Howard Roberts Lamar, *Dakota Territory, 1861-1889* (New Haven, Conn., 1956), pp. 96-97, 112-16, 120-24, 233.

30. The numbers represent paired agreement scores from eight roll call votes.

David G. Browne
100 Walter Cooper
100 100 Alfred Myers
100 100 100 William C. Clark
100 100 100 100 Walter A. Burleigh
100 100 100 100 100 S. S. Hobson
100 100 100 100 100 100 Richard O. Hickman
100 100 100 100 100 100 100 Hiram Knowles
100 100 100 100 100 100 100 100 William M. Bullard
100 100 100 100 100 100 100 100 100 William Parberry
100 100 100 100 100 100 100 100 100 100 Perry McAdow
100 100 100 100 100 100 100 100 100 100 100 Edward Burns
100 100 100 100 100 100 100 100 100 100 100 100 John Ezra Rickards

The eight roll calls are Burleigh's equal rights for women resolution, p. 587; the invitation to the women's suffrage association speaker, p. 80; Joy's literacy test section, p. 449; Bickford's amendment, p. 459; the Marrion substitute to allow only male suffrage, p. 462; the Joy motion to table the McAdow section to allow the legislature to extend suffrage, p. 466; the Kennedy motion to table a women's suffrage proposition, p. 855; and Carpenter's resolution, p. 915. Included with this bloc were Warren C. Gillette, J. E. Kanouse, Timothy Collins, William Muth, Luke D. Hatch, Simeon Bufford, and Edward Aiken with 80 percent minimum agreement scores (Buford and Aiken at 63 percent) (*Boguetab* analysis). The Guttman scaleogram positions the majority of these delegates on the liberal side of center with the exception of delegates like Collins who voted against the Burleigh equal rights resolution. There were 13 Democrats and 7 Republicans in the bloc.

31. The Breen faction also voted against Burleigh's equal rights resolution as it was too extreme for them. This was mitigated by their voting record on more conservative suffrage expansion plans (*Boguetab* analysis). There were eight Republicans

and two Democrats in the faction.

William A. Chessman<br>
100 Francis E. Sargeant<br>
88 88 Charles S. Warren<br>
75 75 88 William H. Watson<br>
71 71 86 86 Milton Cauby<br>
88 88 75 63 86 Peter Breen<br>
88 88 75 63 86 100 Charles Loud<br>
86 86 71 57 67 86 86 Andrew Burns<br>
63 63 50 63 71 75 75 86 O. F. Goddard<br>
63 63 50 63 71 75 75 86 100 William T. Field

32. Proceedings...Montana, pp. 369-71.

33. The conservatives allied with Maginnis included Aaron Witter, Henry Knippenberg, B. Platt Carpenter, Fielding L. Graves, Paris Gibson, and Llewellyn A. Luce with 83 percent minimum agreement scores. Charles S. Marshall, Joseph E. Marion, George B. Winston, Arthur Craven, and Samuel Mitchell agreed with Maginnis a minimum of 75 percent. The Kohrs faction consisted of William W. Dixon, Thomas F. Courtney, Edward Cardwell, William Mayger, and Lewis A. Hershfield with an 86 percent minimum agreement score. William J. Kennedy and John C. Robinson agreed with Kohrs 71 percent and with the other members of the faction 86 percent (Boguetab analaysis). There were six Republicans and six Democrats in the Maginnis faction, and five Democrats and three Republicans in the Kohrs faction. The Guttman scaleogram places both Kohrs and Maginnis in the most conservative voting posture.

34. William Ramsdell's speech best exemplified this attitude. Proceedings...Montana, p. 369.

31. Ibid., pp. 78-80. On Knowles see Hamilton, From Wilderness to Statehood, pp. 331-32, 341-42, 513, 518, 551. For the text of the address to the convention see Proceedings...Montana, pp. 81-88. The conservative opposition to female suffrage also used the outside-agitator device just as Colorado conservatives had during their constitutional convention. See the Colorado Chieftain (Pueblo), January 14, 30, 1876.

36. The text of the literacy test proposal is at Proceedings...Montana, pp. 170 and 331. The debate was lengthy. Charles S. Hartman, a Bozeman lawyer, Thomas F. Courtney, a Butte City grocer, Allan R. Joy, a Livingston lawyer and sponsor of the proposal, Francis E. Sargeant, a Butte City mining secretary, and Peter Breen, the leader of labor in the convention, carried on the proliteracy test offensive. Hiram Knowles and Charles Warren, a Butte mine operator, defended the liberal side of the argument. Breen used the "crazy idiots" phrase, and Warren countered with the nativism charge. The compromise proposal was sponsored by William A. Clark, leader of the mining faction in the convention. Proceedings...Montana, pp. 330-59.

37. Ibid., p. 363.

38. Daily Inter Mountain (Butte), August 23, 1889. Also see Ibid., July 11, 1889. Helena Daily Herald, July 16, 20, 26, 30, 31, August 14, 1889.

39. For an example see Collins' speech. Proceedings... Montana, p. 404.

40. Ibid., p. 369.

41. Ibid., p. 369 (Joy amendment), p. 373 (Clark), pp. 374-75 (Bickford); the abdication substitute lost 29 to 34, p. 373. Helena Daily Herald, July 31, 1889. On Toole see Hamilton, From Wilderness to Statehood, pp. 528-39, 545-55, 568-69.

42. Proceedings...Montana, p. 404. Timothy Collins' speech was indicative of the attitude. "Women have had the right to vote in school elections for a number of years under the laws of the Territory. Women have also had the right to be candidate for county office under the laws of this Territory. This constitutional enactment or section takes away part of the rights they have had before. Now, I believe that instead of taking away part of those rights we should add some to them."

43. Ibid., pp. 404-5.

44. Ibid., p. 915.

45. Leonard J. Arrington, Great Basin Kingdom, pp. 360-61.

46. See Dennis L. Thompson, "Religion and the Idaho Constitution," 58 Pacific Northwest Quarterly 169-78 (October 1967). Merle W. Wells, "The Idaho Anti-Mormon Movement, 1872-1908" (Ph.D. dissertation, University of California, Berkeley, 1950). Proceedings and Debates of the Constitutional Convention of Idaho (Caldwell, Idaho 1912), pp. 129-46 (polygamy debate and unanimous vote against polygamist political participation). Also see the debates of the convention for the general flavor of argument; Ibid., pp. 183-200.

47. Laws...Idaho, 4th session, pp. 65, 138.

48. Ray v. Ray (1874), 1 Idaho 566.

49. Laws...Idaho, 10th session, p. 21; 13th session, p. 194. The 1889 territorial legislature also validated the election of female county school superintendents. Laws...Idaho, 15th session, p. 11.

50. James Wesley Reid, Augustine Sinnot, and G. W. King supervised the suffragists' floor maneuvers. Proceedings... Idaho, pp. 907-14. Their voting records also put them on the liberal side of the Guttman scale.

51. Proceedings...Idaho, p. 907.

52. Ibid., pp. 912-14. The Idaho World (Idaho City) thought that women's suffrage could jeopardize the constitution's chance at the polls. The paper made a direct connection with the temperance issue and supported those advocating future legislative action. Idaho World, July 26, 1889.

53. Proceedings...Idaho, pp. 375-92, 382 (Lewis).

54. Idaho Daily Statesman, July 21, 1889.

55. Based on six roll calls involving the suffrage issue and the division of counties by voters, the cluster blocs reveal extremely high agreement scores for most Republicans. The liberals were small factions with similarily high agreement scores. For example, the Reid faction:

Henry Armstrong, Labor party
100 Solomon Hasbrouck, Republican
100 100 Henry Melder, Republican
100 100 100 J. S. Whitton, Republican
100 100 100 100 Isaac Coston, democrat
83 83 83 83 100 Alexander Mayhew, Democrat
83 83 83 83 100 100 John Hogan, Democrat
83 83 83 83 100 100 100 James Wesley Reid, Democrat

The Republicans formed larger blocs and had high percent agreement between blocs.

Weldon B. Heyburn
100 A. J. Pinkham
100 100 W. H. Claggett
100 100 100 W. C. B. Allen
100 100 100 100 John A. Myer, Democrat
100 100 100 100 100 James M. Shoup
83 83 83 83 83 83 Charles M. Hays
67 67 67 67 67 67 83 Fred Campbell
67 67 67 67 67 67 83 100 H. S. Hampton

John Lewis headed a bloc of nine delegates; two were Democrats. They included Albert B. Moss, James I. Crutcher, Edgar Wilson, W. C. Maxey, Willis Sweet, John L. Underwood, Stephen S. Glidden, and A. D. Bevan. Their minimum agreement score was 100 percent. The Lewis bloc agreed with the first six of th Heyburn bloc above 100 percent. James Beatty, J. W. Ballentine, John Lemp, O. B. Batten, William H. Savidge, Drew S. Standrod, and Samuel Prichard agreed with Lewis 100 percent. Batten and Standrod were Democrats (Boguetab analysis). The Guttman scaleogram placed all these delegates on the conservative end of the scale. The Democrats who joined the Republicans were often from the same county delegations.

56. Proceedings...Idaho, p. 918 (Parker), p. 931 (Ainslie).

57. The "tricky Mormon" phrase was continually used in and out of the convention. For example see Ibid., pp. 962-65 (Lewis). The Idaho Daily Statesman, July 21, 1889, reminded the delegate that "the Mormons excel in cunning evasion."

58. See Proceedings...Idaho, pp. 619-29 for Ainslie's fight to obtain time for a Democratic caucus on suffrage.

59. The partisan debates were extensive. See Ibid., pp. 947-49, 950-52 for Reid's attack on the Republicans for their shabby treatment of the Democrats; pp. 953-59 for Standrod's call back to the issues; and pp. 980-98 for the Reid-Claggett debate on strictly partisan politics.

60. Ibid., p. 1030 (text of two sections), pp. 1033-34 (Ainslie characterization of Republican sponsored section), p. 1035 (Parker), p. 1048 (Ainslie).

61. Idaho Constitution, Art. 6, sec. 3, 4.

62. Thomas F. O'Dea, The Mormons (Chicago, 1957), p. 249.

63. The basic statutes involving women's rights are in Compiled Laws of Utah (1888), II, section 2528. The Utah territorial supreme court gave judicial sanction to these provisions in Warr

v. Honeck (1892), 8 Utah 61. On suffrage see O'Dea, Mormons, p. 249.

64. Arrington, Great Basin Kingdom, pp. 360-61. Also see Thomas G. Alexander, "An Experiment in Progressive Legislation: The Granting of Woman Suffrage in Utah in 1870." 38 Utah Historical Quarterly 20-30 (Winter 1970). Jean B. White, "Gentle Persuaders: Utah's First Women Legislators," 38 Utah Historical Quarterly 31-49 (Winter 1970). Beverly Beeton, "Woman Suffrage in Territorial Utah," 46 Utah Historical Quarterly 100-120 (Spring 1978).

65. Proceedings and Debates...Utah (Salt Lake City, 1898), p. 1782 (Evans), p. 1783 (Varian), p. 1782 (Howard). For biographical information see Salt Lake Tribune, March 4, 1895.

66. Salt Lake City Daily Tribune, March 4, 1895.

67. See Ibid., March 4, 12, 15, 19, 20. Deseret Evening News, March 7, 25, 28, 29, 30, April 1, 2, 1895. For an example of the petitions received by the convention see Proceedings...Utah, pp. 142-43.

68. Ibid., p. 559. Snow defined hell as "to want to and can't." "They [Republicans] want to oppose the insertion of an equal suffrage plank in the Constitution, but they cannot because they are bound down by a party chain and they are surrounded with flame that has no end, and the worm that dieth not," he said.

69. The voting patterns are based on an analysis of seven roll calls. Proceedings...Utah, pp. 685-86 on a motion to cut debate on women's suffrage (52 to 43), p. 703 on a motion to postpone debate (42 to 51), pp. 732-33 on a motion to recess (44 to 52), pp. 736-37 on a motion of the previous question (51 to 39), p. 765 on a motion to recommit (42 to 52), p. 767 on section one containing female suffrage (75 to 14), and p. 804 on final passage of the suffrage article (75 to 16). The procedural votes identify the general delegate groupings, while the substantive votes identify ideologues on the issue (Boguetab analysis). The Roberts-Mackintosh bloc contained 34 delegates with a minimum bloc agreement of 71 percent.

70. The following delegates formed a bloc with 100 percent agreement scores: Rufus A. Allen, Andrew S. Anderson, John R. Barnes, John S. Boyer, William Buys, Chester Call, George M. Cannon, Louis L. Coray, Elmer Corfman, William Creer, George Cunningham, William Driver, Andreas Engberg, Francis A. Hammond, Charles Hart, John Holladay, William Howard, Andrew Kimball, Hyrum Lemmon, William Loew, James P. Low, George Miller, Elias Morris, Edward Partridge, J. D. Peters, Alonzo Raleigh, Jasper Robertson, Joseph Robinson, Willis Robison, John H. Smith, Edward Snow, Charles Symons, Ingwald Thoreson, Samuel Thurman, Franklin Richards, Joseph Murdock, Karl G. Maeser, Joseph Jolley, Samuel Francis, John Chidester, Theodore Brandley, Robert Heybourne, Henry Hughes, Christen Larsen, Peter Lowe, and Joseph Thorne. The four Gentiles were Corfman, Larsen, Miller and Symons.

71. Proceedings...Utah, p. 407. The report was signed by Richard Mackintosh, Fred J. Kiesel, and Robert McFarland.

72. Ibid., p. 412.

73. Ibid., pp. 421-29.

74. Ogden Standard, March 29, 1895. Salt Lake Argus, March 30, 1895. Salt Lake Tribune, March 12, April 2, 1895. These editorials were cited by Roberts in an April 2 speech. Proceedings...Utah, pp. 592-94.

75. Ibid., p. 556 (Evans), p. 559 (Snow), pp. 429-31. (Chidester), p. 431 (Snow), p. 434 (Thurman), p. 437 (Richards).

76. Ibid., pp. 459-73, 582-98 (Roberts), pp. 505-13 (Whitney).

77. Ibid., pp. 457-58 (Ivins), p. 553 (Cannon).

78. Ibid., p. 535.

79. Ibid., p. 561 (Maeser), pp. 564-66 (Smith, p. 567 (Larsen), p. 573-74 (Partridge), p. 582-98 (Roberts).

80. Ibid., p. 680 (Squires proposed separate submissions), pp. 688-89 (Van Horne supported), p. 697 (Evans), p. 705 (Eichnor section proposal), pp. 705-9 (Eichnor amendment ruled out of order, chair sustained, 59 to 35), p. 709 (Wells amendment), p. 711 (Maloney amendment).

81. Ibid., p. 735 (Allen motion, 51 to 39), p. 758 (adjournment rejected), p. 765 (recommitment rejected 42 to 52).

82. Richard G. Gambert ably expressed this apprehension in the convention. "I am led to think that in those propositions are too much legislation. We are here to formulate fundamental principles, and the balance should be left for the legislature to arrange in the future. We are not here to enact the laws that are necessary, but simply to formulate that fundamental principle upon which laws shall be founded." Ibid., p. 553.

83. See Deseret Evening News, March 7, 1895.

84. Robert W. Larson, New Mexico's Quest for Statehood 1846-1912 (Albuquerque, 1968), p. 279.

85. Edward D. Tittman, "New Mexico Constitutional Convention: Recollections," 27 New Mexico Historical Review 182 (July 1952). Robert W. Larson, "Statehood for New Mexico, 1888-1912," 37 New Mexico Historical Review 194 (July 1965).

86. Reuben W. Heflin, "New Mexico Constitutional Convention," 21 New Mexico Historical Review 67 (January 1946).

87. "Mrs. D. H. Carnes to Delegates of Constitutional Convention," MSS, University of New Mexico Archives.

88. Murdock, Constitutional Development of Arizona, p. 18. Also see Mattie L. Williams, "History of Woman Suffrage in Arizona," 1 Arizona Historical Review 69-73 (No. 4, 1928).

89. Arizona Gazette, November 1, 1910. "Verbatim Report...Arizona," morning, November 11, 1910, pp. 11-12. On prohibition and suffrage see Tombstone Epitaph, October 30, 1910. Arizona Citizen and Weekly Tribune (Tucson), October 28, 1910. Arizona Journal-Miner, October 29, 1910, November 18, 1910. Arizona Republican, November 18, 1910. Arizona Daily Star, October 29, 1910. On the Democratic split see Arizona Republican, November 18, 1910. Also see Cunniff's speech, "Verbatim Report...Arizona," morning, November 11, 1910, p. 11, for an example of the split of philosophy forced by the issue.

90. See "Wood Notes," MSS, University of Arizona, proposition number 74. "Verbatim Report...Arizona," Vol. 1, afternoon, October 29, 1910, p. 1; Vol. 2, morning, November 11, 1910, pp. 9-12. On Wills see Arizona Journal-Miner, November 1, 1910. On

convention disposal of the issue see Arizona Sentinel (Yuma), November 10, 1910. Arizona Daily Star, November 18, 1910. Arizona Republican, November 17-18, 1910. For examples of suffragist arguments see Arizona Republican, November 3, 1910. Arizona Daily Star, November 27, 2910.

91. Alan P. Grimes, The Puritan Ethic and Woman Suffrage (New York, 1967), p. xi. For other general studies of the subject see Beverly Beeton, "Woman Suffrage in the American West, 1869-1896" (Ph.D. dissertation, University of Utah, 1976). T. A. Larson, "Emancipating the West's Dolls, Vassals, and Hopeless Drudges: The Origins of Woman Suffrage in the West," in Roger Daniels, ed., Essays in Western History (Laramie, Wyo., 1971). T. A. Larson, "Woman Suffrage in Western America," 38 Utah Historical Quarterly 1-19 (Winter 1970). Beeton's dissertation is also in book form. Beverly Beeton, Women Vote in the West: The Woman Suffrage Movement, 1869-1896 (New York, 1986). In her 1985 introduction, she summarized her causal factors in the suffrage success of women in Wyoming, Colorado, Idaho and Utah as regional advertisement, territorial politics, reaction to black enfranchisement during Reconstruction, recruitment of Eastern support for statehood, and the lack of territorial political opposition to a safe experiment.

## CHAPTER 9

1. This conclusion about 19th century legal and constitutional concepts may concern recent legal theorists who believe that a major change took place in the 19th century. Followers of Morton Horwitz would claim that an 18th-century legal paradigm existed that was "built around concepts of community, solidarity, and equity that was replaced by a 19th-century paradigm that gave prominence to economic progress, atomistic competition, and individuality." Stephen B. Presser, "Some Realism About Orphism or the Critical Legal Studies Movement and the Great Chain of Being," 79 Northwestern University Law Review 869-99, 878 (December 1984/February 1985). Historians seem to take "critical legal studies" less seriously than do law professors, perhaps because most of the debate printed in law reviews seldom is noted by historians or perhaps because critical legal studies advocates have produced so little scholarly research based on primary sources. Law professors, on the othe hand, find theory and argument compelling, forgetting perhaps that appellate advocacy or any closing argument should have a factual basis derived from admissible evidence. Going to the heart of the argument, the assumption that the American people in the 19th-century rejected a market system, property law, and contract as a capitalist conspiracy is diametrically opposed by John P. Reid in his Law for the Elephant (San Marino, Calif., 1980). Rather, Americans released from the bonds of legal institutions on the overland trail embraced traditional concepts of property and contract.

Students of American history should understand that legal history is too important to be left to advocacy and should enter the lists to deal with primary source research. While critical-legal-studies advocates write numerous book reviews challenging scholars to engage them on theory, perhaps it is time for more critical-legal-studies researchers to engage in the tedious process of researching legal history and writing books distinguishing the complexities of the past and the problems of the present.

TABLE 1: NEVADA DELEGATION

COW-COUNTY:

| | | | | | | | | | | |
|---|---|---|---|---|---|---|---|---|---|---|
| J. H. Kinkead | | | | | | | | | | |
| 100 | George A. Nourse | | | | | | | | | |
| 100 | 100 | G. N. Folsom | | | | | | | | |
| 100 | 100 | 100 | H. B. Brady | | | | | | | |
| 100 | 95 | 95 | 95 | W. W. Belden | | | | | | |
| 84 | 100 | 89 | 89 | 90 | James H. Sturtevant | | | | | |
| 83 | 89 | 87 | 87 | 78 | 87 | J. W. Haines | | | | |
| 83 | 89 | 88 | 88 | 89 | 84 | 93. | A. J. Lockwood | | | |
| 77 | 85 | 81 | 81 | 80 | 85 | 89 | 89 | Goerge L. Gibson | | |
| 80 | 80 | 79 | 79 | 71 | 70 | 80 | 80 | 86 | Albert T. Hawley | |
| 79 | 95 | 85 | 85 | 85 | 77 | 73 | 83 | 80 | 85 | J. Neely Johnson |

MINERS:

| | | | | | | | | | | |
|---|---|---|---|---|---|---|---|---|---|---|
| H. G. Parker | | | | | | | | | | |
| 85 | Charles E. DeLong | | | | | | | | | |
| 80 | 96 | J. G. McClinton | | | | | | | | |
| 70 | 88 | 93 | B. S. Mason | | | | | | | |
| 84 | 92 | 89 | 85 | Frank H. Kennedy | | | | | | |
| 90 | 95 | 91 | 83 | 96 | George A. Hudson | | | | | |
| 75 | 76 | 85 | 75 | 70 | 87 | Frank Tagliabue | | | | |
| 67 | 65 | 77 | 78 | 64 | 78 | 96 | Nelson E. Murdock | | | |
| 60 | 64 | 74 | 79 | 63 | 74 | 89 | 100 | William Wetherill | | |
| 57 | 71 | 82 | 82 | 63 | 71 | 88 | 93 | 94 | Charles W. Tozer | |
| 37 | 46 | 58 | 59 | 44 | 55 | 74 | 86 | 82 | 100 | J. H. Warwick |

| | | | | | | | | | | | |
|---|---|---|---|---|---|---|---|---|---|---|---|
| Josiah Earl | | | | | | | | | | | |
| 77 | Samuel A. Chapin | | | | | | | | | | |
| 73 | 79 | E. F. Dunn | | | | | | | | | |
| 73 | 74 | 93 | James A. Banks | | | | | | | | |
| 76 | 88 | 76 | 76 | J. S. Crosman | | | | | | | |
| 50 | 69 | 44 | 47 | 86 | Lloyd Frizell | | | | | | |
| 56 | 65 | 53 | 69 | 60 | 80 | Thomas Fitch | | | | | |
| 67 | 67 | 59 | 62 | 52 | 56 | 69 | Cornelius M. Brosnan | | | | |
| 67 | 65 | 73 | 72 | 74 | 60 | 44 | 76 | Almon Hovey | | | |
| 63 | 72 | 80 | 71 | 61 | 50 | 57 | 68 | 78 | F. M. Proctor | | |
| 73 | 71 | 64 | 63 | 68 | 69 | 65 | 74 | 65 | 56 | John A. Collins | |
| 50 | 33 | 50 | 48 | 32 | 42 | 59 | 52 | 36 | 38 | 58 | Israel Crawford |

Note the low agreement scores of the miners bloc. Not only did the bloc not have high agreement scores, but also the agreement scores with the cow-county delegates indicate support for that bloc. All of the last seven delegates but Proctor were from Storey County.

## TABLE 2: WYOMING

| YYYNNN | |
|---|---|
| +++ | Melville C. Brown |
| +0+ | George C. Smith |
| +0+ | Herman G. Nickerson |
| ++0 | John M. McCandlish |
| +++ | Henry Hay |
| +++ | Elliott S.N. Morgan |
| +++ | Caleb Organ |
| ++ + | Hubert E. Teschemacher |
| +++ | Frederick Harvey |
| ++0 | Mark Hopkins |
| + + + | John W. Hoyt |
| +++ | Mortimer Grant |
| +0+ | James A. Casebeer |
| ++0 | William C. Irvine |
| +++ | Charles H. Burritt |
| ++0 | Charles N. Potter |
| ++0 | Anthony C. Campbell |
| +++ | George W. Baxter |
| +++ | James A. Johnston |
| ++0 | John K. Jeffrey |
| +++ | Henry Asa Coffeen |
| +0+ | Louis J. Palmer |
| ++0 | William E. Chaplin |
| ++0 | Alexander J. Sutherland |
| ++0 | Thomas R. Reid |
| ++0 | Jonathan Jones |
| ++0 | Asbury B. Conway |
| +++ | John Russell |
| +0+ | Charles W. Holden |
| +++ | Jesse Knight |
| +++ | Frank Foote |
| +++ | Clarence D. Clark |
| +++ | John A. Riner |
| +++ | Henry Elliott |
| ++0 | Douglas Preston |
| +0+ | George W. Fox |

TABLE 3: IDAHO

PART I

MAYHEW-HARRIS BLOC<br>
Weldon B. Heyburn<br>
100 John Hogan<br>
100 100 James M. Shoup<br>
100 100 100 A. D. Bevan<br>
100 100 100 100 John S. Gray<br>
100 100 100 100 100 Alexander Mayhew<br>
100 100 100 100 100 100 W. C. Maxey<br>
100 100 100 100 100 100 100 Charles Hays<br>
100 100 100 100 100 100 100 100 Robert Anderson<br>
75 75 75 75 75 75 75 75 100 Edgar Wilson<br>
75 75 75 75 75 75 75 75 100 100 H. S. Hampton<br>
75 75 75 75 75 75 75 75 100 100 100 Frank Harris<br>
75 75 75 75 75 75 75 75 100 100 100 100 Henry Melder<br>
75 75 75 75 75 75 75 75 100 100 100 100 100 A. J. Pinkham

(9 Republicans & 5 Democrats)

TABLE 3: IDAHO

PART II

CLAGGETT BLOC

Fred Campbell
100 James I. Crutcher
100 100 H. B. Kinport
75 75 75 Edward S. Jewell
75 75 75 100 Solomon Hasbrouck
75 75 75 100 100 W. H. Claggett
75 75 75 100 100 100 Thomas Pyeatt
75 75 75 100 100 100 100 John L. Underwood
67 67 67 100 100 100 100 100 J. W. Ballentine
50 50 50 75 75 75 75 75 100 G. W. King
50 50 50 75 75 75 75 75 100 100 Willis Sweet

(7 Republicans & 4 Democrats)

MORGAN-LEWIS BLOC

Charles A. Clark
100 William McConnell
100 100 James Wesley Reid
75 75 100 A. S. Chaney
75 75 100 100 J. S. Whitton
75 75 100 100 100 Isaac Coston
75 75 100 100 100 100 John H. Myer
75 75 100 100 100 100 100 Frank P. Cavanah
75 75 100 100 100 100 100 100 Augustine M. Sinnott
100 100 100 100 100 100 100 100 100 Abel John Pierce
67 67 100 100 100 100 100 100 100 100 John Lewis
100 100 100 100 100 100 100 100 100 100 100 John T. Morgan

(6 Democrats & 5 Republicans)

TABLE 4: NEVADA (IMPEACHMENT AND REMOVAL)

| Y | Y | Y | Y | N | N | N | N | |
|---|---|---|---|---|---|---|---|---|
| + | + | + | + | | | | | W. W. Belden |
| + | + | + | + | | | | | H. B. Brady |
| + | + | + | + | | | | | Lloyd Frizell |
| + | + | + | + | | | | | G. N. Folsom |
| + | + | + | + | | | | | George Gibson |
| + | + | + | + | | | | | Albert T. Hawley |
| + | + | + | + | | | | | A. J. Lockwood |
| + | + | + | + | | | | | Nelson E. Murdock |
| + | + | + | + | | | | | George A. Nourse |
| + | + | + | + | | | | | James H. Sturtevant |
| + | + | + | + | | | | | Frank Tagliabue |
| + | + | + | + | | | | | J. H. Warwick |
| + | + | + | + | | | | | William Wetherill |
| + | + | + | + | | | | | J. Neely Johnson |
| | + | + | + | 0 | | | | J. S. Crosman |
| | | + | + | + | + | | | John A. Collins |
| | | | | + | + | + | + | F. M. Proctor |
| | | | | 0 | + | + | + | J. G. McClinton |
| | | | | + | + | + | + | B. S. Mason |
| | | | | + | + | + | + | Frank H. Kennedy |
| | | | | + | + | + | + | Almon Hovey |
| | | | | + | + | + | + | E. F. Dunn |
| | | | | + | + | + | + | Charles E. DeLong |
| | | | | + | + | + | + | Cornelius M. Brosnan |
| | | | | + | + | + | + | James A. Banks |

TABLE 5: NEVADA (PACIFIC RAILROAD)

| Y | Y | Y | Y | N | N | N | N | |
|---|---|---|---|---|---|---|---|---|
| + | | + | + | | + | | | James A. Banks |
| + | | + | + | | + | | | J. O. Crosman |
| + | | + | + | | + | | | Almon Hovey |
| + | | + | | | + | | + | J. H. Warwick |
| | + | | + | + | | + | | H. B. Brady |
| | + | | + | + | | + | | Israel Crawford |
| | + | + | | + | | | + | Josiah Earl |
| | + | | + | + | | + | | G. N. Folson |
| | + | + | + | + | | | | Albert T. Hawley |
| | + | 0 | + | + | | | | J. H. Kinkead |
| | + | | + | + | | + | | H. G. Parker |
| | + | | + | + | | + | | J. Neely Johnson |
| | | + | + | + | + | | | Cornelius M. Brosnan |
| | | + | + | + | + | | | Samuel A. Chapin |
| | | + | + | + | + | | | John A. Collins |
| | | + | + | + | + | | | E. F. Dunn |
| | | + | + | + | + | | | William Wetherill |
| + | | | + | | + | + | | Thomas Fitch |
| + | | | + | | + | 0 | | Lloyd Frizell |
| | | | + | + | + | + | | Charles A. DeLong |
| | | | + | + | + | 0 | | J. W. Haines |
| | | | + | + | + | + | | George A. Hudson |
| | | | + | + | + | + | | Frank H. Kennedy |
| | | | + | + | + | + | | A. J. Lockwood |
| | | | + | + | + | + | | B. S. Mason |
| | | | + | + | + | + | | J. G. McClinton |
| | | | + | + | + | 0 | | F. M. Proctor |
| | | | + | + | + | + | | James H. Sturtevant |
| | | | + | + | + | + | | Frank Tagliabue |

## TABLE 6: NEVADA MINING TAXATION

### HAWLEY COW-COUNTY BLOC

| | | | | | | | | | | |
|---|---|---|---|---|---|---|---|---|---|---|
| J. H. Kinkead | | | | | | | | | | |
| 100 | George Nourse | | | | | | | | | |
| 100 | 100 | G. N. Folson | | | | | | | | |
| 100 | 100 | 100 | H. B. Brady | | | | | | | |
| 100 | 100 | 100 | 100 | J. H. Sturtevant | | | | | | |
| 100 | 93 | 93 | 93 | 93 | W. W. Belden | | | | | |
| 90 | 93 | 93 | 93 | 93 | 85 | J. N. Johnson | | | | |
| 90 | 92 | 92 | 92 | 92 | 83 | 100 | A. J. Lockwood | | | |
| 83 | 89 | 89 | 89 | 89 | 78 | 89 | 88 | J. W. Haines | | |
| 91 | 86 | 86 | 86 | 86 | 79 | 77 | 83 | 89 | George L. Gibson | |
| 82 | 79 | 79 | 79 | 79 | 71 | 85 | 92 | 89 | 93 | A. T. Hawley |

### JOHN A. COLLINS MODERATE BLOC

| | | | | | | |
|---|---|---|---|---|---|---|
| Thomas Fitch | | | | | | |
| 82 | John A. Collins | | | | | |
| 70 | 85 | Cornelius M. Brosnan | | | | |
| 73 | 64 | 85 | George A. Hudson | | | |
| 82 | 71 | 77 | 93 | Frank Kennedy | | |
| 64 | 64 | 80 | 91 | 82 | H. G. Parker | |
| 64 | 64 | 80 | 91 | 82 | 82 | Charles E. DeLong |

TABLE 6: NEVADA MINING TAXATION

PART II

CHAPIN MINER BLOC

| | | | | | | | | | | | | | |
|---|---|---|---|---|---|---|---|---|---|---|---|---|---|
| B. S. Mason | | | | | | | | | | | | | |
| 100 | J. G. McClinton | | | | | | | | | | | | |
| 100 | 100 | F. M. Proctor | | | | | | | | | | | |
| 93 | 93 | 100 | N. E. Murdock | | | | | | | | | | |
| 93 | 93 | 100 | 100 | F. Tagliabue | | | | | | | | | |
| 93 | 93 | 100 | 100 | 100 | Charles W. Tozer | | | | | | | | |
| 93 | 93 | 100 | 100 | 100 | 100 | J. H. Warwick | | | | | | | |
| 93 | 93 | 100 | 100 | 100 | 100 | 100 | William Wetherill | | | | | | |
| 79 | 79 | 83 | 86 | 86 | 86 | 86 | 86 | Josiah Earl | | | | | |
| 71 | 71 | 75 | 79 | 79 | 79 | 79 | 79 | 93 | James A. Banks | | | | |
| 79 | 79 | 83 | 86 | 86 | 86 | 86 | 86 | 86 | 93 | E. F. Dunn | | | |
| 79 | 79 | 83 | 86 | 86 | 86 | 86 | 86 | 86 | 93 | 100 | Samuel Chapin | | |
| 85 | 85 | 83 | 85 | 85 | 85 | 85 | 85 | 85 | 92 | 100 | 100 | J. S. Crosman | |
| 92 | 92 | 91 | 85 | 85 | 85 | 85 | 85 | 69 | 62 | 69 | 69 | 75 | Almon Hovey |

TABLE 7: IDAHO WATER RIGHTS

| Y | Y | N | N | |
|---|---|---|---|---|
| + | + | | | Stephen S. Glidden |
| + | + | | | John S. Gray |
| + | + | | | Weldon B. Heyburn |
| + | + | | | Alexander Mayhew |
| + | + | | | Abel J. Pierce |
| + | + | | | James M. Shoup |
| + | + | | | J. S. Whitton |
| | + | + | | George Ainslie |
| | + | + | | A. D. Bevan |
| | + | + | | W. H. Claggett |
| | + | + | | James I. Crutcher |
| | + | + | | John Lewis |
| | + | + | | A. J. Pinkham |
| | + | + | | James W. Reid |
| | + | + | | John L. Underwood |
| | | + | + | Edgar Wilson |
| | | + | + | Willis Sweet |
| | | + | + | Augustine M. Sinnott |
| | | + | 0 | William H. Savidge |
| | | + | + | Thomas Pyeatt |
| | | + | + | Albert B. Moss |
| | | + | + | John H. Myer |
| | | + | + | Henry Melder |
| | | + | + | William J. McConnell |
| | | + | + | W. C. Maxey |
| | | + | + | J. W. Lamoreaux |
| | | \| | \| | H. B. Kinport |
| | | + | + | G. W. King |
| | | + | + | Edward S. Jewell |
| | | + | + | John Hogan |
| | | + | + | Charles M. Hays |
| | | + | + | Solomon Hasbrouck |
| | | + | + | H. S. Hampton |
| | | + | + | Isaac N. Coston |
| | | + | + | Charles A. Clark |
| | | + | + | A. S. Chaney |
| | | + | + | Fred Campbell |
| | | + | + | Henry B. Blake |
| | | + | + | J. W. Ballentine |
| | | + | + | Henry Armstrong |
| | | + | + | Robert Anderson |
| | | + | + | W. C. B. Allen |

## TABLE 8: ARIZONA WATER RIGHTS

### PART I

GOLDWATER BLOC

| | | | | | | | | | | | | | | | |
|---|---|---|---|---|---|---|---|---|---|---|---|---|---|---|---|
| C. M. Roberts | | | | | | | | | | | | | | | |
| 100 | J. J. Keegan | | | | | | | | | | | | | | |
| 100 | 100 | Homer R. Wood | | | | | | | | | | | | | |
| 100 | 100 | 100 | Henry Lovin | | | | | | | | | | | | |
| 100 | 100 | 100 | 100 | Albert M. Jones | | | | | | | | | | | |
| 100 | 100 | 100 | 100 | 100 | M. G. Cunniff | | | | | | | | | | |
| 83 | 83 | 83 | 83 | 83 | 100 | John Bolan | | | | | | | | | |
| 83 | 83 | 83 | 83 | 83 | 100 | 100 | Thomas Feeney | | | | | | | | |
| 80 | 80 | 80 | 80 | 80 | 100 | 100 | 100 | R. B. Sims | | | | | | | |
| 67 | 67 | 67 | 67 | 67 | 80 | 83 | 83 | 100 | John Langdon (Republican) | | | | | | |
| 67 | 67 | 67 | 67 | 67 | 80 | 83 | 83 | 100 | 100 | Mit Simms | | | | | |
| 67 | 67 | 67 | 67 | 67 | 80 | 83 | 83 | 100 | 100 | 100 | Morris Goldwater | | | | |
| 67 | 67 | 67 | 67 | 67 | 80 | 83 | 83 | 100 | 100 | 100 | 100 | A. M. Tuthill | | | |
| 75 | 75 | 75 | 75 | 75 | 75 | 75 | 75 | 100 | 100 | 100 | 100 | 100 | W. T. Webb | | |
| 50 | 50 | 50 | 50 | 50 | 60 | 67 | 67 | 80 | 83 | 83 | 83 | 83 | 75 | George Pusch (Republican) | |
| 60 | 60 | 60 | 60 | 60 | 60 | 60 | 60 | 75 | 80 | 80 | 80 | 80 | 75 | 100 | Jacob Weinberger |

TABLE 8: ARIZONA WATER RIGHTS

PART II

REPUBLICANS

| | | | | | | | | | | |
|---|---|---|---|---|---|---|---|---|---|---|
| Lamar Cobb (Democrat) | | | | | | | | | | |
| 80 | Carlos C. Jacome | | | | | | | | | |
| 67 | 100 | P. F. Connelly (Democrat) | | | | | | | | |
| 67 | 100 | 100 | E. W. Coker (Democrat) | | | | | | | |
| 67 | 100 | 100 | 100 | Samuel L. Kingan | | | | | | |
| 67 | 100 | 100 | 100 | 100 | William F. Cooper | | | | | |
| 67 | 100 | 100 | 100 | 100 | 100 | Bracey Curtis | | | | |
| 67 | 100 | 100 | 100 | 100 | 100 | 100 | James C. White | | | |
| 50 | 80 | 83 | 83 | 83 | 83 | 83 | 83 | B. B. Moeur (Democrat) | | |
| 60 | 100 | 100 | 100 | 100 | 100 | 100 | 100 | 100 | A. F. Parsons (Democrat) | |
| 50 | 80 | 83 | 83 | 83 | 83 | 83 | 83 | 100 | 100 | A. R. Lynch (Democrat) |

TABLE 8: ARIZONA WATER RIGHTS

PART III

HUNT-STOCKMEN BLOC

| Fred T. Colter | | | | | | | | | | | | | | | | | | |
|---|---|---|---|---|---|---|---|---|---|---|---|---|---|---|---|---|---|---|
| 100 | D. L. Cunningham | | | | | | | | | | | | | | | | | |
| 100 | 100 | A. C. Baker | | | | | | | | | | | | | | | | |
| 100 | 100 | 100 | Lysander Cassidy | | | | | | | | | | | | | | | |
| 100 | 100 | 100 | 100 | James E. Crutchfield | | | | | | | | | | | | | | |
| 100 | 100 | 100 | 100 | 100 | Alfred Franklin | | | | | | | | | | | | | |
| 100 | 100 | 100 | 100 | 100 | 100 | F. A. Jones | | | | | | | | | | | | |
| 100 | 100 | 100 | 100 | 100 | 100 | 100 | John P. Orme | | | | | | | | | | | |
| 100 | 100 | 100 | 100 | 100 | 100 | 100 | 100 | Sidney P. Osborn | | | | | | | | | | |
| 100 | 100 | 100 | 100 | 100 | 100 | 100 | 100 | 100 | Orrin Standage | | | | | | | | | |
| 100 | 100 | 100 | 100 | 100 | 100 | 100 | 100 | 100 | 100 | Fred L. Ingraham | | | | | | | | |
| 100 | 100 | 100 | 100 | 100 | 100 | 100 | 100 | 100 | 100 | 100 | Mulford Winsor | | | | | | | |
| 100 | 100 | 100 | 100 | 100 | 100 | 100 | 100 | 100 | 100 | 100 | 100 | E. E. Ellinwood | | | | | | |
| 100 | 100 | 100 | 100 | 100 | 100 | 100 | 100 | 100 | 100 | 100 | 100 | 100 | James Scott (Republican) | | | | | |
| 83 | 83 | 83 | 83 | 83 | 83 | 83 | 83 | 83 | 83 | 83 | 83 | 83 | 83 | George W. P. Hunt | | | | |
| 83 | 83 | 83 | 83 | 83 | 83 | 83 | 83 | 83 | 83 | 83 | 83 | 83 | 83 | 100 | E. A. Tovrea | | | |
| 80 | 80 | 80 | 80 | 80 | 80 | 80 | 80 | 80 | 80 | 80 | 80 | 80 | 100 | 100 | 100 | William Morgan | | |
| 83 | 83 | 83 | 83 | 83 | 83 | 83 | 83 | 83 | 83 | 83 | 83 | 83 | 67 | 67 | 80 | 80 | C. C. Hutchinson | |
| 67 | 67 | 67 | 67 | 67 | 67 | 67 | 67 | 67 | 67 | 67 | 67 | 67 | 67 | 50 | 50 | 60 | 83 | E. Wells |

C. C. Hutchinson and Ed W. Wells also were Republicans. Both were stockmen, as was James Scott.

TABLE 9: COLORADO

```
YYYYYYNNNNNN

++  +   ++ +      H. P. H. Bromwell
++  +   ++ +      William E. Beck
++ +++  +         Byron L. Carr
++  +   ++ +      A. D. Cooper
+00+++            Daniel Hurd
++  +   ++ +      S. J. Plumb
++ ++   +  +      A. K. Yount
++ +++  +         William Lee
+0  +   ++ +      W. C. Stover
+ ++ + +  +       George G. White
 + ++++ +         L. C. Rockwell
 + ++++ +         W. W. Webster
 + ++++ +         J. C. Wilson
 + +++0 +         J. S. Wheeler
  +++++0          William M. Clark
  ++ +++  +       L. C. Ellsworth
  ++++++          C. P. Elder
  + + ++ + +      William James
  ++++++          Alvin Marsh
  ++ +++  +       Henry C. Thatcher
  ++++++          William H. Cushman
  ++ +++  +       John S. Hough
  +0+00+          George Pease
  ++ +++  +       Robert A. Quillian
  ++ +++  +       Wilbur Stone
  + ++++ +        Agapeta Vijil
  ++ +++  +       J. W. Widderfield
   + ++00++       F. J. Ebert
   +0++00         LaFayette Head
   +0++00         William H. Meyer
   +0++00         George Boyles
 +  +++ ++        Robert Douglas
 +  +0+ +0        W. B. Felton
 +  +00 +0        William R. Kennedy
  +  +++ ++       Henry Crosby
+ +    + +++      E. T. Wells
```

TABLE 10: COLORADO DELEGATION

PART I

MODERATES

| | | | | | | | | | | | | |
|---|---|---|---|---|---|---|---|---|---|---|---|---|
| L. C. Ellsworth | | | | | | | | | | | | |
| 100 | Henry C. Thatcher | | | | | | | | | | | |
| 100 | 100 | Robert A. Quillian | | | | | | | | | | |
| 100 | 100 | 100 | Wilber Stone | | | | | | | | | |
| 100 | 100 | 100 | 100 | J. W. Widderfield | | | | | | | | |
| 100 | 100 | 100 | 100 | 100 | John S. Hough | | | | | | | |
| 83 | 83 | 83 | 83 | 83 | 83 | C. P. Elder | | | | | | |
| 83 | 83 | 83 | 83 | 83 | 83 | 100 | Alvin Marsh | | | | | |
| 83 | 83 | 83 | 83 | 83 | 83 | 100 | 100 | William H. Cushman | | | | |
| 67 | 67 | 67 | 67 | 67 | 67 | 83 | 83 | 83 | Agapeta Vijil | | | |
| 83 | 83 | 83 | 83 | 83 | 83 | 67 | 67 | 67 | 83 | Henry R. Crosby | | |
| 50 | 50 | 50 | 50 | 50 | 50 | 67 | 67 | 67 | 83 | 67 | William James | |
| 80 | 80 | 80 | 80 | 80 | 80 | 100 | 100 | 100 | 80 | 60 | 60 | William Clark |

TABLE 10: COLORADO DELEGATION

PART II

GRANGERS

| | | | | | | | | | | | | |
|---|---|---|---|---|---|---|---|---|---|---|---|---|
| J. S. Wheeler | | | | | | | | | | | | |
| 100 | W. W. Webster | | | | | | | | | | | |
| 100 | 100 | J. C. Wilson | | | | | | | | | | |
| 100 | 100 | 100 | L. C. Rockwell | | | | | | | | | |
| 100 | 83 | 83 | 83 | William Lee | | | | | | | | |
| 100 | 83 | 83 | 67 | 100 | Byron L. Carr | | | | | | | |
| 80 | 83 | 83 | 83 | 67 | 67 | Robert Douglas | | | | | | |
| 80 | 67 | 67 | 67 | 83 | 83 | 50 | A. K. Yount | | | | | |
| 100 | 100 | 100 | 100 | 75 | 75 | 100 | 75 | W. B. Felton | | | | |
| 60 | 50 | 50 | 50 | 67 | 67 | 67 | 83 | 75 | H. P. H. Bromwell | | | |
| 60 | 50 | 50 | 50 | 67 | 67 | 67 | 83 | 75 | 100 | A. D. Cooper | | |
| 60 | 50 | 50 | 50 | 67 | 67 | 67 | 83 | 75 | 100 | 100 | S. J. Plumb | |
| 60 | 50 | 50 | 50 | 67 | 67 | 67 | 83 | 75 | 100 | 100 | 100 | William Beck |

TABLE 11: ARIZONA--CORPORATIONS

| YYYYNNNN | |
|---|---|
| + ++ + | Fred T. Colter |
| ++++ | D. L. Cunningham |
| ++++ | E. A. Tovrea |
| ++ +   + | J. J. Keegan |
| ++ +   + | Alfred Kinney |
| ++ +   + | John Langdon (Republican) |
| ++++ + | Lamar Cobb |
| + ++ + | A. R. Lynch |
| + ++ + | Mit Simms |
| + ++ + | A. M. Tuthill |
| ++++ | W. T. Webb |
| +0+0 | A. C. Baker |
| + ++ + | John P. Orme |
| +0++ | Orrin Standage |
| ++++ | Henry Lovin |
| + +0 + | E. E. Ellinwood |
| + ++ + | C. C. Hutchinson (Republican) |
| + +  + + | Samuel L. Kingan (Republican) |
| + +  + + | William F. Cooper (Republican) |
| + +  + + | Carlos C. Jacome (Republican) |
| + + ++ + | George Pusch (Republican) |
| + +  + + | James C. White (Republican) |
| + +  + + | E. W. Wells (Republican) |
| ++++ | John Bolan |
| ++++ | S. B. Bradner |
| + ++ + | P. F. Connelly |
| ++++ | Thomas Feeney |
| ++++ | A. F. Parsons |
| ++++ | C. M. Roberts |
| + ++ + | George W.P. Hunt |
| ++++ | Jacob Weinberger |
| ++++ | Lysander Cassidy |
| + ++ + | James E. Crutchfield |
| + ++ + | F. A. Jones |
| +0+0 | B. B. Moeur |
| + ++ + | William Morgan |
| + ++ + | E. W. Coker |
| ++++ | M. G. Cunniff |
| ++++ | Morris Goldwater |
| + ++ + | Albert M. Jones |
| ++0+ | A. A. Moore |
| + ++ + | Homer R. Wood |
| + ++ + | Fred L. Ingraham |
| + ++ + | E. L. Short |
| + ++ + | Mulford Winsor |
| +++0 | R. B. Sims |
| ++00 | Sidney P. Osborn |
| + ++ + | James Scott (Republican) |
| ++++ | Bracey Curtis (Republican) |
| +0+0 | Thomas N. Wells |
| +    ++0 | Alfred Franklin |

TABLE 12: ARIZONA--CORPORATIONS

PART I

GEORGE W. P. HUNT BLOC

| | | | | | | | | | | | | | | | |
|---|---|---|---|---|---|---|---|---|---|---|---|---|---|---|---|
| George W. P. Hunt | | | | | | | | | | | | | | | |
| 100 | James E. Crutchfield | | | | | | | | | | | | | | |
| 100 | 100 | E. W. Coker | | | | | | | | | | | | | |
| 100 | 100 | 100 | Albert M. Jones | | | | | | | | | | | | |
| 100 | 100 | 100 | 100 | Homer R. Wood | | | | | | | | | | | |
| 100 | 100 | 100 | 100 | 100 | Fred L. Ingraham | | | | | | | | | | |
| 100 | 100 | 100 | 100 | 100 | 100 | Mulford Winsor | | | | | | | | | |
| 100 | 100 | 100 | 100 | 100 | 100 | 100 | P. F. Connelly | | | | | | | | |
| 100 | 100 | 100 | 100 | 100 | 100 | 100 | 100 | F. A. Jones | | | | | | | |
| 100 | 100 | 100 | 100 | 100 | 100 | 100 | 100 | 100 | William Morgan | | | | | | |
| 100 | 100 | 100 | 100 | 100 | 100 | 100 | 100 | 100 | 100 | E. L. Short | | | | | |
| 100 | 100 | 100 | 100 | 100 | 100 | 100 | 100 | 100 | 100 | 100 | B. B. Moeur | | | | |
| 75 | 75 | 75 | 75 | 75 | 75 | 75 | 75 | 75 | 75 | 75 | 100 | John Bolan | | | |
| 75 | 75 | 75 | 75 | 75 | 75 | 75 | 75 | 75 | 75 | 75 | 100 | 100 | T. Feeney | | |
| 75 | 75 | 75 | 75 | 75 | 75 | 75 | 75 | 75 | 75 | 75 | 100 | 100 | 100 | Lysander Cassidy | |
| 75 | 75 | 75 | 75 | 75 | 75 | 75 | 75 | 75 | 75 | 75 | 100 | 100 | 100 | 100 | C. M. Roberts |

TABLE 12: ARIZONA--CORPORATIONS

PART II

GOLDWATER BLOC

| | | | | | |
|---|---|---|---|---|---|
| R. B. Sims | | | | | |
| 100 | Jacob Weinberger | | | | |
| 100 | 100 | Morris Goldwater | | | |
| 100 | 100 | 100 | M. G. Cunniff | | |
| 100 | 100 | 100 | 100 | A. F. Parsons | |
| 100 | 100 | 100 | 100 | 100 | A. A. Moore |

TABLE 12: ARIZONA--CORPORATIONS

PART III

REPUBLICAN-CORPORATION DEMOCRATS

| | | | | | | | | | | | | | | | | |
|---|---|---|---|---|---|---|---|---|---|---|---|---|---|---|---|---|
| C.C. Hutchinson | | | | | | | | | | | | | | | | |
| 100 | Fred T. Colter | | | | | | | | | | | | | | | |
| 75 | 75 | Samuel L. Kingan | | | | | | | | | | | | | | |
| 75 | 75 | 100 | William F. Cooper | | | | | | | | | | | | | |
| 75 | 75 | 100 | 100 | Carlos C. Jacome | | | | | | | | | | | | |
| 75 | 75 | 100 | 100 | 100 | James C. White | | | | | | | | | | | |
| 100 | 100 | 100 | 100 | 100 | 100 | A. C. Baker | | | | | | | | | | |
| 100 | 100 | 75 | 75 | 75 | 75 | 100 | Lamar Cobb | | | | | | | | | |
| 100 | 100 | 50 | 50 | 50 | 50 | 100 | 100 | Sidney P. Osborn | | | | | | | | |
| 75 | 75 | 50 | 50 | 50 | 50 | 100 | 75 | 100 | E. A. Tovrea | | | | | | | |
| 100 | 100 | 75 | 75 | 75 | 75 | 100 | 100 | 100 | 75 | A. M. Tuthill | | | | | | |
| 100 | 100 | 67 | 67 | 67 | 67 | 100 | 100 | 100 | 100 | 100 | Orrin Standage | | | | | |
| 100 | 100 | 75 | 75 | 75 | 75 | 100 | 100 | 100 | 75 | 100 | 100 | John Orme | | | | |
| 100 | 100 | 75 | 75 | 75 | 75 | 100 | 100 | 100 | 75 | 100 | 100 | 100 | A. Lynch | | | |
| 100 | 100 | 100 | 100 | 100 | 100 | 100 | 100 | 100 | 67 | 100 | 100 | 100 | 100 | E. E. Ellinwood | | |
| 100 | 100 | 50 | 50 | 50 | 50 | 0 | 100 | 100 | 50 | 100 | 100 | 100 | 100 | 100 | Thomas N. Willis | |
| 75 | 75 | 50 | 50 | 50 | 50 | 50 | 75 | 100 | 50 | 75 | 67 | 75 | 75 | 67 | 100 | Bracey Curtis |

TABLE 13: ARIZONA--LABOR

| YYYYNNNN | |
|---|---|
| ++ + + | D. L. Cunningham |
| ++++ | A. F. Parsons |
| ++++ | J. J. Keegan |
| ++++ | Alfred Kinney |
| +0++ | Jacob Weinberger |
| ++ + + | Mit Simms |
| +0 + + | W. T. Webb |
| +00+ | B. B. Moeur |
| ++ + + | Thomas N. Wills |
| +0++ | E. L. Short |
| ++++ | E. E. Ellinwood |
| + + + + | James Scott |
| ++++ | John Bolan |
| ++++ | S. B. Bradner |
| ++++ | P. F. Connelly |
| ++++ | Thomas Feeney |
| ++++ | R. B. Sims |
| +0+0 | E. A. Tovrea |
| ++++ | George W. P. Hunt |
| ++++ | John Langdon |
| + +0 + | A. M. Tuthill |
| ++++ | Lysander Cassidy |
| ++++ | James E. Crutchfield |
| ++++ | Henry Lovin |
| ++++ | William Morgan |
| ++++ | E. W. Coker |
| ++++ | M. G. Cunniff |
| ++++ | Albert Jones |
| ++++ | A. A. Moore |
| ++++ | Homer R. Wood |
| ++++ | Fred L. Ingraham |
| ++++ | C. M. Roberts |
| +0+0 | A. C. Baker |
| +++0 | F. A. Jones |
| ++++ | Morris Goldwater |
| ++++ | Mulford Winsor |
| + + ++ | Lamar Cobb |
| + + ++ | Alfred Franklin |
| + + ++ | John P. Orme |
| + + ++ | Sidney Osborne |
| ++0+ | Fred T. Colter |
| + +++ | C. C. Hutchinson |
| + +++ | Samuel L. Kingan |
| + +++ | William F. Cooper |
| + +++ | Carlos Jacome |
| + +++ | George Pusch |
| + +++ | E. W. Wells |
| + ++++ | Bracey Curtis |
| 0+0+ | James C. White |
| 0++0 | Orrin Standage |

# Bibliographical Notes

Any specialized study must deal substantially with primary sources. Here the primary sources are numerous if not always helpful. For the conventions, the official reports, excepting New Mexico's, were the most useful. They supplied the researcher with a record of debate, procedure, and limited voting data. The newspapers occasionally offered another dimension of behavior. Editorials and reports of convention activity yielded a perspective on attitudes and internal bargaining. However, after reading those cited and numerous other newspapers, this researcher was impressed by the fact that aside from convention-city newspapers, the press paid little attention to delegate activities. To many editors statehood, rather than the constitution, was crucial. Not surprisingly, manuscript collections yielded a similar ore. Although several cited in the notes provided useful information, most contained low-grade. For example, the Kohrs papers give the convention little space amid a glory-hole of material on cattle ranching. One is left then with resort to basics--the official records complemented by corroborative evidence. However, like public opinion research, the voting behavior of delegates proved the best evidence of attitude and causation.

Among the secondary sources cited in the notes, some require additional comment. The territorial period has been expertly surveyed by several historians. Earl S. Pomeroy's *The Territories and the United States, 1861-1890* (Philadelphia, Pa., 1947) remains a basic work. Jack Eblen's *The First and Second United States Empires* (Pittsburgh, Pa., 1968) is a detailed study of selected aspects of the territorial system. Most important for the region's territorial experience is Howard R. Lamar's *The Far Southwest* (New Haven, Conn., 1966). Primarily a political history, Lamar's work provides valuable insights into the politics of the conventions and the territorial period. The basic work on the constitutional conventions continues to be John D. Hicks' 1923 study entitled The Constitutions of the Northwest States (Lincoln, Neb., 1923). Limited to the conventions of 1890, Hicks does provide a topical context. The best study of legal and political development leading to statehood is Robert W. Larson's New Mexico's Quest for Statehood (Albuquerque, N.M., 1968). Among the useful state histories are T. A. Larson's History of Wyoming (Lincoln, Neb., 1965) and Lewis Gould's Wyoming, A Political History, 1868-1896 (New Haven, Conn., 1968) and Carl Ubbelohde's, Maxine Benson and Duane A. Smith's A Colorado History (Boulder, Colo., 1972).

The most analytical political histories are James E. Wright's The Politics of Populism (New Haven, Conn., 1974) and Robert W. Larson's New Mexico Populism (Boulder, Colo., 1972). The best book on regional Populism is Robert W. Larson's Populism in the Mountain West, (Albuquerque, New Mexico, 1986). Professor Larson persuasively argues that Rocky Mountain Populism was not a one-issue party in the free coinage of silver camp. Rather Rocky Mountain Populism included strong support for antimonopolism, workingmen's conditions, women's rights, direct legislation, and Chinese exclusion.

On issues of justice, individual rights and the role of the U.S. Constitution and judicially-defined rights several books stand out as required reading. John Rawls' A Theory of Justice (Cambridge, Mass., 1971) set off a spirited discussion of individual rights. Ronald Dworkin gave the debate much of its spirit with Taking Rights Seriously (Cambridge, Mass., 1977) and A Matter of Principle (Cambridge, Mass., 1985). Rex Martin has refined and revised some of the philosophical and legal issues in Rawls and Rights (Lawrence, Kansas, 1985).

Lawrence M. Friedman's A History of American Law (New York, N.Y., 1985) still stands as the only comprehensive legal history of the American experience. It must be read with the works of Willard Hurst, particularly Law and Economic Growth (Cambridge, Mass., 1964), Law and the Conditions of Freedom in the Nineteenth-Century United States (Madison, Wis., 1956), The Growth of American Law (Boston, Mass., 1950), A Legal History of Money in the United States, 1774-1970 (Lincoln, Neb., 1973), and The Legitimacy of the Business Corporation in the Law of the United States, 1780-1970 (Charlottesville, Va., 1970). Perhaps the most important legal history of the decade of the 1980s is John Phillip Reid's Law for the Elephant: Property and Social Behavior on the Overland Trail (San Marino, Calif., 1980). Importantly for our understanding of the 19th-century American experience, Reid found that emigrants on the trail "respected the legal principles vesting in the individual exclusive enjoyment of property lawfully possessed." For this study, that taught, learned, and accepted law grounded in morality helps explain the delegate respect for property ensconced in constitutions.

The critical legal studies movement questioning the Friedman-Hurst-Reid structure of legal history has generated less literature. The most important early book is Morton J. Horwitz's The Transformation of American Law, 1780-1860 (Cambridge, Mass., 1977). More recently, whole issues of law reviews have been dedicated to the debate. A particularly useful one is The Yale Law Journal vol. 90 (April 1981). Stephen B. Presser's "Some Realism about Orphism or The Critical Legal Studies Movement and the New Great Chain of Being: An English Legal Academic's Guide to the Current State of American Law," 79 Northwestern University Law Review 869-99 (1985) is a good summary of the interpretative positions and critique of the arguments. Until the debate moves to the firmer ground of research in original sources, it may remain confined primarily to law reviews.

Perhaps the most exciting work in legal history is being done on women rights issues. Norma Basch's 1982 study of 19th-century New York family and property law impacting women, In the Eyes of the Law (Ithaca, N.Y., 1982), and Ellen Carol DuBois' Feminism and Suffrage (Ithaca, N.Y., 1978) made contributions to our knowledge of the feminist movement as well as legal history. Richard H. Chused's "Married Women's Property Law: 1800-1850," 71 Georgetown Law Journal 1359-1425 (1983) demonstrated that the expansion of married women's property rights was a legislative recognition of the rapidly expanding role of women in family affairs. Paula Baker provides the political perspective on the women's movement and legal change in "The Domestication of Politics: Women and American Political Society, 1780-1929," 89 American Historical Review 620-647 (June 1984). Focusing primarily on the eastern experience, this growing literature is nonetheless important context for the demands of women on the legal system of the 19th-century west.

# Index

## About the Author

GORDON MORRIS BAKKEN is Professor of History at California State University, Fullerton. He is the author of *The Development of Law on the Rocky Mountain Frontier* and *The Development of Law in Frontier California* (Greenwood Press, 1983, 1985).